The Mother's Philosophy of Education

Dr. G. Ranjit Sharma

Published by

ATLANTIC

PUBLISHERS & DISTRIBUTORS (P) LTD

7/22, Ansari Road, Darya Ganj, New Delhi-110002
Phones : +91-11-40775252, 40775214, 23273880, 23275880
Fax : +91-11-23285873
Web : www.atlanticbooks.com
E-mail : orders@atlanticbooks.com

Printed & bound in India by Atlantic Print Services

In memory of
Mrs Pishak Devi,
Mr Nabakishwar Sharma
and
Mrs Akashimi Devi

— The unfortunate author

Preface

Contemporary Indian philosophy of education may be characterised as integral approach to education. However, the most significant and satisfactory integral approach has been presented by The Mother. It is an irony that while researches have been conducted upon the philosophies of education of Swami Vivekananda, Rabindranath Tagore, Sri Aurobindo, M.K. Gandhi and even Dr. Sarvapalli Radhakrishnan, no research has been conducted on The Mother's philosophy of education. Sri Aurobindo Society, Pondicherry, has published The Mother's writings in 16 volumes. Besides, all the journals and magazines published by Sri Aurobindo Ashram, abound in the teachings of The Mother. Besides this theoretical literature available for research, Sri Aurobindo International University and The Mother's schools at Pondicherry and Delhi are living monuments of her practical contribution to the evolution of an integral scheme of education for free progress of the educand, in a spiritually free atmosphere. Therefore, the author has discovered that The Mother's philosophy of education needs systematization and critical evaluation.

The purpose of the present research is therefore two-fold. It will first gather material on various topics of education and its philosophical, psychological and sociological foundations from the teachings of The Mother as published in journals and books. This will be collaborated and enriched by relevant comparisons with the philosophies of education of East and West. Secondly, the Mother's philosophy of education will be critically evaluated particularly from the point of view of internal consistency. Thus, the author will utilise the primary and secondary sources for a construction through criticism.

Thus, the present work aims at presenting an integral philosophy of education and also pointing out its present limitations and future possibilities. It has been left to future researchers to further explore the horizons. Education is a subject which requires persistent enquiry, revaluation, reconstruction and redirection in the context of changing circumstances. Therefore, the researcher has a duty to reinterpret and evaluate the important philosophies of education with an eye to find solutions of everyday life in various fields of education. It is left to the educationists, the administrators and the policy makers to work out details and give it a practical form. While today most of the educationists and political leaders are talking of new scheme of education, it is their duty to evolve it out of the fundamental thought presented by Indian philosophers of education. It is so since philosophical approach is a synoptic vision, a synthesis of sciences and arts.

In the progress of the present work the author is profoundly grateful to Dr. P.B. Vidyarthi, formerly Professor and Head of the Department of Philosophy, Ranchi University, for giving constant inspiration and encourage to march ahead whenever the author felt disappointed. The author also expresses his heartfelt gratitude to Dr. R.N. Sharma, retired Professor of Philosophy, for his helpful advice with a sense of involvement. Besides the author is indebted to Dr. R.S. Srivastava, formerly Professor & Head of the Department of Philosophy, Ranchi University, for his guidance in finalising the synopsis of the present work. For giving valuable suggestions about the scheme of the present research the author is further indebted to Dr. I.P. Atreya, retired Professor of Philosophy and Dr. Ramjee Singh, Professor & Head of the Department of Gandhian Studies, Bhagalpur University. Besides, these stalwarts the author has been fortunate in receiving guidance and inspiration from a host of scholars both in philosophy and education. The author feels immense sense of gratitude for all of them.

The author cannot but remember with profound feelings of piety and gratitude of his mother who created in him a passion for knowledge and democratic ideals. The author lost his mother while he was seriously studying for the present work. Despite this severe set back the author continued to study more seriously to timely accomplish the work in honour of the departed soul.

Formal though it may look the author must expresses his appreciation to his wife Dr. A. Nungshitombi Devi, Department of Home Science, G.P. Women's College, Imphal, without whose help and cooperation, both domestic and academic, it would have not been possible for him to accomplish the work in the present form.

Last but not the least, the author desires to express his gratitude to all those who have contributed to the present work in one way or another.

G.R. Sharma

Contents

1

Introductory

"The Mother comes in order to bring down the supramental and it is the descent which makes her full manifestation here possible."[1]

— **Sri Aurobindo**

Mirra Alfasa (The Mother) was born on 21 February, 1878 in Paris, France. Her father was a banker. She was born in a rich family. Eight from the beginning she used to experience spiritual phenomena. She has herself described her early spiritual experiences on so many occasions. At the age of 16 she used to practise painting with a devotion. At this age she organised a group of mystiques in Paris called, "Cosmic", whose activities have been described in the book *Words of Long Ago*. In due course she received training in *Tantra* from a famous Algerian Tantric expert. Her Tantric powers have been admitted by Sri Aurobindo.[2] Besides, she also experienced various spiritual levels. In 1912 she declared that our aim should be to manifest a progressive world harmony. In other words, our aim is to establish human unity by experiencing kingdom of God on earth which is already within us.[3] She was particularly attracted to India and used to feel that in India she will find her mentor. Her husband Paul Richard came to Pondicherry to meet Paul Rlusom, a representative of French Chamber. He met Sri Aurobindo who interpreted a spiritual symbol given by Mirra to Paul Richard. Mirra knew that he who will interpret this symbol will be her mentor. Paul Richard also met Rabindranath Tagore in Japan. On 29th March 1914 Mirra along with her husband arrived at Pondicherry. She met Sri Aurobindo soon after her arrival She immediately felt that Sri Aurobindo was her mentor. However, soon she had to leave Pondicherry for Paris. She finally arrives at Pondicherry on 24th April, 1920. During this period of 6-year she was in occasional correspondence with Sri Aurobindo. Her spiritual ascent was continued. At Pondicherry she started living in house No. 1 on Second Line Beach Now she regularly visited Sri Aurobindo. Gradually she shifted to live with Sri Aurobindo. Now the entire management of Sri Aurobindo's group developed around her. Sri Aurobindo himself initially called her by name but gradually started calling her The Mother. The 24th November 1926 was Sri Aurobindo's day of realisation. This was exactly after 6 years of The Mother's coming to Sri Aurobindo's residence. After the day of realisation Sri Aurobindo severed all contacts from the external world and lived for almost 24 years in complete solitude. The entire management of Sri Aurobindo Ashram was entrusted to The Mother now onwards. After it Sri Aurobindo Ashram developed fast. More and more buildings were occupied around the centre which consisted of a meditation house, a secretariat, rosery and a library house. The Ashram gradually extended to more than two hundred buildings which house besides *Yoga* centre, library, press, physical education centre, studio, motor workshops, various centres for small scale industries, diary, laundry, various factories, playgrounds, swimming pools, gardens and guest house etc. A significant growth of the Ashram complex was extended in the form of Auroville. The press and publication department regularly publishes books by Sri Aurobindo and The Mother. Thus thousands of men and women flocked around The Mother at Sri Aurobindo Ashram.

Sri Aurobindo on the Mother

In order to understand the importance of the Mother's philosophy of education it is necessary to analyse the close collaboration of Sri Aurobindo and The Mother. The above mentioned brief review of the meeting of these two great persons is only an introduction to this collaboration. Sri Aurobindo has himself described the role of The Mother in his work in very clear terms. To the question "Do you not refer to the Mother (Mirra Alfasa) in your book, The Mother'. He said, "Yes".[4] He hailed The Mother as an *Avatar* of Divine *Sakti* He said, "The Divine puts on an appearance of humanity assumes the outward human nature in order to tread the path and show it to human beings, but does not cease to be the Divine. It is a manifestation that take place, a manifestation of growing divine consciousness, not human turning into divine. The Mother was inwardly above the human even in childhood. So the view upheld by 'many' is erroneous".[5]

He clearly maintained that The Mother has come to pursue the same aims and objectives which he is pursuing. Both of them were engaged in the mission of bringing down the supramental force on earth. In the words of Sri Aurobindo, "The Mother comes in order to bring down the supramental and it is the descent which makes her full manifestation here possible."[6] Thus, The Mother came to earth for spiritual transformation of humanity and worked for the establishment of Divine power on the earth. In the words of Sri Aurobindo, "There is one divine Force which acts in the universe and in the individual and is also beyond the individual and the universe. The Mother stands for all these, but she is working here in the body to bring down something not yet expressed in this material world so as to transform life here —it is so that you should regard her as the *Divine Sakti* working here for that purpose. She is that in the body but in her whole consciousness she is also identified with all the other aspects of the Divine."[7]

For the aspirants in Sri Aurobindo's *Yoga* God's grace is the most helpful phenomenon. The Mother represented God's grace on the earth. As Sri Aurobindo said, "It is the work of the Cosmic Power to maintain the cosmos and the law of the cosmos. The greater transformation comes from the Transcendent above the universal, and it is that transcendent Grace which the embodiment of The Mother is there to bring to action."[8] Therefore, Sri Aurobindo asked every *Sadhak* to follow the dictates of The Mother. There was no Ashram at first, only a few people came to live near Sri Aurobindo and practise *Yoga*. It was only sometime after The Mother came from Japan that it took the form of the Ashram, more from the wish of the *sadhakas* who desired to entrust their whole inner and outer life to The Mother than from any intention or plan of hers or of Sri Aurobindo. The Mother was doing *Yoga* before she knew or met Sri Aurobindo; but their lines of *Sadhana* independently followed the same course. When they met, they helped each other in perfecting the *Sadhana*. What is known as Sri Aurobind's *Yoga* is the joint creation of Sri Aurobindo and The Mother; they are now completely identified — the *Sadhana in* the Ashram and all arrangement were guided directly by The Mother, Sri Aurobindo supported her from behind. All who came to Ashram for practicing *Yoga* had to surrender themselves to The Mother who helped them always and building up their spiritual life.

The Mother on Sri Aurobindo

When The Mother met Sri Anrobindo for the first time she wrote in her diary, "It matters not if there are hundreds of beings plunged in the densest ignorance. He whom we saw yesterday is on earth; His presence is enough to prove that a day will come when darkness shall be transformed into light, when Thy reign shall be indeed established upon earth."[9] Since then she joined Sri Aurobindo's path in search of Divine. She followed Sri Aurobindo's aim of life. In her own words, "My only aim is to give a concrete form to Sri Anrobindo's great teaching and in his teaching he reveals that all the nations are essentially one and meant to express the Divine Unity upon earth through an organised and harmonious diversity".[10] She hailed Sri Aurobindo's advent upon this earth as a decisive action direct from the Supreme. She said, "What Sri Aurobindo represents in the world's history is not a teaching, not even a revelation; it is a decisive action direct from the Supreme".[11] Explaining the meaning of Sri Aurobindo's birth in the history of the universe The Mother said, "The sentence can be understood in four different ways on four ascending planes of consciousness:

1. Physically, the consequences of the birth will be of eternal importance in the world.

2. Mentally, it is a birth that will be eternally remembered in the universal history.

3. Psychologically, a birth that recurs forever from age to age upon earth.

4. Spiritually, the birth of the Eternal upon earth."[12]

Spiritual Collaborators

Thus Sri Aurobindo and The Mother were close spiritual collaborators. As The Mother said, "Without Him. I exist not, without me, He is unmanifest."[13] Again, "When in your heart and thought you will make no difference between Sri Aurobindo and me, when to think of Sri Aurobindo will be to think of me and to think of me will mean to think of Sri Aurobindo inevitably, when to see one will mean inevitably to see the other, like one and the same person, – then you will know that you begin to be open to the supramental force and consciousness."[14] The same idea was expressed by Sir Aurobindo in very clear terms like this: "The Mother's consciousness and mine are the same, the one Divine

Consciousness in two, because that is necessary for the play. 'Nothing can be done without her knowledge and force, without her consciousness — if anybody really feels her consciousness, he should know that I am there behind it and if he feeds me it is the same with hers. If a separation is made like that (I leave aside the turns which their minds so strongly put upon these things), how can the Truth establish itself — for the Truth there is no such separation."[15] However, from the point of view of the Sadhakas the supramental light of Sri Aurobindo was pale blue and that of The Mother white or golden. Thus both helped the Sadhakas in achieving supramental plain and divine realisation. Both followed the following aims:

1. *Realisation of supramental consciousness:* According to Sri Aurobindo, "When we speak of The Mother's Light or my light in a special sense, we are speaking of a special occult action — we are speaking of certain lights that come from the Supermini"[16] As The Mother said about Sri Aurobindo, "Sri Aurobindo came to announce the creation of tomorrow: the coming of the supramental being."[17]

2. *Liberation while living*: Against the Advaita Vedanta of Samkara Sri Aurobindo considered the world as the real *lila* of the divine. Along with The Mother he decided to work for liberation of the entire humanity on the earth. As The Mother maintained, "Sri Aurobindo came to tell us 'One need not leave the earth to find the Truth, one need not leave the life to find his soul, one need not abandon the world or have only limited beliefs to enter into relation with the Divine. The Divine is everywhere, in everything if He is hidden, it is because we do not take the trouble to discover him."[18]

Thus both The Mother and Sri Aurobindo worked for the establishment of the kingdom of God on earth. Both were the proof that this aim can be realised. Both claimed to be the incarnations of divine power. Both worked for spiritual transformation of humanity. In this transformation while Sri Aurobindo presented the example, The Mother assured the possibility of its realisation by promising constant help to not only the disciples and the devotees but also to those who doubled and revolted. She maintained constant touch with the people around her. She allowed three choices to everyone in the endless variety of man-God relationships and she promised to help everyone. In her own words,

"And this tie between you and me is never cut. There are people who long ago left Ashram, in a state of revolt, and yet I keep myself informed of them, I attend to them. You are never abandoned."[19]

However, the identity does not mean overlapping roles. In the mission to realise the supramental force upon earth while Sri Aurobindo concentrates upon developing the technique and presenting the theory. The Mother organised the movement. This collaboration may be compared to that of *Purusa* and *Prakrti* in Sankhya philosophy. After 1926 Sri Aurobindo used to appear in public only four times a year and it was left to The Mother to attend to the management of the Ashram as well as to the everyday needs of the *Sadhakas* including guidance in their spiritual pursuits. With a rare combination of spirituality and management skill The Mother developed various activities at the Ashram and made it a multisided flowering of a spiritual community. She was responsible for the growth of international university at Pondicherry. She was also responsible for the growth of Sri Aurobindo society and the international city known as Auroville. She guided and presided over the evolution of dozens of associations and institutions around Sri Aurobindo Ashram. And last but not the least she managed to keep Sri Aurobindo free from all worldly difficulties and totally devoted to her work in complete solitude. Since The Mother personally looked after educational activities in the Ashram she had more intimate experience of the difficulties and their solution. She gilded not only the teachers but also the students. In every aspect of educational activity therefore, while Sri Aurobindo's philosophy of education was a result of intense thinking and philosophical excellence. The Mother's philosophy of education developed more out of practical experience. Therefore, in a way her philosophy of education may be called more practical though fundamentally she agrees to Shri Aurobindo's philosophy of education.

Again with the characteristic sympathy and empathy of a woman The Mother particularly developed the philosophy of child education, she made important discoveries in the field of child psychology, teaching methods, methods of evaluation, methods of discipline, school management and almost all the activities concerning education. She extensively spoke and wrote about almost every aspect of education such as aims and ideals, principles, aspects, guiding principles and types of education, influence of parents, personality traits of the ideal teacher, suitability of various syllabi at various ages, laws of development of physical, vital and psychic etc. She made important suggestions concerning teaching of various subjects to the children. She gave valuable guidance about the moral education of children. By her personal experience in the field of education and spirituality she personally supervised every aspect of educational activity at the Ashram. Along with Sri Aurobindo she drew the blueprint of education for Indian nation. She outlined India's role in human community and showed how it may be achieved. She was a cosmopolitan, a humanist and a votary of world unity. However, she everywhere advocated unity in and through diversity. Therefore right from the individual child to the Human Unity her principle was the evolution of the unit to evolve the whole. In her integral approach she found a place forevery ism in the history of philosophy of education. One finds a rare example of a synthesis of idealism and realism, naturalism, pragmatism and existentialism in her philosophy of life. Before she took over charge of Sri Aurobindo Ashram at Pondicherry, she was invited by Rabindranath Tagore, when they met in Japan, to take up the charge of the educational activities at Santiniketan. But since she was a devotee of Sri Aurobindo no less than a collaborator, she chose to work at Pondicherry.

While Sri Aurobindo outlined a national system of education, a model to realise his scheme was developed by The Mother in the form of Sri Aurobindo international university at Pondicherry. It was developed as a new centre of education to experiment for the realisation of the aims outlined by Sri Aurobindo. The curriculum, the teaching methods, the system of evaluation and all the other details were formed with this central aim. The fundamental principle underlying the model was freedom since freedom is the only essential spiritual principle working anywhere. As has been already pointed out, this ideal control of education not only aimed at realization of Sri Aurobindo's aim in India but also in humanity. All the aims of education outlined earlier were practiced here. Children were admitted from a very early age. They gathered from all the parts of the country as well as from different countries in the world to make it a true representative of world cultures. The natural scenery, dress, games, sports, industries, food, art etc., were developed on the principle of unity and diversity. An effort was made to realise a cultural synthesis.

Students of different nations were placed at different places with their own groups so that while they may develop international culture, no rigid timetable, classes, curriculum, teaching method or system of evaluation and examination was insisted. This was left upon individual choice of the educand himself. The idea was to give full freedom to the individual growth of the educand. The experiment fared very well but did not grow elsewhere due to a model for a new system of education which may be hoped to develop in India and also in parts of the world.

The Mother had devised a scheme of education which is followed in the Centre of Education. This is based on her spiritual philosophy. According to her everybody has in him something divine, something of his own and the task is to find and develop it. Thus, the main purpose of education is to draw out the inner capacities of an individual and use them for a noble cause. This shows that the key to knowledge is within. The spark is within. So, the soul has to be awakened. The duty of the parent or the teacher is to help the student to educate himself, to develop his own intellectual, moral and practical capacities. So, the system of "free progress education" is followed at the Centre of Education. Thus, the students are free to choose what subjects they like. They take some subjects at one level, and other subjects at another level. They are also free to take examination when they deem fit. Thus, at the Centre of Education, the student is motivated and inspired to rely on his soul. The approach, the motivation and the aspirations are different at the Centre of Education from the outside world. So, this is a journey towards self-discovery. The Mother has maintained that free progress is progress guided by the soul and not enslaved by habits, conventions and pre-conceived ideas. One should not think that there is no discipline in the "free progress system". Discipline may not be imposed from without, but there is an inner law which prescribes the norm of behaviour. This is better than the mechanical regulations.

Now how is this system to be implemented? In this case, the teacher is the heart of the structure. In the education of tomorrow, the emphasis is on the teacher and his methods rather than anything else. He should act as a friend, philosopher and guide and offer counsel to the student when he needs it. He should maintain separate dossier for each student. He should present the subject in such a way that the student's interest is stimulated and he is encouraged to undertake further study. Thus, the philosophy of education at the Centre is 'integral' and ideal. According to this, it is important to develop the faculties of mind and body under the direction of the soul within. The earlier we follow this philosophy, better it would be for our nation.

The Mother has presented a complete and integral philosophy of life and has shown the way to the maximum good of all. She brings within our ken, a future far greater than anything realised so far, fulfilling man's greatest dreams and even beyond. Her practical philosophy appeals to all who have tried to see life in its totality. Her views of this great future can be summed up as follows:

(a) *Individual* — Accelerated evolution from man to the supramental being through the practice of Integral *Yoga* and the evolution of super mind.

(b) *Social Transformation* — Evolution of spiritual communities, where the basic needs of all will be provided free, and all people would choose work that they can do best according to their own aptitudes and do it free in a spirit of Divine perfection and service. The collective life will provide to the growth of the individual.

(c) *National* — Realisation of nation-soul and reorganisation of collective national life-law, education and all other activities — aiming them at freedom, truth and maximum good of all and each nation, finding and playing its true role in the world.

(d) *World* — Human Unity in freedom and organised diversity.

But all these goals are interconnected and interdependent and can be realised only through the growth of consciousness. It may be noted that the aim of The Mother's teaching is not only to realise the Divine, not only to carry out the Divine commands, but to transform the life by a descent of the Divine consciousness in the mind, life and body of man and its manifestation through a transformed collective life. It is a vision of "a life divine" on earth.

Sri Aurobindo Society was established to spread the teachings of Sri Aurobindo and The Mother and to work for their practical realisation all over the world. At present, there are about 450 Sri Aurobindo Centres in India and about 50 Centres abroad.

In order to assist these Sri Aurobindo Centres to render effective services in their respective areas, it has been found necessary to develop certain facilities at the national level, namely preparation of talks and documentary films on various subjects, training of workers and organisers, establishment of a Convention Centre, Extension Services for Spiritual Community Development etc. Some of the activities have already been taken in hand. A more forceful perusal of these goals is yet to be undertaken. However, for the growth of the Society and its effective functioning, a National Council works as a cohesive group to realise the teachings of Sri Aurobindo and The Mother.

Auroville

Auroville is established, developed and managed by Sri Aurobindo Society to realise mainly the following of the Society's objectives:

(a) to provide a place for the practice of integral *yoga* for its members and their friends;

(b) to provide a model of spiritualised society;

(c) to locate its various projects for realising human unity and other teachings of Sri Aurobindo;

(d) to be the seat of:

- (i) The Academy of the Future
- (ii) National Cultural Pavilions
- (iii) Children's World.

At present, there are about 2,000 acres of land under the project and several services have been organised, namely, agricultural farms, schools, community kitchens, health centres, transport services etc.

Unfortunately, some of the residents have forsaken the solemn undertaking given by them at the time of admission, and have started indulging in promiscuous sex, drugs, alcohol, and even violation of the laws of the country. This problem has assumed an acute shape during the years 1975-76 as some politicians, with vested interests, began to encourage the troublemakers with a view to controlling the administration and eventually taking over Auroville itself.

The Society submitted a Memorandum to the Education Ministry apprising it of the correct situation. Finally, the Government has taken over the administration of this proposed international city.

World Assembly for Human Unity

Human unity in freedom and diversity, based on the realisation of the Divine consciousness, is one of the major visions of Sri Aurobindo. While The Mother was in her physical body, a proposal for the World Assembly for the Human Unity was placed before her. Not only did she approve of it enthusiastically, but she wrote, "It would help India to play its true role in the world." Sponsored by Sir Aurobindo Society, the World Assembly for Human Unity has been established as a result of two international conferences and a seminar held by the Society. The World Assembly is proposed to be a permanent body with its headquarters in Auroville, Pondicherry. Its first meeting was held in Madras in 1978.

The organisation of its work consists of:

(a) Preparation of a draft of the Charter on Human Unity placed for adoption by the Assembly.

(b) To clarify the concept of Human Unity and the ways to realise it.

(c) Setting up of commissions on various subjects such as law, education, economic services, youth, etc. from the angle of human unity. The Commissions set up during the Assembly were served till the next Conference was held in London in 1980.

(d) To promote projects for leadership training, audo-visual education, World Research and Information, Integrated Health Sciences, Communities as models of Human Unity *viz.* Auroville. The list is illustrative and can be expanded.

(e) To make regular use of mass media for creating awareness for the need of human unity and programme of the World Assembly.

(f) To institute annual awards for significant contribution to the cause of human unity.

(g) To establish in Auroville a Convention Centre for holding regular conferences and seminars as well as cultural pavilions of various countries.

(h) To work in close collaboration with the International Institute for Human Unity, London, and other similar organisations.

(i) To set up an International Fund for Human Unity.

(j) To maintain a Register of those who want to work actively for human unity.

The Assembly works towards strengthening the United Nations and the principles it stands for.

The Programme of Commissions 1978-1979

Social transformation and an accelerated individual evolution go hand in hand in the yoga of Sri Aurobindo, each helping the other. Hence, Sri Aurobindo Society set up various commissions with multiple objectives. The Commissions were to provide Karma Yoga for those who will be working on them and services for the community to bring about progressive perfection — social transformation, economic stability, a new and integral outlook within newly created helpful and congenial environment.

The programme of the Commissions was outlined as follows:

Commissions	*Proposed Programme for 1978-79*
1. Education	(a) An experimental model school in Auroville. (b) Teachers Training. (c) Publications and production of audio-visual materials. (d) Implementation of the Programme suggested by the National Education Committee (constituted by the National Committee for celebrating The Mother's Birth Centenary).
2. Physical Education	(a) Publication of "Body of Light". (b) Various designs for stadiums. (c) Training in *Asanas* and *Pranayams,*
3. Public Life (Sri Aurobindo's Approach to Leaderrship)	(a) Leadership training. (b) Extension Service for Community Development. (c) National Planning. (d) District and State Planning. (e) Country-wide seminars on India's true role in the world.
4. Economic Services (Employment,	(a) Publications. (b) Research Studies.

Training & Rural Development)	(c) Registration of a National Trust for giving comprehensive services, *viz.* marketing services, consultancy etc. (d) Local trusts for local work. (e) Development of S.C. Institute of Business Management in Pondicherry.
5. Women	(a) Booklet on "Women". (b) Setting up a Home Science and Craft Centre and a Girls Hostel in Auroville. (c) Setting up of a Youth Centre in Auroville.
6. Youth	Setting up to a Youth Centre in Auroville.
7. Environmental Planning	Booklet on "Model Environmental Planning".
8. Health	(a) Experiments on Spiritual dealing. (b) Booklets on Illness (Comprehensive). (c) Seminar on "Death, Longevity & Immortality".
9. Organisation	To achieve the target of 600 Sri Aurobindo Centres in India, including the existing ones, and services for their development.

The Mother's Contribution to Education

The Mother was a spiritual companion of Sri Aurobindo. In her own however, she was as much a thinker, a spiritual seeker and a religious *sadhak* as Sri Aurobindo. She has written extensively on almost all the subjects concerning philosophical thought particularly in the fields of practical application of philosophy to human life. Her thought had been collected in sixteen volumes and published by Sri Aurobindo Ashram Trust in the centenary year 1978. These works contain her comments on the questions asked by *sadhaks,* written and verbally, in everyday life. Her message on different occasions were also full of deep thought. Sri Aurobindo Ashram Trust has published briefs of her views on different aspects of education in the three parts of the booklet, *Sri Aurobindo and The Mother on Education.*

The Mother's contribution to education has been accepted by all the illustrious persons in India and abroad. The government and the national leaders have acclaimed her contribution to education. She was not only a great educationist and a philosopher but also a source of inspiration to almost all the important national leaders of her time. Therefore, it is in the fitness of things that her philosophy of education should be made subject of research.

Purpose of the Present Work

The purpose of the present work is to enquire into the fundamentals of philosophy of education, to visualize the philosophy of education suitable to meet the demands of our age, to systematise the Mother's philosophy of education and to evaluate and examine it in the light of the criteria, of an ideal system of education for humanity. The aims and objectives of the study are: To present a systematic outline of the philosophy of education; to work out salient features of The Mother's philosophy of education; to show how far this philosophy of education indicates the ideal outlines for future; and finally to assess The Mother's contribution in transforming the character of Indian education through a critical analysis of the challenging view expressed in the sixteen volumes of her selected works.

Methods of Study

The method and procedure of this study will be that of construction through criticism which is the characteristic method of philosophy of education. Primary and secondary sources will also be scanned, scrutinized and studied. They will be subjected to careful internal and external criticisms. The interpretation will be based upon the analysis of data and synthesis of various conclusions.

References

1. *Sri Aurobindo and The Mother On Themselves*, Part II (Pondicherry: Sri Aurobindo Ashram, 1973), p. 13.
2. *Words of long ago*, 3rd imp. (Pondicherry; Sri Aurobindo Ashram, 1974), pp. 11-12.
3. *Talks with Sri Aurobindo*. II, p, 160.
4. Sri Aurobindo, *The Mother* (Centenary Ed. Vol. 25), p. 47.
5. *Ibid.*, p. 48.
6. *Ibid.*
7. *Ibid.*, pp. 49-50.
8. *Ibid.*, p. 50.

9. *Sri Aurobindo and The Mother On Themselves*, Part I (1973), p. 8.
10. *Message given by The Mother* on 15.8.54.
11. *Sri Aurobindo and The Mother On Themselves*, Part I, p. 8.
12. *Ibid.*
13. *Message given by The Mother* on 4.3. 58.
14. *Ibid.*
15. *Sri Aurobindo On Himself* (Centenary Ed. Vol. 26), p, 455.
16. *Sri Aurobindo, The Mother* (Centenary Ed. Vol. 25), p. 83.
17. *Bulletin* (1972 August), p. 25.
18. *Bulletin* (1972 February), p. 49.
19. *Sri Aurobindo and The Mother On Themselves*, Part II, p. 19.

2

Aims and Ideals of Education: Western

"The aim of education is not to prepare a man to succeed in life and society but to increase his perfectibility of its utmost."[1]

—The Mother

The aims of education are determined by human life. Putting it differently, the aims of education are formulated after deciding the kind of life we want human beings to lead. In addition to this, the aims of education are also determined by the kind of life human beings live. It can thus be said that the aims of education are based upon human nature. Since the basic form of human nature has remained unchanged over many centuries, the aims of education have also remained the same while humanity has passed through many centuries. For example, the human being is constituted not only of the reason and intellect, but also of emotions and the body. Any system of education which seeks to fulfil its aims must provide for the development of all these aspects. In view of the complex social and economic structure of human society, every adult human being is faced with the necessity of earning his bread and of fulfilling his various needs. In view of this permanent necessity of human life, one of the aims of education has always been to equip the individual to earn his livelihood. Man has to fight with Nature to ensure his own existence, and in this process he needs his physical abilities and powers. For this reason children are taught to maintain their health, not only in civilized societies but even in the most primitive ones. Education is also made to conform to the changing environment of a particular social group so that its later generations may be able to adjust better. For this reason one finds distinct differences in the pattern of education in societies living near the coast and societies living inland.

The Aim of Life

Thus the aim of education is deduced from the aim of life.

The aim of life is the sure philosophical foundation of the aim of education. That life should have an aim was long back said by Socrates in pointing out that an unexamined life is not worth living. Since then every thoughtful person worth the name, supported this principle. As The Mother said, "Life without an aim is a life without joy."[2] The need of joy needs no reasoning since it is very much instinctive. If there is an aim one may follow quietly the way that leads towards the aim. The aim is an ideal, an enrichment, The aim gives a meaning, a reason for existence to life. This reason implies an effort and the effort results in joy. It has been said long ago that only the brave succeeds in life. To quote The Mother again, "People essentially lazy will never have joy — they have not the strength to be joyful. It is effort that gives joy. Effort makes the being vibrate to such a degree of tension that enables you to feel the joy."[3] Thus the aim gives direction to the efforts. Aimless life is an irresponsible life. Man's birth has a responsibility. This responsibility requires following the aim. One should have a firm resolution to follow the aim of life.

Now, what is this aim of life? Different thinkers have answered this question differently. This may be seen in the case of the idealists, the realists, the materialists, the existentialists, the positivists and other philosophers. The Mother's philosophy is idealist. According to her, "The aim of human life is to discover the Divine and to manifest it. Naturally this discovery leads to happiness but this happiness is a consequence, not an aim in itself. And it is this mistake of taking a mere consequence for the aim of life that has been the cause of most of the miseries which are afflicting human life."[4] Thus The Mother condemns hedonism though she also shuns asceticism. Her is an integral approach to life. Her philosophy is progressive and enlightened. The aim of life is not pleasure but spiritual progress. In the words of The Mother, "In the world, as it actually is, the goal of life is not to secure personal happiness, but to awaken the individual progressively towards the truth-consciousness."[5] Thus life has a purpose and that purpose is to serve the Divine, In other words, life aims as perfection since the divine is perfect. The Mother does not distinguish between the aims of individual and social life. Man aims at superman. Superman however, aims at the realisation of the kingdom of God upon earth. The philosophy of The Mother is based upon an undaunted optimism in the evolutionary purpose of life, she maintains that man has evolved with a particular goal of life.

According to The Mother the advent of mail upon, this earth is a sign of the descent of God upon earth. As she pointed out, "For the mere fact that man stands upright is symbolic of the capacity to look at things from above. He dominates what he sees instead of always having his nose to the ground. Of course, it may be said that birds fly, but with wings if is difficult to have a means of intellectual self-expression!"[6] The aim of a particular form of life follows from its structure. Since the stricture of man is very much different from the structures of all other living beings, his aim of life is different from those of other animals. His upright position is symbolic and a sign of his superior status. According to The Mother, "The whole structure of the human body is made to express' a mental life."[7] Human brain lies in the head, it is at the apex. Therefore, man's life is primarily mental. Hence, he has been defined as a rational animal. This size of his brain, its weight and complexity is much more than that of any other animal. Man is much more intelligent than other animals. Animals do use some sort of instrument and exhibit rudimentary signs of intelligence. Man's intelligence is not only more in quantity but much more in quality. Even the human hand is a marvel of nature. Hence man's skill in physical manipulation very much surpasses all the other animals. Due to the central position of brain in human mind the purpose of his life is certainly an intelligent purpose. Intelligence leads to learning. Therefore, the possibility of man's education is unlimited. As The Mother said, "Man has a power to educate: his body can be developed and educated. He can increase certain faculties."[8] Therefore, most of the educational systems have laid importance upon physical development. Again, intelligence leads to constant progress. A life without progress is not a human life. This may be seen in the unprecedented growth in man's control over nature in our time. And the progress of science is becoming more and more fast. Progress of all sides of human life is an aim which directly follows from man's intelligent nature. Stressing this fact The Mother said, "Man is certainly, in an organised way, the first progressive animal who can augment his capacities, his possibilities, increase his faculties and acquire things that he did not have spontaneously. There is not one animal which can do that"[9] Man's power over nature, his progress in science and various fields of knowledge has been due to tie above-mentioned characteristics, his purposive nature, his dynamic body, his brain, his intelligence, his educability and above all his progressive nature. The mental qualities of intelligence, observation, comprehension and reduction are responsible for unprecedented growth of all knowledge. As The Mother said, "And with this possibility of expressing intelligence, observation, comprehension, deduction — all the mental qualities — man has gradually learnt to understand the laws of Nature and tried not only to understand them but master them."[10]

It is an old principle that nothing can come out of nothing. Whatever evolves must be involved. The ascent is correlative to descent. Therefore the above-mentioned characteristics of human nature symbolically express what nature seeks through man. Nature again, expresses what Divine seeks through nature. Therefore, in the ultimate analysis, man's life aims at the expression of Divine, in other words man has to express what Divine seeks through him. To quote The Mother, "All progress, all perfection is the result of an inner effort of 'something' that is present and seeks to manifest."[11]

The above analysis is not applicable only to the human individual but also to human society. The Mother believes in a parallelism of the individual and society since both are equally the expressions of Divine. Therefore, human society also aims at the expression of Divine. As Sri Aurobindo puts it, "All life is only a lavish and manifold opportunity given us to discover, realise, express the divine."[12] As against Sankara's negation of the world The Mother affirms life. Her attitude to life is even more affirmative than that of the positivist, the realist, the materialist and the meliorist. The aim of individual and society is the perfection of man. This perfection, however, requires transformation, spiritualisation, psychisisation and divinisation of human life. This is what has been sought through Yoga. This has been the aim of all great religions. The achievement of this aim requires sincerity, hope, effort, surrender, fearlessness and resolutions. The Mother has always asked the aspirants to keep an absolute faith and confidence in God and to be honest to oneself. According to her, it is the law of god that one is given whatever he sincerely, seeks to achieve. As you want so you become. As you make effort so you get. Therefore if man seeks to transform the earth, it is possible. Liberation is not a phenomenon after death. It is possible in this very life, In fact nature seeks liberation through man. Contradicting the world-negating philosophy of *Advaita Vedanta* The Mother said, "Samkara said — and others with him — that the world is not worth, living in, that you must look upon it as an illusion and leave it as soon as possible, for you can do nothing with it. I tell you on the contrary, that it is because the world is very bad, very obscure, very ugly, very unconscious, full of misery and pain that there exists in if the possibility of becoming the supreme Beauty, the supreme Light, the supreme Consciousness and the supreme Delight."[13]

In coherence with her philosophy of man and society The Mother has interpreted the aim of Indian Nation in the world immunity. As a great individual leads other members of society similarly a great nation has to lead the world. This leading however, can be only through example and not by the application of any force from outside. Unity in diversity is the fundamental postulate of The Mother's philosophy. In mankind different nations have to evolve according to their genius. India has been the spiritual teacher of mankind and that is her mission in the world. Like other contemporary Indian philosophers The Mother was not satisfied with the overall progress India has made since independence. The only creditable sign was her yearning for Truth. Her greatest fault was insincerity to her goal. Therefore, The Mother advised, "Prepare her children for the rejection of falsehood and the manifestation of Truth."[14] This incidentally, lays down the goal of national education in India. This goal can be achieved by making matter ready to manifest the Spirit. According to The Mother, India's true genius and destiny is, "To teach to the world that matter is false and important unless it becomes the manifestation of the Spirit".[15] Even technological and scientific development in the country should aim at this goal. This spiritual goal however, is not life negating. It affirms life and seeks after the realisation of the kingdom of God upon earth. Our chief defects were ignorance, fear and falsehood. Indians have to overthrow their egoistic personalities and become worthy children of The Mother India.

This national goal however, is complementary to the aim of world unity. According to The Mother the world unity is not a dead uniformity. It is a unity in diversity since that is the law of the divine everywhere. Therefore, in order to realise world unity each nation must realise its own unity. Thus national integration is the first duty of every Indian, a duty not only to our nation but to humanity. As The Mother said, "The unity of all the nations is the compelling future of the world. But for the unity of all nations to be possible, each nation must first realise its own unity."[16]

The Mother deplored the almost exclusive importance that is being given to success, career and money as aims of education in contemporary India. She asked the educators to get out of convention and to insist on the growth of the inner soul. She pointed out that national integration can be achieved only through catching and insisting upon India's soul. Spelling out her *Mantra* for national integration she said, "It is only India's soul who can unify the country. Externally, the provinces of India are very different in character, tendencies, culture, as well as in language, and any attempt to unify them artificially could only have disastrous results. But her soul is one, intense in her aspiration towards the spiritual truth, the essential unity of the creation and the divine origin of life, and by uniting with this aspiration the whole country can recover a unity that has never ceased to exist for the higher consciousness."[17]

Various Aims of Education

In her interpretation of the aims of education The Mother has explained its different aspects in details. The following are the different aims of education according to her:

1. *Perfection*: Decrying the present aims of education in India The Mother said, "Do not aim at success. Our aim is perfection. Remember you are on the threshold of a new world, participating in its birth and instrumental in its creation. There is nothing more important than the transformation. There is no interest more worthwhile."[18] The Mother was a perfectionist. She was never satisfied with partial remedies. It is hence that she decided to pursue a more perfect method of realisation of perfection of human racer. It is hence that she presented solution not only of the individual needs but also of the social and political problems facing nations and humanity. This perfectionism is the strength and this again is the weakness of The Mother's philosophy of education. In tune with the Indian concept of human nature she considered the individual as a growing soul. The aim of education, therefore, is to realise these capacities and grow into a fullness of being. As

The Mother said, "The aim of education is not to prepare man to succeed in life and society, but to increase his perfectibility to its utmost."[19]

2. *Harmony*: Harmony is the key to understand The Mother's thought everywhere. Those who complain about the difficulty in understanding her writings lack this inherent urge to harmony. On the other hand those who seek harmony easily understand her messages. As she said, "All urge of rivalry, all struggle for precedence and domination should disappear giving place to a will for harmonious organisation, for clear-sighted and effective collaboration."[20]

In her philosophy of education, as in her metaphysics, epistemology, political philosophy and social philosophy, The Mother searches after the principle of harmony of the individual, community and humanity and aims at its realisation. She seeks to achieve harmony of the individual by the growth and evolution of his different aspects such as physical, vital, mental and psychic etc. For this she proposes a scheme of physical, vital, mental, moral, religious and spiritual education. She also seeks harmony of different individuals in a community. Compatibility and not uniformity is the law of collective harmony. The roles of the male and female, the different types of individuals in a community are not identical but diverse and therefore complementary. Thus The Mother proposes an educational system in which details must be planned according to individual differences. This is particularly true about the women's education, the education of backward classes and the education of below normal, abnormal and supernormal children.

3. *Evolution:* The edifice of The Mother's philosophy is based upon his theory of evolution. It stands and falls with the truth of evolution. Evolution, however, has been felt and realised by almost all the thinkers of our age. Therefore, The Mother aim at the evolution of the individual, nation and humanity through education. As The Mother said, "Collective progress and individual progress are interdependent. Before the individual can take a leap forward, it is necessary that something of an antecedent progress is achieved in the collective life. A way has therefore to be found whereby the two-fold progress can go on simultaneously."[21] This evolution will be continued and spiral. It is hence that The Mother aims at nothing less than supramental education. Evolution involves not

only adjustment but a more intimate harmony. In the words of N.C Dowsett, The Mother's education aims, "to educate the true individual potential within each student, to help him to manifest that within him which is uniquely his, so that he may find that as a perfection to be offered to life as his individual contribution to a collective perfection which is the evolving spirit of man and true heritage to which he aspires,"[22] This evolution can be achieved by man's opening and uniting with the universal divine. In other words, this requires divine perfection.

4. *Humanisation*: Education, according to The Mother, as according to Swami Vivekananda, aims at man-making. The individual and the nation have to grow as members of one humanity. The Mother's system of national education ultimately aims at evolution of humanity. Describing the aims of Sri Aurobindo's international university at Pondicherry, The Mother declared, "It is in answer to this pressing need that Sri Aurobindo conceived the scheme of his International University, so that the elite of humanity may be made ready who would be able to work for the progressive unification of the face and who at the same time would be prepared to embody the new force descending upon earth to transform it."[23]

5. *Harmony of the individual and collectivity*: While most of the thinkers in social political field have either laid emphasis upon the individual or the collectivity, Tie Mother aims at realisation of harmony between individuals and also between nations. Her scheme of education, therefore, is truly international. It is not only for India but also for the world. Explaining this ideal, The Mother said, "For all world organisation, to be real and to be able to alive, must be based upon mutual respect and understanding between nation and nation as well as between individual and individual. It is only in the collective order and organisation, in a collaboration based upon mutual goodwill that lies the possibility of man being lifted out of the painful chaos where he is now. It is with this aim and in this spirit that all human problems will be studied at the University Centres and their solutions will be given in the light of the Supramental knowledge which Sri Aurobindo has revealed in his writtings."[24]

6. *Building the innate powers*: The central aim of education, according to The Mother, is the building of the powers of the

human mind and spirit. To the question what should be the guiding principle of the new ideal of education? She replied, "Truth, harmony, liberty." Again, to the question what is the way of making the consciousness of human unity grow in man? she said, "Spiritual Education, that is to say, an education which gives more importance to the growth of the spirit than to any religious or moral teaching or to the material so-called knowledge,"[25] The child is born with certain innate powers of the body, the vital, the mini and the spirit The aim of the school and the teacher is to develop these powers to their perfection. For this a programme of sense training, body building, character formation, development of logical and other mental faculties, religious education and finally a training of integral yoga is necessary. Moral development and aesthetic development should go side by side. Explaining this integral aim of education The Mother said, "Education to be complete must have five principal aspects relating to the five principal activities of the human being: the physical, the vital, the mental, the psychic and the spiritual. Usually these phases of education succeed each other in a chronological order following the growth of the individual This, however, does not mean that one should replace another but that all must continue, completing each other, till the end of life."[26]

7. *Cultivation of values*: The present crisis of man is due to a chaos of value. Old values have been challenged while new values have not firmly taken their place. One finds momentum towards crude materialism of what Sri Aurobindo has called the economic man. Pointing out the need of cultivation of higher values The Mother said, "In a general way, education, culture, refinement of the senses are the means of curing movements of crude instinct and desire and passion. To obliterate them is not curing them; instead they should be cultivated, intellectualised, refined. That is the surest way of curing them. To give them their maximum growth in view of the progress and development of consciousness, so that one may attain to a sense of harmony and exactitude of perception is a part of culture and education for the human being."[27] The values to be cultivated should be physical mental as well as spiritual Character formation very much depends on value. The supreme value in The Mother's thought is harmony. Other values are: spirituality, divinity, evolution, ascent, transformation etc. All these must be cherished and developed. But the most important value required for all growth is sincerity. Once that is

developed the rest follows. Eight emotions and *sanskaras*, *svabhava* and nature are the foundation of The Mother's scheme of education. The Mother not only aims at moral status but at going beyond it, rising above virtue and vice. This is the supramental status aimed at by both the individual and collectivity in The Mother's thought.

Individual Aims of Education

Sri Aurobindo has aptly pointed out that "The true basis of education is the study of human mind because any system of education founded on theories of academic perfection, which ignore the instruments of study is more likely to hamper and impair intellectual growth than to produce a perfect or perfectly equipped mind."[28] Clarifying the value of the individualist aim of education The Mother said, "The first aim then will be to help individuals to become conscious of the fundamental genius of the nation to which they belong and at the same time to put them in contact with the modes of living of other nations so that they may know and respect equally the true spirit of all the countries upon earth."[29] Thus the individualist aim of education is to make a person a true unit of the nation as well as humanity. This is so since nation and humanity are the wider expressions of the Divine in man. Otherwise, The Mother agrees with the age old wisdom that sole aim of education is 'know thyself.' The educational aim of the parents and the teachers is to help the educand to know himself. To quote The Mother, "Fundamentally the only thing you must do assiduously is to teach them to know themselves, and to choose their own destiny, the way they want to follow. Teach them to look at themselves, to understand themselves — and to will by themselves. This is much more important than to teach them what happened upon earth once upon a time or even how the earth is built, or even...."[30]

Explaining the meaning of knowing oneself in more details The Mother said, "To know oneself means to know the motives of one's actions and reactions, the why and the how of all that happens in oneself".[31] While the first *sutra* of the individual aim of education is 'know thyself' the other is 'be thyself,' The Mother explained, "To master oneself means to do what has decided to do, to do nothing but that, not to listen to or follow impulses, desires or fancies."[32]

Thus to be oneself one requires transformation. In her philosophy of education The Mother has brought to light the ultimate principles of life with balanced appreciation of the multifarious values of life. The educative system based on it must start with a penetrative insight into the meaning of life, The aphoristic premise of The Mother's theory of integral education is that all has to be accepted but all has to be transformed. But if any transformation is to be brought it can possibly be achieved only by the full emergence of the spirit, its power of super mind, it means that it must make inconscient conscious, it must change the mental into the supramental being, spiritualize our material substance and erect its laws gnostic consciousness in our whole evolutionary being and natures. This process which makes the supramental evolution possible is called "education" in The Mother's terminology. *Prima facie*, if body, life and mind are not taken up in their wholeness and transformed there can be no evolution in any field either education or any other. "To recapitulate in brief: one must gain a full knowledge of one's character and then gain control over one's movements so that one may achieve perfect mastery and transformation of all the elements that have to be transformed."[33]

There can be no doubt that a true education would be an integral process by which individualisation, universalisation and transcendentalisation occurs since the educational philosophy will depend on its concept of man and the values which it considers worthy of human pursuits. Thus there is a vast variation in the prevailing concepts of education and the corresponding aims towards which it works to lead. An empiricist like Locke would advocate that mind is an empty chamber, a *tabula rasa* which has nothing in it, except a power to receive passively impressions from the outside world. Accordingly, education was taken as the process of learning through experience with the outside world and working towards the realisation of individual happiness through the senses. Similar view is held by great educationist Johann Friedrich Herbart that experience is the source of knowledge. Accordingly, the environment in which a child is placed is of greater importance because it is the environment from where he receives impressions to fashion his personality. It is for the teacher to determine which impressions the educand should receive.

The Mother advocates her theories of education in favour of

striving for freedom from imitations and the progress of individuality. She repudiates the apotheosis of the law of the guiding principles of evolution since the conquest which supplies the chief dynamic element in culture advance. It means that education according to The Mother must be helpful for the free untrammelled low of the life current, since according to her view, "spiritualty respects the freedom of human soul, because it is itself fulfilled by freedom, and the deepest meaning of freedom is the power to expand and grow towards perfection by the laws of one's own nature, dharma."[34] However, The Mother warns, "Do not mistake liberty for licence and freedom for bad manners. The thoughts must be pure and the aspiration ardent."[35]

The Mother said, "The business of both parent and teacher is to enable and to help the child to educate himself, to develop his own intellectual, moral, aesthetic and practical capacities and to grow freely as an organic being, not to be kneaded and pressured into form like an inert plastic material."[36] When the aim of education, according to The Mother, is to make explicit the potentialities of the individual, importance should be attached to the individuality of the learner. In the first phase of manifestation of the Absolute, the inconscient matter gives rise to that separative consciousness that provokes the individual ego to realise its differences from all the individual centres. But at a higher stage of evolution these barriers of individuality are to be broken so that education may lead to the perfection of the individual in his powers. Here The Mother seems to have come closer to Rousseau who holds that the object of education is not to make a soldier, magistrate or a priest but to make a man in all other things being only bye-products of aiming at the improvement of his inner worth as an end in itself. However, it is necessary to realize that the purpose of education is to liberate an individual from the bondage of environment without destroying connection with it and in this process, the individuals are of supreme worth. Thus the hallmark of education of The Mother is a quest for freedom, but freedom has a very wide connotation as it covers the freedom of man, unity of mankind, divinity of man and a will to perfection. It means that the ultimate aim of life is spiritual which can be realised through a knowledge of unity and identity and it becomes a fundamental principle of the educational theory of The Mother that the individual may be lifted from narrow individuality to richer perspective and harmony of life through the value appreciation and make him one with the universal This is the real freedom. To this point The Mother would agree with the doctrine of making an individual realise that the essence of individual is to be one with the universality.

The individual aim of education does not imply that it is intended for one individual alone, because, in view of the close relationship between them, the individual and society cannot be dissociated from each other. But when we talk of the individual aims of education, we imply those objectives of education which seek to benefit the individual alone. It is possible that these may even go against the interests of society. The first, individual aim of education is to fit the individual to earn his livelihood so that he can earn money and satisfy his own and his family's normal needs. The second individual objective is the individual's mental development. Without this, he finds it difficult to understand and to solve the problems of his life. Mental development includes education through a formal syllabi, Knowledge of language enables the individual to exchange ideas with other people and to take advantage of the social heritage, secure in the form of books. It is said that the body is the only means of achieving fulfilment. Hence, another aim of education is to develop the body. In addition to mental and physical development, education must also allow for moral and spiritual development, because without these no individual can even dream of complete development.

Social Aim of Education

Emphasising the social aim of education The Mother said, "For all world organisation, to be real and to be able to live, must be based upon mutual respect and understanding between nation and nation as well as between individual and individual. It is only in the collective order and organisation, in a collaboration based upon mutual goodwill that lies the possibility of man being lifted out of the painful chaos where he is now."[37] Man lives in society and acquires socialization through his contact with his family, his relatives, his neighbours and friends. He learns the ways of moving in society of talking to people, of mutual behaviour. Through these contacts with others he satisfies his own physical and psychological needs. Hence it would not be out of place to say that if education does not fulfil the social aims, it is incomplete. From the social standpoint, education must aim at developing those qualities in the individual which will help him to adjust with other members of society. Such qualities are sympathy, service, kindness, love, brotherhood, equality, etc. By developing such qualities an individual can become a useful member of society.

The aim of education in society will be determined by the nature of society and man we cherish. "The educational system which we attempt to set up" says Cole, "must depend on the kind of society we mean to live in, on the qualities in men and women on which we set the highest value and on the estimates which we make of the educability both of those who are endowed with the higher intellectual or aesthetic capacities and of ordinary people."[38] The Mother cherishes a divine society and a divine man. Hence her scheme of education aims at the achievement of the divine perfection of man as well as human society. In her philosophy of education The Mother has tried to arrive at an integral synthesis of the ideals of the East and the finding of the West. She maintains with ancient Indian seers that the ultimate aim of education is the fullest and most perfect realisation of the Divine in man. Education has always been regarded in India, "as a source of illumination and power which transforms and ennobles our nature by the progressive and harmonious development of our physical, mental, intellectual and spiritual powers and faculties."[39] In the tradition of ancient Indian system of education The Mother favours an integral education. Man aims at an integral self-realisation and education is useful to him to the extent it serves this purpose.

Meeting of East and West

Thus the aim of education in The Mother's philosophy happens to be the meeting ground of the East and West. Brought up in the West The Mother had the firsthand knowledge of the western system of education. Like Swami Vivekenanda and R.N. Tagore she was also conversant with the advantages of European system of education. Though one of the greatest admirers of ancient Indian thoughts The Mother was a votary of the synthesis of whatever is good in East and West. This synthesis is visible everywhere in her thought. Therefore, while presenting a scheme for Indian education, she advocated synthesis of Indian educational ideals along with the Westers methods and techniques.

In West education has been defined as an all-round development of the child leading to his proper adjustment in society. In Republic, Plato points out that "true education, whatever that may be, will have the greatest tendency to civilise and humanise them in their relation to one another and to those who are under their protection",[40] This humanist definition of education propounded by Plato is still the most widely accepted meaning of education in the West Education everywhere has been taken as a process of inculcating values. As Plato said, "Now I mean by education that training which is given by suitable habits to the first instincts of virtue in children."[41] These views of Plato have been universally accepted in West as well as in the East. Education has been defined differently by the idealists, the pragmatists, the naturalists and the realist philosophers. However, its meaning has been generally idealistic. Without some sort of idealism there can be no education worth the name. In the words of Robert R. Rusk, "We may accept that the aim of education is the enhancement or enrichment of personality the differentiating feature of which is the embodiment of universal values."[42] The western educational philosophers have generally agreed that the growth of the human child is the essence of education. In the words of A.G. Hughes, "The essence of discipline is, thus, not forced subordination to the will of the hatred tyrants, but submission to the example of admired superiors." In the middle ages Comenius declared education to be a process whereby an individual developed qualities relating to religion, knowledge and morality, and thereby established his claim to be called a human being, "The fundamental principles of education", according to F.A. Froebel, "instruction and teaching should be passive and protective not directive and interfering."[43] The principle of liberty has found most eloquent expression in the definition of education given by J.J. Rousseau when he said, "Let us obey the call of Nature. We shall see that her yoke is easy and that when we give heed to her voice we find the joy in the answer of a good conscience,"[44]

Others have laid emphasis upon the social meaning of education whereby it aims at making an individual fit in the society. It was in this sense that Aldous Huxley said, "A perfect education is one which trains up every human being to fit into the place he or she is to occupy in the social hierarchy, but without in the process, destroying fats or her individuality."[45]

All the foregoing definitions have stated that education is the process of development. It, therefore, becomes necessary to discover what is implied in this development Although the ability to learn depends upon development, but development is not synonymous with education. Development means the gradual and continuous progress of mind and body. Through this development the child acquires the following, elements:

1. Knowledge of the environment by which he is surrounded;
2. The necessary motor control to fulfil his individual needs;
3. Linguistic abilities to enable him to converse;
4. Some knowledge of individual and collective relationships.

The development of all these elements begin at home itself.

The educator's task is to continue this process and to encourage it while the child is at school.

In fact, this process of development continues right through an individual's lifetime. Consequently, it is accepted that education in its general sense continues throughout a man's natural span of life. Even the successful teacher or educator himself remains a student throughout his life. He teaches certain things to some people but at the same time he learns something from them. All the successful educators experience that the development undergone by their thoughts, personalities and abilities would have been impossible otherwise. In much the same way, people other than the educators, teach and learn, simultaneously.

In her detailed instructions and expeditions concerning the education of the child The Mother has agreed to the above-mentioned meaning of education. In her new method of teaching children she has asked the teachers to have sufficient knowledge, through intellectual and intuitive attitude, mental silence and a sympathetic attitude to the child. Both the educand and the educator must grow together. Advising the teachers she said, "Only a discerning affection that is firm yet gentle and an adequate practical knowledge will create the bonds of trust that are indispensable for you to be able to educate your child effectively. And do not forget that you have to control yourself constantly in order to be equal to your task and truly fulfil the duty which you owe your child by the mere fact of having brought him into the world."[46]

References

1. *Collected Works of The Mother (C.W.M.), Centenary Edition*, Vol. 12 (1977), p. 120.

2. *Bulletin of Physical Education* (November, 1950), p. 41
3. *Ibid,* (November, 1965), pp. 48-49.
4. *Ibid* (April, 1970), p. 41.
5. *Ibid* (April, 1072), p. 45.
6. C.W.M. Vol. 9 (1979), p. 218.
7. *Ibid.*, pp. 218-219.
8. *Ibid.*, p. 219.
9. *Ibid.*
10. *Ibid.*, p. 220.
11. *Ibid.*, p. 221.
12. Sri Aurobindo, *Collected Works*, Birth Centenary Edi., Vol. 15, p. 138.
13. *Sri Aurobindo and The Mother on The Aim of Life*, Part I (1973), p. 30.
14. *Answers given by The Mother* on 5.8.65.
15. *Sri Aurobindo and The Mother on India* (1973), p. 30.
16. *Ibid.*, p. 31.
17. *Ibid.*, pp. 32-33.
18. *C.W.M.*, Vol. 12 (1978), p. 120.
19. *Ibid.*
20. *Sri Aurobindo and The Mother On Education*, Part I (1973), p. 26.
21. *Ibid.*, p. 25.
22. Dowsett, N.C., *The Psychology for Future Education* (Pondicherry: Sri Aurobindo Ashram, 1977), p. 13.
23. *Ibid.*, pp. 25-26.
24. *Sri Aurobindo and The Mother On Education*, Part I (1973), p. 23.
25. *Ibid.*, p. 3.
26. *Ibid.*, p. 5.
27. *C.W.M.*, Vol. 12 (1978), p. 121.
28. Sri Aurobindo, *A System of National Education*, p. 11.
29. *Sri Aurobindo and The Mother on Education*, Part I (1973), p. 28.
30. *Bulletin of Physical Education* (November 1960), p. 29.
31. *Ibid.* (February 1951), p. 17.
32. *Ibid.*
33. *Ibid.* (November 1951), p. 33.
34. Indra Sen, *The Message and Mission of Indian Culture*, pp. 11-12.
35. *Sri Aurobindo and The Mother on Education*, Pt. III (1973), p. 22.
36. *Bullentin of Physical Education* (August 1964), p. 43.
37. *Sri Aurobindo and The Mother on Education*, Part I (1973), p. 28.
38. Cole, G.D.H., *Essays in Social Theory* (London: MacMillan & Co., 1950), p. 47.
39. Altekar, A.S., *Education in Ancient India* (Banaras: The Indian Book Shop, 1934), p. 8.
40. Plato, *Republic*, Jowett, 416.
41. Plato, *Laws*, Jowett, 653.

42. Robert R. Rusk, *The Philosophical Bases of Education* (London: University of London Press, 1956), p. 154.
43. *Froebel's Chief Educational Writings on Education*, Translated by Dr. Fletcher, p. 32.
44. Rousseau, J.J. *Emile* (London: J.M. Dents & Sons, 1950), p. 151.
45. Huxley, A., *Proper Studies* (London: Chatto & Windus, 1928), p. 136.
46. *C.W.M.*, Vol. 12 (1978), p. 11.

3

Aims and Ideals of Education: Indian

Meaning of Education in India

Turning to the Indian approach, it becomes necessary to include the spiritual aspect also because it is accepted as a part of the development by education. In fact, Indian thinkers have placed special emphasis upon this. Yajnavalkya opined that only that is education which gives a sterling character to an individual and renders him useful for the world. Sankaracharya said that education is that which leads to salvation. Even the more recent educationists have stressed the importance of the spiritual aspect. It may be seen in the works of contemporary Indian philosophers of education in their integral approach, synthesis of idealism and pragmatism, rationalism and humanism, diversity in unity and harmony of the individual and society. It was due to this emphasis on the spiritual meaning of education that Swami Vivekananda said, "Religion is the innermost core of education."[1] In the words of Sri Aurobindo, "The child's education ought to be an outbringing of all that is best, most powerful, most intimate and living in his nature, the mould into which the man's action and development ought to run is that of his innate quality and power. He must acquire new things but he will acquire them best, most wholly, on the basis of his own developed type and inborn force."[2] M.K. Gandhi expressed the same idea when he defined education by saying, "By education I mean an all round drawing out of the best in child and man, body, mind and spirit. Literacy is not the end of education not even the beginning. It is one of the means whereby man and woman can be educated. Literacy in itself is no education."[3] In keeping with the ancient Indian ideal of education as liberation (*Sa Vidya Ya Vunuktaya*), The Mother has said, "To pursue an integral education that leads to the supramental realisation, four austerities are necessary, and with them four liberations."[4] However, Sri Aurobindo international university itself was an example of the meeting of East and West. Explaining why the university has been called international The Mother said. "Therefore, the International University Centre will be international not because students from all countries will be admitted here, nor because the education will be given in their own mother tongue, but particularly because the cultures of the different regions of lie earth will be represented here in such a way as to be accessible to all, not merely intellectually in ideas, theories, principles and languages, but also vitally in habits and customs, in art under all forms — painting, sculpture, music, architecture, decoration — and physically too through natural scenery, dress, games, sports, industries and food."[5] Advocating the meeting of East and West in more clear terms. The Mother said, "India has or rather had the knowledge of the Spirit, but she neglected matter and suffered for it. The West has the knowledge of matter but rejected the Spirit and suffers badly for it. An integral education which could, with some variations, be adapted to all the nations of the world, must bring back the legitimate authority of the Spirit over a matter fully developed and utilised,"[6]

Supramental Aim

True education again, is ultimately supramental' education, that which leads to our evolution towards the supramental. This supramental evolution however, will necessarily pass through and only after the evolution of the physical, the vital, the mental and the psychic. Physical education is the education of the body. It includes the order, discipline, plasticity and receptivity of the body. Its principal aspects are: "(1) Control and discipline of functions; (2) a total, methodical and harmonious development of all the parts and movements of the body; and (3) rectification of defects and deformities, if there are any."[7] The vital education is indispensable, though difficult. It is so since the nature of vital has been often misunderstood. In the words of The Mother the vital education involves two principal aspects, "The first is to develop and utilise the sense organs, the second is to become conscious and gradually master of one's character and in the end to achieve its transformation."[8] Thus vital education includes sense training and the development of character. This character again will be developed according to individual differences. It requires redirection and transformation of the instincts and emotions, drives and propensities. Describing the mental education The Mother has laid down the following five phases:[9]

1. Development of the power of concentration, the capacity of attention.

2. Development of the capacities of expansion, wideness, complexity and richness.

3. Organisation of ideas around a central idea or a higher ideal or a supremely luminous idea that will serve as a guide in life.

4. Thought control, rejection of undesirable thoughts so that one may, in the end, think only that one wants and when one wants.

5. Development of mental silence, perfect calm and a more and more total receptivity to inspiration coming from the higher regions of the being.

While the physical, vital and mental education are the means to develop the personality, the psychic education alone leads to the future evolution of man. The Mother's system of education does not aim only at the adjustment and normal development of the human personality but its total growth and transformation. The idea of psychic education has not been developed in any existing philosophy of education. It is so since psychic element was never considered and understood by the Western educationists. In India also in spite of the importance of psychic element found in Yoga, its nature has been seldom understood. The core of the psychic principles in us. This may be reached by psychological, religious or mechanical methods. Everyone will have to find out the method best suitable to him and his aspiration. The psychic education requires sincere and steady aspiration, a persistent and dynamic will, concentration, meditation, revelation and experience. In the words of The Mother, "Only one thing is absolutely indispensable: the will to discover and realise."[10] This is in fact the field of occult and yoga which will be discussed in detail in sequence.

Thus the supramental education requires the above steps as a prelude to its realisation. It is only so far as one gets through the physical, vital, mental and psychic education and realises a certain transformation that one can enter into supramental education. To quote The Mother again, "Then will begin also a new education which can be called the supramental education; it will by its all-powerful action work not only upon the consciousness of individual beings, but upon the very substance of which they are built and upon the environment in which they live,"[11] The idea of supramental education like that of the psychic education is The Mother's significant contribution to the field of education. This is more important at the present juncture when most of the educationists are realising the need for an educational system aiming at man-making. According to The Mother humanity today has already reached what has been called by hint a subjective stage. The future evolution has to be above the mental level. This will require great and persistent efforts.

Integral Education

True education, according to The Mother, is not only spiritual but also rational, vital and physical. In other words, it is an integral education. This integral education has been explained by The Mother, in these words, "Education to be complete must have five principal aspects relating to the five principal activities of the human being: the physical, the vital, the mental, the psychic and the spiritual. Usually these phases of education succeed each other in a chronological order following the growth of the individual. This, however, does not mean that one should replace another but that all must continue, completing each other, till the end of life."[12] The Mother's scheme of education is integral in two senses. Firstly, it is integral in the sense of including all the aspects of the individual being, physical, vital, mental, psychic and spiritual. Secondly, it is integral in the sense of being an education not only for the evolution of the individual alone but also of the national and finally of the humanity.

Explaining the integral aim of education, The Mother said, "Your aim should be high and wide, generous and disinterested; this will make your life precious to yourself and to others. But whatever your ideal, it cannot be perfectly realised unless you have realised perfection in yourself. To work for your perfection, the first step is to become conscious of yourself, of the different parts of our being and their respective activities".[13] Thus integral education includes physical education, vital education, mental education, moral education, religious education and finally spiritual education. She has discussed these in great details. Therefore, in the present work, each of these has been dealt with in a separate chapter. For the present, it may be noted that integral education aims at perfection. Perfection is achieved through unification of the various constituents of the human individual and collectivity. Therefore, integral education requires purification and unification. It is based upon a four-fold discipline, the four austerities. In other words, the method of integral education is the method of fourfold discipline. This four-fold discipline aims at a four-fold perfection. This four-fold perfection results in four-fold liberation. In the words of The Mother, "When we reach this degree of perfection which is our goal, we shall perceive that the truth we seek is made up of for major aspects: Love, Knowledge, Power and Beauty. These four attributes of the Truth will express themselves spontaneously in our being. The psychic will be the vehicle of true and pure love, the mind will be the vehicle of infallible knowledge, the vital will manifest an invincible power and strength and the body will be the expression of a perfect beauty and harmony."[14]

The Four Austerities and the Four Liberations

The Mother has written, "To pursue an integral education that leads to the supramental realisation, four austerities are necessary, and with them four liberations."[15] Incidentally, this aim of education agree with the ancient Indian definition of education as that which leads to liberation. The Mother has however explained liberation more integrally, as the liberation of psychic, the mental, the vital and even the physical in the individual and collectivity. Life on earth, according to her, aims at perfection. Therefore, from the philosophical viewpoint, education should naturally aim at perfection. This perfection, however, is not asceticism. The Mother has deplored self-mortification as unhealthy and sadistic. She wrote, "In reality, these things are very far removed from all spiritual life, for they are ugly and base, dark and diseased; whereas spiritual life, on the contrary, is a life of light and balance, "beauty and joy".[16] Thus, like Gautama Buddha The Mother rejected all ascetic practices as cruel and abnormal. She supported equanimity and serenity. Therefore, the meaning of the word austerity or *Tapasya* should be taken in a positive sense. This positive approach is marked by harmony, purity and balance and rejects asceticism, over-indulgence and cruelty.

Outlining her four-fold discipline for the achievement of fourfold liberation The Mother said, "This is why we shall have recourse to the four austerities which will result in four liberations within us. The practice of these austerities will constitute a four-fold discipline or *tapasya* which can be defined as follows:

1. *Tapasya* of love
2. *Tapasya* of knowledge
3. *Tapasya* of power
4. *Tapasya* of beauty"[17]

Thus austerity of beauty leads to physical perfection, austerity of power leads to vital perfection, austerity of knowledge leads to mental perfection and finally austerity of love leads to psychic perfection. All these result in corresponding liberations. It should be remembered here that The Mother has identified perfection with liberation. Liberation is the result of perfection. For example, if the body has achieved perfection, the man will be liberated from all physical limitations, difficulties, deformities and bondages. Similarly in order to achieve liberation of vital one must realise perfection of the vital. While the physical perfection aims at beauty, the vital perfection aims at power. Similarly, mind can be liberated only through knowledge and the psychic can be liberated only through love. In this scheme the means of liberation are positive. Explaining further her four-fold discipline, The Mother wrote, "These terms have been listed from top to bottom, so to say, but their order should not be taken to indicate anything superior or inferior, or more or less difficult, or the order in which these disciplines can and ought to be practised. The order, importance and difficulty vary with, each individual and no absolute rule can be formulated. Each one must find and work out his own system according to his personal needs and capacities."[18] Thus integral perfection should not be understood in sequence. It is a simultaneous process. Love, knowledge, power aid beauty are achieved simultaneously and not successively. There is no sequence or order in these four aims. However, psychologically the order of these will vary according to individual differences. It has been an old belief in India that different persons should adopt different paths to their perfection according to their inherent nature and capacities. Thus while the *Brahmins* pursued knowledge, the *Kshatriyas* pursued power. Man, according to The Mother, is a complex whole involving at least the physical, the vital, the mental and the psychic components of personality, These again, vary in different individuals.

It has been accepted by modern science that human beings differ in these aspects of personality. While different races differ in physical and mental characteristics, within the same race also human beings show a large variation of physical and mental characteristics. For example, in the sub-continent that is called India one finds all shades of complexion, type of hair, structures of body and other physical characteristics. Same is the case with vital and mental characteristics. Therefore, it is now generally agreed that all growth and evolution should take into consideration the primary fact of individual differences. Hence The Mother does not claim any finality in her statements. She has however, tried to make her system more and more complete. As she puts it, "Accordingly, only an overall view will be given here, presenting an ideal procedure that is as complete as possible. Each one will then have to apply as much of it as he can in the best possible way."[19]

In the above-mentioned four austerities the actual growth starts from the lowest and proceeds to the highest. Therefore, The Mother has explained the four austerities in the sequence of bottom to top.

1. *Tapasya of Beauty:* Explaining the first step in the goal of liberation The Mother wrote, "The *Tapasya* or discipline of beauty will lead us, through austerity in physical life, to freedom in action. Its basic programme will be to build a body that is beautiful in form, harmonious in posture, supple and agile in its movements, powerful in its activities and robust in its health and organic functioning."[20]

In the discipline of beauty, material life should be organised with the help of regular routine and corresponding habits. One must however, avoid being slave to one's habits. The Mother has advised flexibility in life. This flexibility leads to endurance. The Mother has cautioned that the body should not be unnecessarily over-burdened. Otherwise, as she puts it, "A physical culture which aims at building a body capable of serving as a fit instrument for a higher consciousness demands very austere habits: a great regularity in sleep, food, exercise and every activity."[21] The quantity of sleep, food, exercise and every activity will be determined by each individual himself. But once a rule is made, no exceptions should be allowed to violate the rule. Thus The Mother condemns all weakness and escapade. She recommends a sensible and regular life concentrating attention on building a perfect body. And the old rule that excess is always bad, should be followed. The consumption of the slow poisons like tobacco and alcohol must be eschewed. It is an old belief in India that as yon eat so you become. In the case of sleep also everybody should follow his own rule. Moderation and not excess however, is the general principle. The Mother suggests that the quality of sleep is more important than its quantity. The activities of the day and night should be sensibly organised. About the exercises The Mother prescribes, "With regard to exercises each one will choose the ones best suited to his body and, if possible take guidance from an expert on the subject, who knows how to combine and grace the exercises to obtain a maximum effect."[22] The choice and execution of the physical exercises should not be governed by fancy, amusement, ostentation, distinction or any other mundane aim. Similarly, in work also perfection should be aimed. Explaining the austerity of work, The Mother said, "Whatever occupation or task falls to your lot, you must do it with a will to progress: whatever one does, one must not only do it as best one can but strive to do it better and better in a constant effort for perfection."[23] This leads to liberation in action since it makes one free from all social conventions and moral prejudices. About sex, The Mother has supported the ancient ideal of *Brahmacharya*, advocated by almost all the contemporary Indian philosophers of education. With them, she agrees that the only reason for sexual act is the birth of the child and never physical pleasure. Therefore she prescribes, "Countenance is therefore the rule for all those who aspire for progress."[24] This countenance should lead to total voluntary abstinence and transformation. The sexual impulses and desires should be totally eliminated from the physical, the vital and the mental level. Then alone, a total physical transformation may be achieved. This approach may appear impractical and ascetic. It should be however, remembered that The Mother's aim of education was not pleasure, success or adjustment but perfection. Therefore, he has asked for renunciation from all pleasure seeking. As she puts it, "One must refuse pleasure if one wants to open to the delight of existence, in a total beauty and harmony."[25] It should be noted here that this is not a negative approach. On the contrary, it is more positive than other approaches since pleasure has been negated to achieve the more positive ideals of delight, beauty and harmony. In fact. The Mother's system of education requires transvaluation of all values hitherto presented by the educationists. Education, for her, seeks' total transformation. Therefore her prescriptions should be viewed from the point of view of perfection and liberation.

2. *Tapasya of Power: Tapasya* of power is the austerity of the vital being. The vital being is the seat of power. It has three successes of subsistence: from the physical energies through sensations, by contact with the universal vital forces and finally, by the infusion and absorption of spiritual forces and inspiration. The Mother strongly condemns the interchange of vital forces among human beings which has been ordinarily called love, but which, according to her, is only infatuation. According to her, "It is by enlightening, strengthening and purifying the vital, and not by weakening it, that one can contribute to the true progress of the being."[26] Therefore, the senses should be made perfect. They should aim at harmony, beauty and good health. Sensations are the food for vital and the vital should not be starved. He Mother condemns all negative approach, all repressions and suppressions. She, on the other hand, asks for refinement and transformation. As she puts it, "It is by educating the vital, by making it more refined, more sensitive, more subtle and, one should almost say, more elegant, in the test sense of the word, that one can overcome its violence and brutality, which are in fact a form of crudity and ignorance, of lack of taste."[27] Thus one should aim at a cultivated and illumined vital. This is characterised by perseverance and sincerity. The vital education aims at substituting petty satisfactions by divine delight.

3. *Tapasya of Knowledge:* Tapasya of knowledge is the austerity of the mind. It aims at mental perfection. This, first of all, requires control of one's speech. The Mother has decried the tendency of using speech for various unrefined purposes, She shows a rare insight in psychology when she points out that too much speaking, gossiping, useless arguing, vain speeches are the signs of weak mental power. Those who are born orators say what they want to say and say it well There should be no ideal talking. Various categories of spoken word should be classified according to their need in physical domain, social life and speaking about others. As a general rule, the less one speaks of others the better it is. One must never speak ill of others. Speech should never be used

for favour or opposition since, as The Mother points out, "He, the divine workers, is free from all preferences and all attachment; he has broken down the limits of his ego and is now only a perfectly pure and impersonal instrument of the supramental action upon earth."[28]

The Mother even condemns argumentation and the so called academic discussion, since they are mostly guided by narrow and petty aims. One must observe balance and moderation in one's speech. One must reject all sectarianism, Lastly, in teaching itself brevity is the soul of communication. The Mother rejects all speech on the part of the teacher, for relaxation, amusement and entertainment. The teacher should not unnecessarily describe even his spiritual experiences. Silence is the golden rule both for the teacher and the disciple. Even the Divine is subject to the same law. To quote, the beautiful words of The Mother, "Thus even the embodied god cannot be perfect on earth until men are ready to understand and accept perfection. That day will come when everything that is now done out of a sense of duty towards the Divine will be done out of love for Him. Progress will be a joy instead of being an effort and often even a struggle. Or, more exactly, progress will be made in joy, with the full adherence of the whole being, instead of by coercing the resistance of the ego, which entails great effort and sometimes even great suffering."[29]

4. *Tapasya of Love:* The fourth austerity is concerning love. This is the most difficult and yet the most important since it aims at perfection of the psychic. It is the austerity of feelings and emotions. Since ancient times love has been an important force in human life. Methods have been suggested for controlling its force but the rules were broken again and again. According to The Mother, the power of love cannot be disciplined by mental or social rules. In integral psychology, propounded by Sri Aurobindo and The Mother, each component of human personality has its own liberty, its own laws. Each must develop and evolve. No one should suppress, repress and even control the other. Thus only a higher emotion can control a lower emotion. This is the theory of sublimation and evolution. The old practice of trying to control the infarctional element by rational principles involves repression and consequent abnormalities. Therefore, the western psychologists have agreed to keep man in the middle. The concept of normality, according to contemporary abnormal psychology involves the

average. The psychologist is busy raising the below normal to normal but also pulling down the super normal to normal. Against this psycholop of leveling down integral psycholop maintains freedom and equality of all the elements in human personality. Thus the body is now low, neither should it be subjected to mortification. It too may be transformed. Similar is the case with feelings and emotions. There, The Mother said, "Only love can rule over love by enlightening, transforming and exalting it For here too, more than anywhere else, control does not consist of suppression and abolition but of transmutation — a sublime alchemy. This is because, of all the forces at work in the universe, love is the most powerful, the most irresistible. Without love the world would fall back into the chaos of inconscience."[30]

Explaining the nature of love The Mother said, "Love is, in its essence, the joy of identity; it finds its ultimate expression in the bliss of union. Between the two lie all the phases of its universal manifestation"[31] Love starts between two complementary poles. Psychologically, it involves attraction as well as surrender. It is the meeting of consciousness. It involves physical and vital nature and is therefore corrupted. In animals it involves instinctive life. Among human beings however, it is enlightened and therefore expresses in sacrifice. The purpose of Nature behind the force of love is to help creative evolution. This purpose however, has been degraded by confusing love with sex. The Mother traces the history of love in human society and points out that it is the basis of group formations such as families, clans, tribes, castes, classes and even the nations. This process of union should inevitably lead to human unity through love. Thus love ultimately aims at human unity. It is here that its circle is completed. This is the divine love, the highest evolution of feelings and emotions. All lesser expressions must be rejected. In the words of The Mother, "For one who has known love for the Divine, all other forms of love are obscure and too mixed with pettiness and egoism and darkness; they are like a perpetual haggling or a struggle for supremacy and domination, and even among the best they are full of misunderstanding and irritability, of friction and incomprehension."[32] As you love so you become. Thus in order to become Divine one must love Divine. This should be an absolute surrender. All lesser attachments must be subordinated to this highest love. It requires absolute consecration and integral identification. In the words of The

Mother, "In seminary, austerity in feelings consists them of giving up all emotional attachment, of whatever nature, whether for a person, for the family, for the country or anything else, in order to concentrate on an exclusive attachment for the Divine Reality. This concentration will eliminate in an integral identification and will be instrumental to the supramental realisation upon earth,"[33]

Four-fold Liberation

As has been already pointed out, the four-fold austerities are the four-fold discipline leading to four-fold perfection and fourfold liberation. Thus the austerities of love, knowledge, power and beauty respectively lead to the liberation of psychic, mental, vital and physical. This has been explained, by The Mother as follows: "This leads us quite naturally to the four liberations which will be the concrete forms of this achievement."[34] These four-fold liberations are as follows:

1. *Psychic Liberation:* This is the liberation from suffering. It leads to a total realisation of the supramental oneness.

2. *Mental Liberation*: This is the liberation from ignorance. It leads to the mind of light or gnostic consciousness.

3. *The Vital Liberation*: This is the liberation from desire. It gives the individual the power to identify itself perfectly and consciously with the divine will. It brings constant peace and serenity as well as the power resulting from peace and serenity.

4. *Physical Liberation*: This is the liberation from the law of material cause and effect. It results in total self-mastery. The man is no more a slave of nature's laws. He is no more forced by subconscious and semi-conscious impulses. One may now take up the path of full knowledge, choose the action freely and march towards the highest will, the truest knowledge, the supramental consciousness.

The concept of four-fold austerities and the resultant four-fold liberation, as advanced by The Mother, has far reaching implications. It lays down the aim of education as a four-fold perfection. This aim is integral since it maintains diversity in unity. Most of the educational aims suffer from one-sidedness. The philosophers of education have subordinated body to mind or mind to body, feelings to reasoning or reasoning to feelings. Different philosophers have supported knowledge, love, power or beauty or subordinated the one to the other. Some decried power, others rejected beauty. The Mother however, allows maximum growth to each component of human personality, the physical, the vital, the mental and the psychic. None of these is subordinated to the other. The educand has not only to attain knowledge but also built up a beautiful body. He has to develop power of the vital being as well as attain divine love and psychic transformation. Not only the aims but also the means of education are four-fold. Four-fold austerities provide the means of education. No single discipline is sufficient as the educand has a diversity of components. While the discipline of beauty leads to physical perfection, mental perfection requires discipline of knowledge. The means of vital perfection is the discipline of power while psychic perfection is attained by discipline of love. Thus the concept of four-fold austerities, four-fold perfection and four-fold liberation provide integral aims and integral means of education through love. It is a complete philosophy of education, both for the educand and the educator, the individual and the group and finally for the nation as well as humanity. It is a blueprint for the establishment of kingdom of God upon earth.

References

1. Swami Vivekananda, Collected Works, Vol. V, p. 161.
2. Sri Aurobindo, *Essays on the Gita* (Calcutta: Arya Publishing House, 1949), p. 319.
3. Gandhi, M.K., Harijan, 31-7-37.
4. *C.W.M.*, Vol.12 (1978), p. 48.
5. *Sri Aurobindo and The Mother on Education*, Part I, pp. 26-27.
6. *C.W.M.*, Vol.12 (1978), p. 251.
7. *Sri Aurobindo and The Mother On Education, Part I*, p. 10.
8. *Ibid.*, p. 11.
9. *Ibid.*, p. 12.
10. *Ibid.*, p. 14.
11. *bid.*, p. 16.
12. *Ibid.*, p. 8.
13. *C.W.M.*, Vol. 12 (1978), p. 3.
14. *Ibid.*, p. 8.
15. *Ibid.*, p. 48.
16. *Ibid.*, p. 49.
17. *Ibid.*, p. 50.
18. *Ibid.*
19. *Ibid.*

20. C.W.M., Vol. 12 (1978), p. 50.
21. *Ibtd.*, p 51.
22. *Ibid.*, p. 53.
23. *Ibid.*
24. *Ibid.*, p. 54.
25. *Ibid.*, p. 55.
26. *Ibid.*, p. 56.
27. *Ibid.*
28. *Ibid.*, p. 60.
29. *Ibid.*, p. 64.
30. *Ibid.*, p. 65.
31. *Ibid.*
32. *Ibid.*, p. 69.
33. *Ibid.*, p. 71.
34. *Ibid.*

4

Philosophical Foundations of Education

Education is an interdisciplinary science. Even the nature of the educand cannot be understood by any single science. It has been explored not only by psychology but also by biology, physiology, anthropology, sociology, political science, economics and a host of other border sciences. The human personality still remains unexplained. It is an old saying that in order to teach Latin to John the educator must know Latin as well as John. In order to know however, he will have to know at least more than half a dozen physical and social sciences. Modern pedagogy has been particularly influenced by psychological foundations. Besides educational psychology, adolescent psychology, physiological psychology, social psychology and almost every other branch of psychology has influenced education. Thus a sound educational theory should have a sound psychological foundation. Morse and Wingo mention four areas of psychological foundation of education: He psychology of learning, development, motivation and group behaviour.[1]

Sociology is a recent addition to human fund of knowledge. It deals with society, the web of social relationships. This web of social relations involves social institutions. The social institutions of family, peer group and state influence the process of education. Sociology explains social interaction, social control and social change. It analyses the social factors in the determinants of the child's personality. It deals with the processes of social structures, its interacting systems and various integrating forces which influence the individual and the society. In education too, we try to equip the man to unfold his self and thereby to develop, improve and modify the society he lives in. Since man lives in a social environment his potentialities are being actualised within this realm. Education tries to cater to the individual as well as the social needs and aspirations. It influences and in turn is very much influenced by the social set up, its values and norms. That is why in the last few decades the sociological foundations of education have come into prominence. Being an emerging concept, it has been quite difficult to demarcate its limits. While giving a concept of education, educationists naturally pain. the picture of the society they want to material. Sociologists define education as "the means by which society prepares within the children, the essential condition of its very existence."[2] But this is not enough. Education working as a sub-system of the total set up, changes and modifies the social behaviour, norms and tie social order. But the participation of the individual in the social consciousness is essential and education has to perform this very function. An educationist, therefore, conceives a society, working of the state and a broad social order.

At last but not the least, besides the psychological and sociological foundations, are the philosophical foundations of education. Philosophy has been the mother of sciences whether natural or social. Whether education is treated as the dynamic side of philosophy or philosophy as both the theory of education, this much is certain that both are closely knit. In the past few decades formal shapes of philosophical, psychological, sociological and economic bases have merged, though there is lack of agreement in their contents, methodology and scope of operation. The economic foundations of education have come into prominence within the last two decades. Educational activities in them are analysed utilising the economic principles. In our study here we will confine ourselves to the three areas—philosophical, psychological and sociological foundations.

Philosophical Foundations

Philosophy deals with the concepts of reality, knowledge and values. These three aspects are denoted as the three branches of philosophy viz., metaphysics, epistemology and axiology. Metaphysics deals with the questions relating to the nature of reality and its manifestations. Cosmology, which deals with the nature of the universe, is treated as a sub-category of metaphysics. The branch which deals with the theory of knowledge, its processes, sources and validation, is known as epistemology. Axiology is concerned with the questions of values. These sub-divisions are not independent but inter-related — one paying the way for the other. Theories of *episteme* and values very much involve the questions of reality.

Every educational activity involves questions of metaphysics, *episteme* and axiology- Not only crucial decisions but also the simple class activities and situations demand an understanding of values, knowing processes, its theories and questions regarding the nature of man and the world, its teleology and the like. Whether we take a decision about the goals of education, its modes and operations, criteria of curriculum formulation, methodology of teaching and learning or the principles involved in the disciplinary measures, evaluation programmes, educational environment within, the campus or the teacher-taught relations, these fundamental questions are to be answered with clarity and precision. We cannot escape even, when we study the educational activities at micro-levels. That is why the philosophical foundations have become a basic need for the study of educational doctrines. Thus philosophical foundations of education may be summarised as follows:

1. *Metaphysical Foundations*: The metaphysics, in brief, deals with reality in man, world and hereafter. This has a close bearing upon the aims and ideals of education. The metaphysical attitude provides the educationists the proper perspective for devising aims and ideals of education. What we want to make out of man depends upon his nature and place in the universe. Again, the concept of self is the basis of the development of character, the central aim of education. Know thyself and be thyself is the universally acknowledged aim of education. The concept of world is directly concerned with the individual's relationships with society and nature. While Indian philosophy emphasises harmony between man and the world the western philosophers have made too much of man's desire to overpower Mature. While the former philosophy has been the foundation of educational institutions like visva-bharati or Sri Aurobindo's International University, the other approach is the philosophy behind the technological and scientific education of today. In fact the more integral is the world view the more multisided will be the education based upon it. In the end, moral and religious education is based upon the metaphysical concept of God. This does not mean that moral education must necessarily be linked to religious education. It only shows that our explanation of the ultimate reality or the total reality, call it God or anything else, his important bearing upon education, particularly its aims and ideals and therefore its means and plans.

2. *Epistemological Foundations*: Epistemology is the branch of philosophy which is concerned with the discussion of the problems concerning knowledge. Its subject matter is the process, methods, objects, characteristics, conditions, validity and fallacies

of knowledge. Epistemology is the philosophical discussion of all these problems. Since epistemology deals with the knowing process, its product, validation and structure, it is bound to affect the structure and spirit of the educational activities. That is why philosophers have always tried to develop a theory of knowledge on which to base the educational processes.

3. *Axiological Foundations*: Education not only inculcate values, but also provides an integral format for values formation. Axiology is that branch of philosophy which deals with values and the process of valuation. It is a pertinent question as to how and what values are to be aimed at. Axiological enquiry provides an answer to these very questions. Normally, its two sub-categories — ethics and aesthetics — are being mentioned. Ethics deals with human conduct and moral order and aesthetics with the norms of beauty and art. In spite of several controversies, this much is true that education and value formation cannot be separated. Hence, the perennial question: how and what values are to be taught?

Epistemology of the Mother

According to the epistemology propounded by the Mother, "There is only one Truth as there is only one Divine."[3] However, the truth is not confined to some particular area. It is global. It is not successive but simultaneous. Agreeing with the ancient Indian approach. The Mother maintained that truth has not to be spoken but lived. She said, "Truth cannot be formulated, it cannot be defined. It is to be lived."[4] This emphasis has the educational implication of pointing out the value of experience. Truth is not a mental formula. It has to be discovered. This discovery, however, is not theoretical but practical. The Mother has everywhere emphasized the importance of encouraging the intuitive power of the educand. Distinguishing between the theoretical and practical aspects of truths she said, "Intellectually, the Truth is the point where all the opposites meet and join to make a unity. Practically, the Truth is the surrender of the ego to make possible the birth and manifestation of the Divine."[5] Thus, The Mother supports the Socratic method of dialectical approach to truth. This admits the value of diversity in unity. In her epistemology as well as in her philosophy of education, The Mother has laid emphasis upon the individual, As she puts it, "Truth is something living, moving, expressing itself each second and it is one way of approaching the Supreme. Everyone has his way of approaching the Supreme."[6] This catholic approach paves the way for meeting of the extremes not only in epistemology but also in politics, religion, ethics and education. In keeping with the ancient Indian tradition, The Mother has called truth, the *Dharma*. Thus she endorses the ancient principle that each has to follow his own *Dharma, Swadharma* and *Swadeshi* are the guiding principles in the life of the individual and the nation. To quote the Mother's words, "It is what one calls here in India, the truth of the being or the law of the being, the *Dharma* of the being, that which is the centre and the cause of the individuality."[7] Thus every child has his own importance. The educator should try to understand the nature and capacity of the individual child and instead of insisting upon his own beliefs and convictions he should pay attention to the abilities of the child. The theory of integral truth incidentally leads to an integral theory of knowledge.

In the integral theory of knowledge all theories, all principles and all statements are only half truths. They are true so far as they go but none of them is the total truth. In the philosophy of The Mother no single theory, statement, formula or expression, aim or means, method or ideal may be called the total truth. Totality is synthesis. It is wholeness, it is integrality, it is multiplicity. It is the whole. Therefore, the true thinker must develop a sense of proportion, a catholic attitude, a vision, tolerance of every view and insight into every expression of truth. As the Mother said, "All theories, all principles, all means are more or less good according to the power they have to express that truth, and as one advances on the ways, if the limits of the world of ignorance are passed, one sees that it is the totality of the manifestation, its wholeness, its integrality that is necessary for the expression of the truth, that nothing can be cut out and nothing is more important or less important. The only thing that seems necessary is the harmonisation of all and that each thing must be at its place in its true relation with the others so that the total Unity may be manifested harmoniously."[8] A complete philosophy of education may be drawn from this statement. It characteristically explains the philosophical method in education. The philosophical method is dialectical. It involves analysis as well as synthesis. To Glaucon who asked, "Who are the true philosophers?

Socrates replied, "those who are lovers of the vision of truth."[9]

While rejecting absolute truth The Mother also rejected absolute falsity, According to her, "There cannot be any absolute falsity. Actually it is not possible, because the Divine is behind everything."[10] This may be easily understood in the philosophical method. As soon as one takes recourse to synoptic vision he finds that truth is multisided. Error is the other aspect of truth. From a certain viewpoint a statement is true while from another standpoint it may lead to error. This however, does not give any license to error and falsehood. The follower of truth has to avoid all errors scrupulously. As The Mother said, "A perfect servant of Truth should abstain even from the slightest inexactitude, exaggeration or deformation."[11] Therefore, she has warned the educand and the educators to abstain from all loose talks, gossips, vain proclamations, propaganda, rumour mongering and even unnecessarily discussing about oneself or the other. This will save a lot of energy and interpersonal relations will improve. A true teacher and a learned scholar is always conscious of relativity of views. As The Mother puts it, "As human consciousness progresses, it has more and more this sense of relativity and, at the same time a kind of feeling, a vague impression that there is a truth which is not perceptible through ordinary means but which must be perceptible somehow."[12] This theory of relativity may be successfully utilised as the guiding principle in the determination of all educational issues concerning methods of teaching, discipline, curriculum, evaluation, school management and last but not the least various isms or theories of educational psychology and educational philosophy.

Like a true philosopher of education The Mother has admitted the utility of both the philosophical and the scientific methods in the field of education. As she puts it, "one can make only an affirmation: all that you know, however fine it may be, is nothing in comparison with that you can know, if you are able to use other methods".[13] The integral method is not merely a synthesis of the opposites, it is a new approach. The Mother's philosophy of education is not only eclectic nor does she support a middle of the road theory or the principle of golden means. Like Sri Aurobindo she has asked for growth, evolution and progress, from the present position so that the contradictories may become complementaries in the supramental methods. Ultimately, both the scholar and the teacher have to rise to the status of a Yoga in vision as well as activities, to quote The Mother, "These positions, the spiritual position and the 'materialistic' position, if one may call it so, are insufficient, not only because they do not admit each other, but because even admitting the two and uniting the two does not suffice to solve the problem. There is something else — a third thing which is not the result of these two, but something that is to be discovered which will probably open the gate of the total knowledge."[14]

Metaphysics of The Mother

As in epistemology so in metaphysics, The Mother is neither absolutist nor relativist Defining God she said, "It is the name man has given to all that surpasses him and dominates him, all that he cannot know, but to which he submits."[15] This agrees with the ancient Indian dictum that Reality is formless and nameless, the one expressed in many. However, as against the *advaita* approach, she maintained that nothing in this world is the sole reality and nothing total appearance. This realistic approach provides a sound basis for a proper philosophy of education. It is a cure against all one-sided approaches. The ultimate reality is mystical and not logical. Logic has its utility only on the mental plane. As one transcends to supramental logic gives place to intuition. Pointing out the limits as well as uses of logic The Mother said, "Logic is the art of correctly deducting one idea from another and inferring from a fact all its consequences. But logic does not itself possess the capacity to discern the truth. So your logic may be indisputable, but if your starting point is wrong, your conclusions will also be wrong, in spite of the correctness of your logic, or rather, because of it."[16] Therefore the teacher requires not logic but reason. As he teaches so he must grow. Constant growth and incessant progress, is necessary both for the educand and the educator.

The ultimate reality has been therefore called "Divine". Explaining the meaning of this term The Mother said, "For those who are afraid of a word: this is what we mean by "Divine": all the knowledge we have to acquire, all the love we have to become, all the perfection we have to achieve, all the harmonious and progressive poise we must make manifest in light and joy, all the unknown and new splendours that are to be realised."[17] This is the solid metaphysical foundation for the four-fold perfections, four-fold liberations and the four-fold austerities forming essentials of The Mother's philosophy of education. Men should seek perfection since the Divine is perfect. As The Mother said, "The Divine is tie absolute of perfection, eternal source of all that exists: of whom we become conscious progressively, all the while being himself for all eternity,"[18] The educational process, its aims and means, all its elements should be for the Divine, of the Divine and within the Divine. Then alone, education may help in the realisation, of the kingdom of God on earth.

The concept of Divine determines the interpretation of Nature. The Mother believes that Divine is the essence of plants, animals as well as human beings. Putting the Divine element in physical Nature in beautiful words The Mother said, "Have 'you never watched a forest with all its countless trees and plants simply struggling to catch the light — twisting and trying in a hundred possible ways just to be in the sun? That is precisely the feeling of aspiration in the physical — the urge, the movement, the push towards the light"[19] Thus heliotropism among plants later on develops 'as religion among human beings. It is hence that The Mother so much appreciates the pedagogical value of flowers and trees particularly in aesthetic education. As is the case of plants so it is about the animals. Pointing out the play of Divine among animals The Mother wrote, "I have seen in the animal all the emotional, affectional, sensational reactions, all those feelings of which men are so proud. The only difference is that they are unable to speak or write of them, so we look upon them as inferior beings, because they cannot flood us with books upon what they have felt."[20] These words provide a solid basis for the educands adjustment with the natural and biological environment. This again justifies the maintenance of ecological balance, both physical and biological. Praising the superiority of the animals The Mother said, "Animals have senses much more perfect than those of men."[21] Thus there is nothing to be proud of rationality. The animals are closer to nature. The Mother supports Rousseau's principle of returning to nature. She endorses the kindergarten philosophy of education. In order to be natural man will have to learn from plants and animals. Perversion is a human malady. It begins with the conscious mind and human species. The man however, cannot return to the presline unity of the animal or even of the savage.

The only course open to him is to forge ahead, to rise to supramental. This alone may give him a real view of things. This alone may dispel ignorance. As The Mother said, "Ignorance is dispelled by a growing consciousness; what you need is consciousness and always more consciousness, a consciousness pure, simple, and luminous. In the light of this perfected consciousness, things appear as they are and not as they want to appear."[22] Thus The Mother's philosophy of education is based upon the metaphysical foundation of the truth of evolution. Evolution is the secret of Nature. It is the principle of the individual as well as collectivity. It is the purpose of creation. As The Mother said, "For the universe is evolving constantly; nothing is at a standstill; everything is changing perpetually, moving forward or backward. Things or acts that take us backward seem bad to us, they are the cause of confusion and disorder. The only remedy for them is a radical movement forward, a progress."[23] Again, "There is an ascending evolution in nature which goes from the stone to the plant, from the plant to the animal, from the animal to man."[24] Therefore, education should be used as an instrument for realisation of change, evolution, revolution and progress in the individual as well as collective being. The theory of evolution provides a basis for The Mother's aim of education. Since the process of evolution so far shows an advance towards more and more perfect expressions, therefore perfection is the aim of education. As animal had to make place for man so man will have to evolve to superman. This evolution is possible through yoga. Therefore, the educational process should lead to yoga and ultimately culminate into it. The teachers must be conversant with the yogic technique so that they may help the educands in adopting it.

From the above discussion of the concepts of ultimate reality, God, world, nature and evolution, it is clear that all these form the metaphysical basis of The Mother's integral theory of education. Integral philosophy of education is based upon integral metaphysics and integral metaphysics is based upon integral epistemology. This is the sound theoretical foundation of The Mother's philosophy of education. Philosophy of education is a theory. The theory is particularly concerned with the internal consistency, though there is no contradiction between consistency and practice. From this viewpoint The Mother's philosophy of education is worth trial. This trial is being conducted at Sri Aurobindo International University at Pondicherry and at The Mother's school at Delhi besides so many other institutions as the aim is lofty, the process of achievement is bound to be slow. However, the philosophy is not so much interested in the results as in the method itself. "The function of philosophy in universities is properly the same as its function in the cultural development of a society to be the intellectual conscience of the community."[25] It can be said without exaggeration that without a philosophical basis, any knowledge is imperfect, because no total picture can be presented without the synthetic function of philosophy. Without this total picture there will always be tension in the field of knowledge which leads to philosophical activities. As Aristotle has said, "Whether we philosophies or not, we must philosophies."[26]

References

1. Morse, W.C. & Wingo, G.M., *Psychology & Teaching* (Bombay; Taraporevala, 1970), p. 4.
2. Durkheim, E., *Education and Sociology*, p. 68.
3. *Sri Aurobindo and The Mother on Truth* (Pondicherry: Sri Aurobindo Society, 1977), p. 1.
4. *Ibid,*
5. *Message given by The Mother* on 6-10-65.
6. *Sri Aurobindo and The Mother on Truth*, p. 2,
7. *Bulletin of Physical Education* (August 1962), p. 12.
8. *Ibid.* (April, 1958), p. 119.
9. Plato, *The Republic*, Book VI, p. 485.
10. *Bulletin of Physical Education* (August, 1961), p. 93.
11. *Sri Aurobindo and The Mother on Truth*, pp. 18-19.
12. *Ibid.*, p. 28.
13. *Bulletin of Physical Education* (August 1965), p. 92.
14. *Ibid.*, (August, 1962), p. 71.
15. C.W.M., Vol. 11 (1980), p. 67.
16. C.W.M., Vol. 10 (1977), p. 68.
17. *Bulletin of Physical Education* (November, 1952), p. 71.
18. *Sri Aurobindo and The Mother on Gods and Divine* (1973), p. 13.
19. *Words of The Mother*, 3rd Series (1951), p. 16.
20. *Bulletin of Physical Education* (November, 1965), p. 33.
21. *Ibid,* (November, 1965), p. 31.
22. *Sri Aurobindo and The Mother on Nature*, p. 34.
23. *Sri Aurobindo and The Mother on Evolution*, p. 17.

24. *Ibid.*, p. 22.
25. Blanshard and Others, *Philosophy in American Education* (New York; Harper & Bros., 1945), p. 80,
26. Quoted by Sharma, G.K. in *Trends in Contemporary Indian Philosophy of Education* (New Delhi: Atlantic Publishers & Distributors, 1987), p. 3.

5

Psychological Foundations of Education

Modern scientific psychology studies man as a living being, acting in an ever-changing world, responding to things and events and other people. He single person is its unit. Man is an organism with various capacities for perceiving, for response, for learning and for symbolization, which he uses to deal with his external environment. Psychology deals with both his behaviour as it appears in his responses and with consciousness as he finds in his immediate experience. Both the elements, experiences and behaviour, depend on the body and its nervous system which includes sensations, perceptions, feelings, emotions, imaginations, memories, thoughts and volitions. As The Mother said, "It is an invaluable possession forevery living being to have learnt to know himself and to master himself. To know oneself means to know the motives of one's actions and reactions, the why and the how of all that happens in oneself"[1]

But this so-called scientific psychology is hardly potent enough to explore the higher levels of awareness beyond mind. All our present psychological knowledge, enormous though it seems, is for the most part limited to relations and interactions of the human personality and the environment. As to what personality exactly is we have no sufficient exploration and systematic study. Dr. C.G. Jung observes that all the usual little remedies and predicaments of psychology fail to explain the true nature of personality. Gardner Murphy fully supports this view and says that nobody knows much about the nature of man. Modern psychology has yet to evolve an established psychological approach to the study of personality as physics has done regarding the study of matter.

According to The Mother, consciousness first emerges from Incontinent Matter as life and then evolves upwards to mind and beyond. There are ranges of consciousness above and below the human range, with which an ordinary human individual has no contact. Regarding ascending evolution in Nature, science tells us that it goes from stone to plant, from plant to animal and from animal to man. But The Mother aids that the process of evolution does not stop here. Man is not the final stage, He is only a transitional being and will be surpassed and his consciousness will grow further to a still higher nature — the Truth Consciousness of the super mind. The quality and richness of his behaviour and experience will then depend on the level of growth his consciousness has reached.

Thus The Mother presents an integral psychology which supplies the missing links in the studies of human personality by Psychology, Sociology, Anthropology and by the constant improvement of the technique of integral yoga, Man, according to The Mother, is a microcosm in macrocosm. Individuality, universality and transcendence are the triple aspects of the human personality. This view emphasizes the non-individualistic and super individualistic aspects of human experience, the universality as well as transcendence.

The Human Goal

According to The Mother, "The condition to be aimed at, the real achievement of *Yoga*, the final perfection and attainment, for which all else is only a preparation, is a consciousness in witch it is impossible to do anything without the Divine."[2] This goal has been explained by The Mother as follows:

1. Have no ambition, above all, pretend nothing, but be at each instant the utmost that you can be.

2. As for your place in the universal manifestation, the Supreme alone will fix it for you.

3. The Supreme Lord has decreed inviolably the place that you occupy in the world concert, but whatever be that place. You have the same right as all others equally to climb the supreme heights up to the supramental realisation.

4. What you are in the truth of your being is decreed in an inviolable manner and nothing and none can prevent you from being that; *but* the way you will take to reach there is left to your free choice-.

5. On the way of ascending evolution, everyone is free to choose the direction he will take: the accent that is swift and sleep towards the summits of Truth, the supreme realisation or, turning one's hack to the peaks, the facile, descent towards termless meanderings of births without end.

6. In the course of lime and even in the course of your present life you can make your choice once for all, irrevocably, and then you have only to confirm it on each new occasion; or you may not lake at the beginning the final decision, and then you have to choose again at each instant between falsehood and Truth.

7. But even when you have not taken at the beginning the irrevocable decision, if you have the good fortune to live at one of those unprecedented instants in universal history when Grace is present, incarnated on earth, she will give you once again, at certain exceptional moments, the possibility of still making a final choice that will lead you straight to the goal."[3]

Types of Man

The structure of man, according to The Mother, "consists of highest self or the spirit, the soul and the psychic being, the physical, vital, mental, psychical and the spiritual sheaths on bodies which enclose the physical body and the ego. Except the ego, all these are the projection of the self for its manifestation on the earth. From the point of view of psychological growth and the capacity to evolve towards the Divine The Mother has classified human beings into four types according to their attitudes in life. As she puts it, "Human beings could be classified under four principal categories according to the attitude they take in life:

1. Those who live for themselves, they look at everything in relation to themselves and act accordingly. The vast majority of men are like this.

2. Those who give their love to another human being and live for him. As for the result everything naturally depends upon the person whom one chooses to love.

3. Those who consecrate their lives to the services of humanity in some activity done not for personal satisfaction but for becoming truly useful to others without any calculation, without expecting any personal gain whatsoever from their work.

4. Those who give themselves wholly to the Divine and live only for Him and through Him. This implies the necessary effort to find the Divine, to be conscious of His will and to work exclusively to serve Him."[4]

Among the other types, the first three are subject to ordinary law for suffering disappointment and pain. It is only the last type of persons, who may follow the Divine, It goes without saying that these will make the process of evolution arrive at a turning point. Till this stage, the process of evolution had developed more or less mechanically without any awareness or responsive co-operation by the evolving units like plants or animals. But here the Nature has found an ally — the active faculty of self-conscious but also conscious of the need and possibility of self-enlarging and self-exceeding. The mini, as it is developed now, is at best, a halfway house. The Mother tells us that there are still higher principles above the psychic and the supramental. These are the principles of self-aware knowledge and self-active power and are to be attained above, evolved within and established in the aspiring consciousness.

The vital has three levels: higher, middle and lower, higher refers to the emotive being, the middle to the sensational and passionate and the lower is concerned with life's small greeds and desires which make up the daily stuff of life. Likewise, the mind is also divided into three parts: the thinking mind, the dynamic mind and the externalising mind. The first is concerned with ideas and knowledge in their own right, the second with putting out of mental forces for realization of the ideas, the third with their expression in life.

Man is normally aware of only a little part of himself. All that he knows is the mind, with which he thinks and acts, the life energy by which he is moved and sustained, and the physical body in which both mind and life are housed. But that is only his external being. He has a vast inner being of which the outer is actually a projection. It has much greater life — being with a more free and larger dynamism. And behind the gross physical frame too, there is a subtle physical body with a wider range. These three beings are governed by this consciousness. It remains involved in the non-living and is gradually evolving in the living. The Mother affirms that all existence is the manifestation of an Eternal and Infinite consciousness which forms a substrate and can be experienced through extension of self-awareness. All manifestation, material or spiritual, has behind it something that is beyond itself.

Planes of Being

In his physical nature, man is yet an animal Nature cannot be satisfied with such an imperfect result; she endeavours to bring out being who will be to man what man is to animal, a being who will remain a man in its eternal form, and yet whose consciousness will rise far above the mental and its slavery to ignorance. With the enlargement and expansion of consciousness, a human individual can transcend his existing mental level. In addition to planes of matter, life and mind which have already evolved, there exist other higher planes like higher mind and super mind.

Our ancient seers have revealed in *Upanisads* that human personality has five '*Kosas*' or sheaths: (1) *Annamaya Kos* — the physical sheath, (2) *Pranmaya Kos* — the vital sheath. (3) *Manomaya Kos* — the mental sheath, (4) *Jnanmaya Kos* — the psychic sheath, and (5) Anandmaya Kos — the spiritual sheath. From the point of view of the growth of consciousness all material objects are at the physical level where consciousness is not yet evolved, the plants and trees and other vegetation are at the vital level where life has just evolved, the animals and men are at the mental level where life has a graded scale. Thus there is a progressive unfoldment and growth of consciousness from inanimate matter to life and then to still higher principle, the mind.

Levels of Consciousness

Integral psychology as propounded by The Mother deals with consciousness and its states and operations in Nature. It studies the living being as it grows through different planes of evolving consciousness — the Inconscient, the Sub-conscient, Conscient and the Super-conscient corresponding to various stages of development *viz.* Matter, Life, Mind and Super mind. Our observable consciousness, that which we call ourselves, is only aware of the movements of our surface nature and superficial nature of other living creatures. Below this small visible part of our being, there are invisible depths and further depths which support and supply it ever widening experiences. What we see at the top is only our ego which we call self.

Below this Conscient nature there is a vast inconscient out of which we come. The Inconscient is greater, deeper, more original, more potent to govern what we are and do with our little conscient nature. If is our sovereign guide and creator. Behind our frontal ego and nature, there is a whole subliminal kingdom of inner consciousness with many planes and provinces. In that kingdom, there are many powers and movements which help to form our surface personality and its operations. This inner self-knows us well and dictates our speech, thought, feelings, emotions and other activities. Besides, the Inconscient or inner' self, there is a circumconscient of which also we are a portion. It is constantly pouring its forces, suggestions, stimuli and compulsions into us.

The greater part of our existence is, therefore, either above or below our mind, of which mind can become aware of only indirectly. The basis of all knowledge is a conscious, half-conscious or sub-conscious participation in the awareness of the Infinite. Both living and non-living together constitute the inner being of man. Deeper than these is still another being, the soul, who is a living spark of the Divine, around which the rest of his being is entered for its life journey, appropriately termed by Sri Aurobindo, the psychic being.

The powers and potentialities of this inner being are much wider than those of the outer surface being. The inner being possesses a separate consciousness of its own called the subliminal. The ranges below it are called subsconscient and those above its level, the Super-conscient. The Mother asserts that these inner ranges of the being can be opened through the psychological discipline of Yoga. The psychic being is a delegate of the Divine, and when fully realised, it gains him an identity with the Divine, which leads to the development of universal or cosmic consciousness within him and he begins to realise his true unity with his fellow beings at the common substratum. The centre of this psychic being is behind the heart and it is through purified emotions that the psychic finds an outlet.

Above the psychic The Mother discovered still other ranges of the Super-conscient before reaching the Supramental plane. She called them, in their ascending order, the higher mind, the illumined mind, intuitive mind and over mind. Each of them is a whole world, vaster and more active than the four levels below the psychological, the vital, the mental and the psychic.

New Concepts of Integral Psychology

"Both for spiritual and philosophical knowledge", says Sri Aurobindo, "it is necessary to be clear and precise in one's own use of terms so as to avoid confusion of thought and vision, by confusion in the words we use to express them,"[5] The Mother has not only developed a whole new knowledge by his yogic experience and exacting introspective analysis and observation, she has also cautiously coined new terms and concepts to explain realities corresponding to different types of experiences. Psychologists and other scientists, in their enthusiasm for physical and biological categories, have often fried to apply item to widely differing experiences. This over-simplification has led to much confusion specially about deeper realities. Confusion in concept leads to confusion in thought and confusion in thought leads to lack of distinction in concepts. Hence the need of clarification in concepts is categorical in every branch of human knowledge, even though the concepts may represent the experiences only approximately.

The Seven Cakras

Subtle bodies, according to The Mother, possess seven main centres called cakras. These centres are located at the base of the spine, over the solar plexus, the spleen, the heart, in front of the throat, between the eyebrows and over the top of the head. This conception has been borrowed by Sri Aurobindo and The Mother from the ancient Hindu psychologists but they tested it by their own personal experience and clarified the specialised action of each of them. Thus the *Muladhara* (base of the spine) governs the sense movements. The *Manipura* (Naval Centre) governs the larger desire movements. The *Anahata* or *Hratpadma* (Heart Centre) governs the expressive and externalizing mind. The Ajna (Centre between the eyebrows) governs the dynamic will, vision, mental formation, the *Sahasradala* (above the head) governs the higher thinking mind. It consists of the higher mind, illumined mind and also the intuitive mind through which the over mind contacts with the rest.

The Subconscient

The subconscient is very valuable and important for the integration of human personality. It must be known and controlled before mm may aspire after integrity. It is indispensable for any transformation of human nature, as the animal and infernal in man has its seat here.

The subconscient however, cannot be known by a direct plunge into it, since it would put man into incoherence or into sleep or a dull trance or a comatose torpor. A mental scrutiny or insight, as in the psycho-analytic method, can give only some indirect and artificial idea of these hidden activities. According to The Mother, the subconscient can be known directly and totally either by drawing back into the subliminal and by extending ourselves into these obscure depths; or by ascending to the superconscient and looking down into the subconscient. This awareness will give us a control ewer the subconscient, which is of utmost importance as the subconscient is the inconscient in the process of becoming conscious.

Higher Mind

The higher mind is less opaque and more free. One at this level, begins to know what joy is in itself. It is not yet a heavy mental substance which catches the light from above and dissolves it in its own substance. As the higher mind gradually accepts its silence, it wins access to the next higher region, the illumined mind.

Illumined Mind

At this level, the consciousness is filled with a flood of light and there comes a sudden awakening as if the entire being were altered and at once plugged into a brand new world, with new values, with new reliefs and one finds a new meaning of life. The access to this new consciousness is accompanied by a spontaneous blossoming of creative capacities, particularly in the poetic field. The Mother has given numerous examples of the illumined mind. The substance of the illumined mind is not transparent but only translucid; *i.e.* its light is diffused.

Intuitive Mind

This region of the superconscient is quite transparent. It is no longer clogged like the Higher mind. It is a domain of flashing consciousness. A point, a sound, a drop of light and a whole world is contained therein. It affords a great gaze — a formidable glance which is seen and known all in the flash of a second. The Mother used to say that intuition is a memory of the Truth. But it has one limit. However crowded with life be our flashes they cannot contain the whole truth. Intuition secs things by flashes, point by point, not as a whole.

Over Mind

This level is the rarely attained submit of human consciousness. It is a cosmic consciousness without a loss of the individual It is the world of gods and the source of inspiration of the great founders of religions. This is also the birthplace of high artistic creations. When consciousness rises to this plane, it no longer sees points by points, but calmly and in great masses. It is no longer the diffused light of the illumined mind, not the isolated flashes of the intuitive mind but, is a mass of stable light. From this emanates continuous universal vision. One experiences universal joy, perceives universal beauty and feels universal love. Over mind is the passage through which one passes from mind to Super mind.

Super Mind

Supramental consciousness, in fact, is not the peak of human consciousness but is another consciousness. This consciousness has an active global vision. The Super mind can perceive not only the whole world of things and beings in a single vision but also discerns the viewpoint of each thing, each being, each force tending towards its absolute. If there were not this absolute at the centre of each one-of is, we would crumble to pieces. Super mind is a truth consciousness and because it sees all, it has omniscient power. This power does not obey our logic and our morality. It sees far into space and time. It is a formidable evolutionary ferment. It does not set truth against truth to see which one will stand and survive, but completes truth by truth in the light of one universal truth of which all are aspects. The Mother calls the working of the Super mind 'thinking spherically. This undivided vision is so real that even the appearance of the physical world changes for the supramental consciousness, that the physical world appears as it really is, the separatist optical illusion in which we live disappears. To the supramental consciousness, nothing seems finite. It sees all in each and each in all. It is an insight in fourth dimension. The material objects to this sight become something different from what we see now; not separate objects in environment but an indivisible part of the unity of all.

The ordinary individual consciousness is like an axis and everything turns round it. If it moves one feels lost. With the growth of supramental consciousness, the axis no more exists. It is free to move in all directions and can develop in a single grip, the past, present and future in their indivisible connections. For such a sight, the Absolute is everywhere and every finite looks infinite. The mind, even the over mind of our prophets is linked to the dualities of right or wrong, good or bad, pleasant or unpleasant. It is argued, if God is above. He is not below, if an object is white, it cannot be black. For the supramental experiences all is round. This consciousness is totally outside the domain of dualities. It can exist in the eternal silence and amidst all tumults. And hence it can truly enjoy life and at the same time master life. For super mind, there is no more a 'passage' no more a 'threshold', from silence to tumulate, from the Divine to the non-divine — the two are fused into one single experience. The kingdom of God exists in this world. The whole secret is to unite the two experiences into one — the infinite in the finite, the timeless in temporal, and the transcendent in the immanent.

The goal of evolution is to rediscover down below this totality up above. It is to find in the midst of dualities, the supreme unity, to feel and experience a proverbial sense of unity in diversity of the Vedas.

Sri Aurobindo and The Mother divide super mind into three layers:

(a) *Interpretive super mind*: What is a possibility on the mental plane becomes a potentiality at this level. It shows the root cause of events that may become true on the physical plane.

(b) *Representative super mind:* It represents the actual movements of potentialities and shows what is in operation. When inspiration is changed into its supramental value, then it becomes representative of Super mind. With the growth of consciousness to this level, one can predict what would happen or say how a certain thing happened.

(c) *Imperative Super mind*: It corresponds to revelation which is always true. Nothing can stand against it is knowledge fulfilling itself by its own inherent power.

The Integral Man

The Integral man is a larger reality. His consciousness is not confined to his outer becoming and importance of his inner true self — the essential being, the superconscious. He is subliminal and the superconscious. His whole way of living, thinking or acting is governed by a vast universal spiritualty. All his existence gets fused into oneness with the transcendent and universal spirit. All his activities originate from and obey the supreme self. His whole life, his feelings, his thoughts and acts are filed with and emanate from the Divine. He feels the presence of the Divine in every centre of his consciousness, in every vibration of his life-force, in every cell of his body. He finds his natural being as the becoming and manifestation of the power of the world-Mother. In this consciousness he Ives and acts in absolute freedom, with a complete joy of the spirit, having identity with the cosmic self and spontaneous sympathy with all in the universe. All beings appear to him his own selves, all ways and powers of consciousness he feels, are the ways and powers of his own universality. He finds no bondage to inferior forces, and no deflection from his own highest truth. The Integral man with his global vision, can be in the world and at the same time can exceed it in his consciousness and live in his self of transcendence above it. His individuality becomes universal because he individualises the universe. He meets the world in its external form by an external contact but inwardly he is in contact with the inner self of things and beings. He meets consciously their inner as well as outer reactions and is aware of that within them of which they themselves are not aware. He not only possesses full power of truth-consciousness to control the physical world, but also full power to transform his vital and mental planes so as to use their forces for the perfection of his mundane existence.

Integral Personality Theory

Modern psychology, which studies mind and its phenomena at their surface values only, will be of no help to us; because it cannot give proper guidance towards deep self-exploration and self-conversion. Our imperfections, limitations, griefs and ignorance are the initial discords of the musicians running. We have to outgrow these limitations to construct perfection and divinise ourselves which is our supreme goal. Integral psychology of The Mother suggests the sure way to open the imperfect human consciousness to the Divine and to live in the inner consciousness more and more while acting upon it on the external life, to bring the in most psychic into the front and by the power of the psychic to purify and change the being so as to make it ready for the transformation. The aim is to universalise the human personality on all the planes, to make it aware of the cosmic being and the cosmic forces. This psychology suggests ways and means to help the individual human consciousness to reach the super-conscious level. All her life The Mother has been an explorer of human consciousness, and the possible height it could reach. She has discovered for us, a process of rapidly and consciously evolving human consciousness to higher levels beyond mental so as to mite and harmonise the two ends of existence: Spirit and Matter.

Everything in existence, she argues, has something in it which seeks to go beyond itself; matter moves towards becoming mind, mind moves towards becoming ideal Truth and ideal Truth rises to become Divine and Infinite spirit. Every symbol being a partial expression of cosmic consciousness, seeks to become its real self by transcending its apparent self. Upward movement is the means towards self-fulfillment. Every nature is a step towards some supernature, something natural to itself but supernatural to what is below it. Man is supernatural to the animal, so is God supernatural to man. Man must, therefore, seek his upward movement towards God. To become Divine in human form itself is our fulfilment. All other pursuits, political, social, literary or intellectual, are only a preparation to this ultimate goal. To achieve this objective, man must transform himself into an integral man and strive to establish a close contact with cosmic consciousness. With an individual, strong in spirit, securing of this touch may indeed be quite rapid. Beyond mind, as we have been, there is supramental or gnostic power which is a dynamic consciousness, full of infinite wisdom and will. It is a far greater consciousness than the highest consciousness proper to human nature. The highest mental level in man is not potent enough to change our live beyond certain narrow limits. But divine superman, or in the words of The Mother, the integral man with a gnostic spirit can lay hands on the mental and physical instruments and standing above and yet penetrating our lower already manifested parts and transform them into something new. The new consciousness, when attained, will be higher in grade and power, always larger, more comprehensive, wider in sight and dominating than the one we possess at the moment. Super manhood is not man climbed to his own natural zenith, not a superior degree of human greatness, knowledge, power, intelligence, will, character, genius, dynamic force, saintliness, purity or perfection. It is, as has already been alluded to above, absolutely a new consciousness – active and global.

Five Psychological Perfections

The Mother recommends five psychological perfections for attaining the goal of education. It may be remembered here that the goal of education, according to The Mother, Ike the goal of every other human activity, is a part of goal of life and even the goal which Nature is seeking through evolution from plant to human life, As The Mother said, "Someone asked me what was this 'psychological perfection' that the Champa lower symbolises. There is not one psychological perfection, but five, like the five petals of this flower. We have said, they are: sincerity, faith, devotion, aspiration and surrender."[6] These have been explained as follows:

1. *Sincerity*: The first condition for any psychological development is sincerity. The Mother calls it transparence. It means sympathy and empathy as well. It is the most necessary requirement for any growth. It means acting according to one's conscience.

2. *Faith*: According to Sri Aurobindo, "Faith is a necessary means for arriving at realisation, because we are ignorant and do not yet know that which we are seeking to realise; faith is indeed knowledge giving the ignorance an intimation of itself previous to its own manifestation, it is the glean sent before by the yet unrisen Sun."[7] According to The Mother faith in Divine Power or Divine Goodness is necessary for evolution in the Divine. This should lead to complete trust. In complete trust there is no doubt of any type.

3. *Devotion*: According to The Mother, "It is the third among the psychological perfection. Yes, Devotion is very essential but unless it is accompanied by many other things, that too may go very wrong and meet with much difficulty."[8] Devotion requires surrender of all egoism to Divine. Therefore, devotion requires gratitude. The sense of gratitude has been recommended by almost all religions as a necessary accompaniment of devotion to Divine. Explaining the sense of gratitude The Mother said, "This feeling of gratitude that the Divine exists, the gratefulness, full of wonder, that truly fills your heart with a sublime delight, because the Divine exists, because there is something in the universe that is the Divine, and there is not merely the monstrosity that we see — because there is the Divine, because the Divine is there."[9]

4. *Aspiration*: According to The Mother aspiration may be called courage that has the taste of a supreme adventure of one

who aspires through himself in search of Divine without any reservation. That is why Indian seers have always insisted upon aspiration as a necessary requirement forevery seeker in the path of knowledge as well as self realisation.

5. *Surrender*: Surrender is a precondition for integral yoga. According to The Mother, it is indispensable for commencing Yoga. She however adds, "But to make your surrender total, all the other qualities are necessary: sincerity, faith, devotion and aspiration."[10] Thus surrender is the culmination of other four types of psychological perfection.

Besides the above-mentioned five types of psychological perfection The Mother also recommends endurance. Endurance is faithfulness to the resolution. It is perseverance. It takes one to the goal without faltering.

Besides the above five-fold psychological perfections The Mother has recommended mastery over desires. Man is made of desires. He can get rid of them by constant vigilance. According to The Mother, "The sign of the true and Divine Consciousness is perfect equality, constant equanimity and peace."[11] Therefore she recommends, "Excitement, irritation, sorrow, depression, upsetting belong all to the physical consciousness and must be surmounted in order to get rid of the falsehood."[12] Self-control and not self indulgence brings self-fulfillment. It is better to conquer a desire than to satisfy it. But, for this it is better to avoid the temptation rather than repression or repression of the desire. The Mother supports Christ's prayer to God — Man should not be tested since he is weak. He requires grace of God. Choice should be made according to highest consciousness. There should be no preference otherwise. Thus psychological perfection is a necessary perfection both for the educator and the educand.

Relevance to Education

The following points may be noted in connection with the relevance of The Mother's psychological findings to education:

1. *Integral personality*: The Mother's explanation of human nature is not only horizontal but also vertical. It not only finds out the physical, the vital and the mental aspects of personality but also explores the influences and possibilities beyond mind. Thus his theory of personality is more integral. This provides a

sound basis for integral education which aims at total evolution of man, not only as a living being but also an evolving being.

2. *Integral curriculum*: By pointing out different aspects of man's mind, its various levels, below reason and above reason. The Mother has given a sold psychological basis for evolving an integral curriculum on different stages of education.

3. *Physical Education*: In the tradition of Indian psychology, The Mother has laid emphasis on body building and physical development since according to her matter too is divine. In her yoga also she presents so many useful suggestions for physical development. In Sri Aurobindo Ashram at Pondicherry one finds a marvellous development of various aspects of physical education.

4. *Aesthetic education*: The most important element in a living being is the vital. The Mother has analysed vital and pointed out its three levels — the lower, the higher and the middle. She lays emphasis upon the need of controlling the lower vital and rising to higher vital. It is here that she lays bare the fundamental principles of aesthetic education. She has given an elaborate theory of art and aesthetics.

5. *Moral Education*: By maintaining the mental level to be above vital and physical, The Mother maintains the value of reason in man's life. No higher life is possible without moral training. Therefore, integral psychology provides a solid basis for the need and planning of moral education.

6. *Spiritual education*: Modern Western psychology stops on the mental level in its explanation of human nature. Some recent eminent Western psychologists have however pointed out to interindividual and trans-individual fields influencing human personality. They have, however, not given any clear explanation of the spiritual aspect of human personality. It is here that The Mother has given an elaborate theory. Beyond mind she explains higher mind, illumined mind, intuitive mind and super mind and analyses their characteristics. She not only gives a description of these higher levels but also builds up a method to ascend to these levels. This method is integral yoga. Thus integral yoga is a method of spiritual education based upon integral psychology.

7. *Integral teaching method*: By explaining the structure of human personality and various influences upon it The Mother has laid down the fundamentals of teacher-taught relationship and the

method of teaching. She analyses education as a spiritual process of which the educator and the educand form two integral poles. Neither of the two should be neglected nor anyone should be overemphasised. Both should grow together as companions in the path of spiritual evolution.

8. *Integral administration*: The educational institution includes the educand, the educator and the educational system. Integral psychology admits the importance of all the three and considers them intimately interconnected. In fact the three together form a spiritual unity. Therefore, the administration should include all the three in a total relationship.

Our discussion of the relevance of The Mother's psychological thinking will be further clarified in the succeeding chapters.

References

1. *Sri Aurobindo and The Mother on Education*, Part II, p. 1.
2. The Mother, *Conversations*, p. 44.
3. *Bulletin of Physical Education* (November, 1959), pp. 53-54.
4. *Ibid.* (April, 1972), pp. 43-45.
5. Sri Aurobindo, *Sri Aurobindo Mandir Annual*, No. 6, p. 43.
6. *Bulletin of Physical Education* (April, 1960), p. 55.
7. *Sri Aurobindo, Letters on Yoga* (Birth Centenary Edn.) Vol. 2, p. 22.
8. *Sri Aurobindo and The Mother on Self Perfection* Part 3 (1973), p. 12.
9. *Ibid.*, p. 13.
10. *Ibid.*, p. 14.
11. *Words of The Mother* (1949), p 217.
12. *Ibid.*

6

Sociological Foundations of Education

It is believed that there is Intimate relationship between the sociological and the psychological foundation in modern education. Such educationists as Pestalozzi, Herbart and Froebel, who encourage the use of psychology in education, also admit the influence of sociological factors in the child's development. Pestalozzi wanted the education of the child to be such that it could lead to the welfare of the family and the nation and society, along with the child's own welfare. According to Herbert, the aim of education is the moral development of the individual, so that he can develop the ability to bring about social welfare. Thus, both Herbart and Pestalozzi wanted to educate the child for social welfare. Even the thinking of Froebel reflects some sociological inclination, for he conceives of the school as a miniature society. In Kindergarten education he has placed special emphasis upon the social aspect of education. Thus, the proponents of the psychological foundation in education believe the social aim to be important, while, at the same time, those in favour of the social objectives of education do not in any way detract from the importance of psychological elements in education Obviously, then, both the tendencies complement each other. In educating the child, it is therefore, important to pay attention to both his psychological and his social condition, for neither is less important than the other. The child enters the world possessed of the psychological elements, but these psychological elements develop in the social environment. Hence both must be studied in child's education.

Like her approach in metaphysics, epistemology and psychology, The Mother's approach in sociology is also integral. Integral sociology conceives social institutions inter-related in the social whole, the society in the cosmos, Thus the same principle harmonises the individuals in social institutions, social institutions in society and the humanity in the cosmos. According to The Mother, "The general aim to be attained is the advent of a progressing universal harmony. The means for attaining this aim, in regard to the earth, is the realisation of human unity through the awakening in all and the manifestation by all of the inner Divinity which is One. In other words, to create unity by founding the kingdom of God which is within us all"[1] On the spiritual level the contradictories become complementaries. Mini divides while the spirit unites. Human, society cannot return to its primitive unity since man has evolved in civilisation. The rational modern man cannot return to the harmony of pre-rational or infarctional stage. Therefore, the only path open to him is to forge ahead. The crisis of the present human society is due to its rational stage. There is nothing to be disheartened by the present chaos. One should never think that infra-rational may be a solution. Evolution cannot turn back. Nature constantly evolves to more and more conscious beings. The present difficulties characteristic of self-conscious man are difficulties of a higher stage in evolution. It is an old saying that an unthinking life is not worth living. It has been generally accepted that the philosophy of satisfaction is a pig philosophy. Only a pig is fully satisfied, man is dissatisfied, and a Socrates dissatisfied is better than a pig satisfied.

Therefore the present difficulties may be solved only by making Divine the principle of life. Even the problems characteristic of political institutions may be solved only by making Divine the principle of political institutions. The characteristic defects and difficulties of the present day democracies are due to the rational stage of the state and government. The principle of reason is impersonal. That is why fraternity could not be realised in the present democratic state. The Mother agrees with Karl Marx that the state cannot deliver the goods since it is an artificial institution. However, by making Divine the principle of democratic states, liberty, equality and fraternity may be realised. To quote The Mother, "Liberty can manifest only when all men will know the liberty of the Supreme Lord. Equality can manifest only when men will all be conscious of the Supreme Lord. Fraternity can manifest only when all men will feel themselves equally born of the Supreme Lord and "One' in his oneness."[2]

Thus like Sri Aurobindo The Mother aimed at the creation of a new society, a Divine society upon earth. This requires a total transformation. This transformation will be both on the individual as well as collective plane. As The Mother said, "The terrestrial transformation and harmonisation can be brought about by two processes which, though opposite in appearance, must combine, must act upon each other and complete each other:

(1) Individual transformation, an inner development leading to the union with the Divine Presence.

(2) Social transformation, the establishment of an environment favourable to the flowering and growth of the individual."[3]

The old social thinking particularly emphasised social change and social reformation or social development. On the other hand the moral philosophers insisted upon the development and growth of the individual alone. But so long as different principles are prescribed for the evolution of the individual and the collectivity, there cannot be a harmony between the individual and society. Therefore, in modern democracies liberty and equality could be realised but not fraternity. On the other hand in modern socialism the individual liberty could not be maintained against the power of the state. "The history of all hitherto existing society," declared Marx and Engels, "is the history of class struggle."[4] Marxist socialism aims at the establishment of a classless society in which the free development of each is the condition for the free development of all. It seeks a government of the proletariat, the people. But "the people" is a vague term and the government of the socialist states is in the hands of a few individuals who constitute a dominant class or party. The class war which led to the abolition of Czardom in Russia again led to the revolution against the personality cult of Stalin, though in a different form. So long as man moves by power-motive of the vital and physical ego, there is no reason to suppose that revolution against Stalinism is the final phase of class war. So long as human nature remains what it is, the classes will always precipitate out of the vague mass of people and class-war will never cease.

As against Marxist materialist sociology, the integral sociology of The Mother makes both the individual and collectivity as two limbs of spiritual transformation. Outlining the aims of the creation of a new society upon earth The Mother said, "This, therefore, is the most useful work to be done:

1. For each individually, to be conscious in himself of the Divine Presence and to identify himself with it.

2. To individualise the states of being that were never till now conscious in man and, by that, to put the earth in connection with

one or more of the fountains of universal force that are still sealed to it.

3. To speak again to the world the eternal world under a new form adapted to its present mentality. It will be the synthesis of all human knowledge.

4. Collectively, to establish an ideal society in a propitious spot for the flowering of the new race, the race of the Sons of God."[5]

In order to create a new society Karl Marx supported revolution. This revolution asked for expropriation of the expropriators. As Marx and Engels said, "This transformation of scattered private property, arising from individual labour, into capitalist private property is naturally, a process. Incomparably more protracted, violent, and difficult, than the transformation of capitalistic private property, already practically resting on socialized production into socialised property. In the former case, we had the expropriation of the mass of the people by a few usurpers; in the latter, we have the expropriation of a few usurpers by the mass of the people."[6] Thus socialist evolution established dictatorship of the proletariat. This means the rule of the collectivity, the rule of the state and the rule of a group of individuals in the name of collectivity. This seeks to transform the individual by the collective power, the power of the state. Therefore, there is a little wonder that in spite of all proclamations of the socialist regime on the contrary, individual liberty, could not be maintained in the communist states. The integral sociology of The Mother, on the other hand, conceives the individual and environment as correlated. Modern sociology accepts the interaction of the individual and society. Therefore The Mother insists upon the development of both the individual and environment side by side. As she puts it, "Since the environment reacts upon the individual and, on the other hand, the value of the environment depends upon the value of the individual, the two works should proceed side by side. But this can be done only through division of labour, and that necessitates the formation of a group, hierarchies, if possible."[7]

Thus spiritual revolution leading towards a new society, requires the action of the groups as well as the individuals. The Mother has clearly outlined the action required from the group as well as the individual Outlining the action of the group she said, "The action of the members of the group should be three-fold:

(1) To realise in oneself the ideal to be attained: to become a perfect earthly representative of the first manifestation of the Unthinkable in all its modes, attributes and qualities.

(2) To preach this ideal by world, but, above all, by example, so as to find out all those who are ready to realise it in their turn and to become also announcers of liberation.

(3) To find a typic society or reorganise those that already exist."[8]

Thus, first of all, every member of a group must himself realise spiritual transformation. That is why in the field of education, The Mother has always insisted upon teaching by example. Wherever spiritual transformation is realised in a small group, it should be organised. Sri Aurobindo Ashram Pondicherry and later on Auroville were intended to be such groups by organising which the spiritual transformation may be realised upon this earth. However, among the group and the individual, the latter is definitely the leader of spiritual revolution. It has been recognised by most of the philosophers of history that revolutions have been always led by individuals. It is so since in the Nature's method, everything is first realised on an individual scale and only later on realised in the group. The world today very much needs spiritual leaders and spiritual individuals. "Our present predicament", said Bertrand Russell, "is due, more than anything else, to the fact that we have learnt to understand and control; to a terrifying extent, the forces of Nature outside us, but not those that are embodied in ourselves."[9] But Russell and other rationalist educational philosophers fail to note that the inner forces cannot be transformed and integrated or even fully controlled by reason. As Sri Aurobindo points out, "Reason and science can only help by standardizing, by fixing everything into an artificially arranged and mechanized unity of material life. A greater whole-being, whole-knowledge, whole-power is needed to weld all into a greater unity of whole-life."[10] Therefore, The Mother prescribes, "For each individual also there is a two-fold labour to be done, simultaneously, each side of if helping and completing the other:

(1) An inner development, a progressive union within the Divine Light, sole condition in which man can be always in harmony with the great stream of universal life.

(2) Aa external action which everyone has to choose according to his capacities and personal preferences. He must find his own place, the place which he alone can occupy in the general conceit, and he must give himself entirely to it, not forgetting that he is playing only one note in the terrestrial sympathy and yet his note is indispensable to harmony of the whole, and its value depends upon its justness."[11]

Educational Implications

The educational implication of integral sociology of The Mother may be particularly found in her concept of national is well as international education. According to her, "Our aim is not a national system of education for India, bit an education for the world at large."[12] His however, does not mean that nationalism has to be sacrificed on the altar of internationalism. This only means that the underlying principle of the individual, the national and the international education should be the same. This is the Divine principle in man which expressed through individuality, communality and essentiality. Every nation has to contribute to Humanity by following its own *swadhamta*. As the growth of the individual leads to the growth of the group similarly the growth of a nation is necessary for the growth of Humanity. Therefore, outlining the role of India in humanity The Mother said, "India has or rather had the knowledge of matter but rejected the Spirit and suffered badly for it. An integral education which could, with some variations, be adapted to all the nations of the world, must bring back the legitimate authority of the Spirit over a matter folly developed and utilised."[13] In August 1965 an Education Commission of the Government of India visited the Ashram to evaluate the ideal and educational methods of the Centre of Education. At that time a group of teachers submitted a series of questions to The Mother. These questions and The Mother's answers to them provide solutions for some basic issues of Indian education. The Mother advised, "Prepare her children for the rejection of falsehood and the manifestation of Truth."[14] To the question about the present concern for national unity in India The Mother said, "The unity of all the nations is the compelling future of the world. But for the unity of all nations to be possible, each nation must first realise its own unity."[15] She pointed out that this unity must be a living fact and not the imposition of an external principle.

She supported the need of a national language though she did not specifically mention as to which language should be the *lingua-franca* criticising the present unhealthy trend of making education literacy and a means to social status. The Mother advised, "Get out of conventions and insist on the growth of the soul,"[16] She maintained that the almost exclusive importance given to success, career and money are the illusions and delusions which beset out educational system today. In order to keep clear of these difficulties she advised, "Insist on the paramount importance of the contact with the Spirit and the growth and manifestation of the Truth of the being "[17] Suggesting modification in the present educational system she advised the government to recognise yoga in the system of education. In her message for the inauguration of a French Institute at Pondicherry on 4 April, 1955 The Mother said, "In any country the best education that can be given to children consists in teaching them what the true nature of their country is and its own qualities, the mission their nation has to fulfil in the world and its true place in the terrestrial concert. To that should be added a wide understanding of the role of other nations, but without the spirit of imitation and without ever losing sight of the genius of one's own country."[18]

Man and Woman

The most natural stratification found in any society is between the man and woman. Though none of them is superior or dominant in all the societies yet their roles are complementary rather than contradictory. In modern times the roles of man and woman in ancient and medieval societies, have been revised. Everywhere the women have clamoured for liberation. The role of woman has been reviewed and equality with the male has been demanded. Therefore, every philosopher of education, worth the name, must examine the relationship of man and woman and prescribe for their education. As a woman, The Mother has been particularly influenced by this question. Condemning the old slavery of woman she said, "the idea that woman should cook for males is against my principles. Are they slaves?"[19] In keeping with her metaphysics of liberation she has supported woman lib movement everywhere. However, going deeper into the problem, she has pointed out that the chief cause of the slavery of women is not men but they themselves. She said, "No law can. liberate women unless they liberate themselves, Whit makes them slaves is:

(1) Attraction towards the male and his strength,

(2) Desire for home life and its security,

(3) Attachment to motherhood.

If they get free these three slaveries, they will truly be the equal of men."[20] Analysing the male-female relationship in the history of human civilisation, The Mother said, "Woman, by the very fact of her passivity, having more easily than man the intuition of the Supreme Power at work in the world, is more often, more naturally humble."[21]

Having a wide knowledge of the women of different countries of Europe and Asia including Japan and India The Mother exhibited a deep understanding of the female nature, her role, problems and destiny. Addressing the women of Japan she said, "True maternity begins with the conscious creation of a being with the willed shaping of a soul coming to develop and utilise a new body. The true domain of women is the spiritual. We forget it but too often."[22] Therefore she asked the woman to create characters of the children so that they may be capable of manifesting the ideal of perfection. For this purpose they should be themselves surrounded by forms of arts and beauty. The woman should develop on different planes, then alone she may fulfil her role in society. In fixture society the woman has to fulfil the role of creating the superman. As The Mother said, "The superman shall be born of woman, this is a big unquestionable truth; but it is not enough to be proud of this truth, we must clearly understand what it means, become aware of the responsibility it creates, and learn to face earnestly the task which is put before us. This task is precisely our most important share in the present world-wide work."[23] In order to fulfil this important task The Mother lays down the following conditions for the woman:

1. They must understand the means by which the present chaos and obscurity may be transformed into light and harmony. So far political social, ethical and religious means have been tried. According to The Mother however, "Only a new spiritual influx, creating in man a new consciousness, can overcome the enormous mass of difficulties barring the way of the workers."[24]

2. In place of reason the woman should utilise intuition to understand the truth concerning Nature, Evolution and Superman.

3. She must conceive the practical result of her spiritual conversion. This makes religious beliefs and cults, secondary. Rules of conduct and conventions lose their importance. The vital will and mental power should equally surrender to the super mind.

4. About the rules of spiritual womanhood The Mother has maintained that she should be no more egoistic and selfish. She should be perfectly disinterested, joyful, peaceful, merging the self into universal divinity.

To conclude The Mother said, "It is by holding firm in our heart and mind the dynamism, the irresistible impetus given by a sincere and ardent aspiration, by maintaining in ourselves a certain state of enlightened receptivity towards the supreme Idea of the new race which wills to be manifested on earth, that we can take a decisive step in the formation of the sons of the future, and make ourselves fit to serve as intermediaries for the creation of those who shall save Humanity."[25]

However, slavery and the need of enlightenment is not required only in the case of woman, According to The Mother men also suffer from so many defects and therefore they also stand in need of reformation if the woman has to get her suitable place in society and fulfil the role of spiritual mother in future society. Pointing out the present defective character of man, The Mother said, "Men also have three slaveries:

(1) Spirit of possession, attachment to power and domination,

(2) Desire for sexual relation with woman,

(3) Attachment to small comforts of married life.

If they get rid of these three slaveries, they can truly become equal of women."[26] Both men and women are bound by vital and material consciousness. However, in comparison to men, the women may more easily discover the inner psychic being and allow it to guide them. According to The Mother, so far as spiritual development is concerned the woman is not inferior to the man in any way. However, she regrets, "There have been many outstanding feminine figures in spiritual life. But on one side women are more interested by action than by mentalisation and intellectual expression, that is why very few women have recorded their spiritual experience and thus they have remained unknown."[27] Fortunately, this has not been the disadvantage with The Mother. Whatever she wrote and said has been recorded and published from Sri Aurobindo Ashram Pondicherry and Sri Aurobindo Society. His her published works have almost no comparison with my distinguished woman in the world.

Like any sane social philosopher The Mother has admitted the complementary nature of male and female. She has supported compatibility in the roles of man and woman in society. As she rightly pointed out, "The true relation of the two sexes is m equal footing of mutual help and close collaboration."[28] His collaboration however, is not confined to the physical or vital plane. On the other hand, The Mother has derogated male-female communication on physical and vital plane. The true collaboration is spiritual, as it was in the case of Sri Aurobindo and The Mother themselves. Chastising the dominance of the male in present day society The Mother pointed out that the men should learn, to be humble and the woman should stop trying to please them. Expressing the eternal principle of male-female relationship The Mother said, "All the universe has been created to express the Divine Power, and human beings, men or women, have their special mission to become conscious of and to manifest that Eternal Divine Essence. Such is their object and none other."[29] Thus the real comradeship between the man and woman is not mutual love, or vital exchange but both serving the role of bringing the kingdom of God upon earth. Hey are companions in the path to Divine values of truth, goodness and beauty. It is in this journey to Divine that they should help each other. Hence as The Mother puts it, "Thus the problem of feminism, as all the problems of the world, comes back to a spiritual problem."[30] And it is in the recognition of this fundamental spiritual equality that can be found the only serious and lasting solution for this problem of the relation of the sexes."[31]

Educational Implications

He is following the implications of The Mother's concept of male-female relationship of society, in the field of education:

1. The boys and girls should be given the same education for perfection of the physical, the vital, the mental and the psychic elements.

2. The female should be provided knowledge not only about physical maternity but also about spiritual Motherhood. They should be taught to make psychic their guide in all walks of life.

3. The boys and girls should be taught to desist from vital communication and physical sex. They should be taught the lesson of celibacy. Thus the Mother has supported the ancient Indian concept of *Brahmacharya* both for the educator and the educand, the boys as well as the girls.

4. The woman should be particularly educated in the field of aesthetic. Hough she should equally value Though and goodness, the pursuit of Beauty is her special vocation.

5. The environment of female education should be particularly surrounded by beauty of forms and expression. This was particularly emphasised by The Mother through her own example.

6. He boys and girls should be taught to be comrades in their march to spirituality.

Marriage and Family

Closely connected to the roles of male and female in society is the question of the functions of social institutions like marriage and family. The mother has written about both these institutions. To the question, "Do You consider this dissolution of the family system indispensable only for the few exceptional individuals who follow some high mental or spiritual ideal or also for the general humanity?", The Mother replied, "Yes, only for the few exceptional individual who follow some high mental or spiritual ideal."[32] Thus those who have to tread the path of mental and spiritual advancement do not require to establish a family. To that extent, the family institution is not compulsory foreveryone.

To the question, "If you advocate a complete dissolution of the family system for the entire humanity, do you consider it advisable for it to happen even before the new process of birth by direct materialisation has teen normalised on earth?", The Mother replied, "More liberty and plasticity in the system are advisable, fixed rules are harmful to evolution."[33] In tune with her spiritual sociology He Mother does not think family institution to be necessary for future society but she warns against all haste in this direction. It is so since evolution in her system, is not linear but spiritual.

In tune with her emphasis upon perfection and liberation as the aims of life The Mother has not accepted the marriage institution as an ideal requirement forevery human being.

According to her the marriage is based upon physical and material unity so that the partners may face together the difficulties and successes of life. This is not a sufficient justification for this institution. Marriage leads to a unity of physical and aesthetic enjoyment. A more appreciable relationship in marriage is based mutual affection and tenderness, tranquility, peace and joy. According to The Mother however, this is not enough. Finally, even about a very high type of marital relationships The Mother has not accepted it as enough. According to her, "In any case, marriage is not a direct way to prepare oneself for *sadhana*. It can be an indirect one if the outward nature needs troubles and disappointments to get rid of all worldly attachments, but in that case the experiment usually ends by separation and often a painful one, at least for one of the two associates. That is all I can tell you on the subject."[34]

The Mother has of course distinguished between lower and higher levels of marital relationships, though she has not considered it necessary for perfection. However, her words may be a pointer for an ideal relationship in marriage. As she said, "To unite your minds, to harmonise your thoughts and make them complementary, to share your intellectual preoccupations and discoveries; in short, to make your sphere of mental activity identical through a widening and enrichment acquired by both at once — that is good, that is absolutely necessary, but it is not enough."[35] In fact The Mother does not support the romantic concept of male-female relationships in which they unite with one another in isolation from the whole world and even God. Ancient Indian social philosophy never supported romantic concept of marriage in spite of the great Kama Sutra of Vatsayana. According to the dominant trend in ancient Indian social philosophy, the male and female unite in marriage only to procreate, the chief ideal of Hindu family is procreation.[36] He birth of a son has been considered to be necessary from the worldly as well as the other worldly viewpoint.[37] According to Manu, a man cannot even renounce the world without procreating a son.[38] In different Vedas, Samhitas and Brahmanas the birth of a son has been declared to be necessary for paying off the debt to the ancestors.[39] The word 'Putra' signifies one who saves a person from the hell of puta'[40]. Thus in Hindu social philosophy the birth of a son is absolutely necessary even for religious and spiritual purposes.

Thus the aim of Hindu marriage was the fulfilment of *Dharma*.

The word '*patni*' signifies that the woman participates with the man in religious ceremonies. No man was permitted to carry out religious celebrations without getting married. Kalidas has called wife as the source of all religious activities. According to Mahabharata "A man's half is his wife, the wife is her husband's best friend; the wife is the source of *dharma*, *artha* and *kama*, and she is also the source of moksa."[41] The *Grhastha-Asrama* has been called the basis of all other Asramas and the chief ideal of the *Grhastha Asrama* is the fulfilment of *dharma*.

In tune with the above-mentioned concept of intimate relationship of male and female in pursuit of Dharma The Mother said, "To be one in aspiration and ascension, to move forward at the same pace on the same spiritual path, that is the secret of a. lasting union."[42] In fact, according to The Mother the bond of social relationships should be neither physical nor spiritual. This however, is not mutual relationship between any two beings, wife and husband, mother and son, brother and sister etc. Instead of establishing social relationships upon mutuality, the Indian philosophers have based it upon the Divine element in all human beings. While this takes away all exclusiveness and therefore conflict, it also provides the widest basis for human relationships. It was in this sense that the sage Yajnavalkya said in Brhadaranyaka Upanisad that it is not for the wife that wife is loved, not for the son that the son is loved but for God. Love, according to Indian philosophy, is not a physical, vital or even mental bond between human beings, it is the communication between different expressions of Divine. Thus ancient Indian social philosophy, in contrast to the Western social philosophy, based social relationships upon God. It is obvious that the future society, as conceived by The Mother, is based upon the ancient Indian concept of human relationships. To quote her words, "Beyond all that, in the depths, at the centre, at the summit of the being, there is a Supreme Truth of being, an Eternal Light, independent of all the circumstances of birth, country, environment, education; That is the origin, cause and master of our spiritual development; it is that which gives a permanent direction to our lives; it is that which determines our destines; it is in the consciousness of That that you must unite."[43]

Thus The Mother has laid down very high ideals for the male-female relationships, including that in marriage. She said, "To be truly a good wife is almost as difficult as to be a true disciple."[44]

This, however, is not based upon exclusive sacrifice on the part of the female. The Mother has openly rebuked all ideas supporting the slavery of woman in any term. However, in tune with ancient Indian concept of rights and duties, she has laid more emphasis upon duties rather than rights. In future society, however, fulfillment of duties will be no longer a matter of sacrifice. It will be natural and spontaneous.

It should be remembered that The Mother has accepted the value of family and marriage as social institutions. To the question: Do you also consider the abolition of the marriage system as equally indispensable as the abolition of the family system for the higher development of humanity? So long as the new process of birth has not been normalised, would not the present manner of sexual procreation continue? In that case, would not some form of marriage relationship be necessary? The Mother replied, "Marriage will always take place, but legal ceremonies must not be enforced, to avoid illegality."[45] In fact, in coherence with her emphasis upon liberty as the principle of spiritual life The Mother has only asked for removal of all bonds, social or legal since spiritual progress requires maximum freedom. She has, however, not supported Plato's hypothesis of bringing up children in the State nurseries. On the other hand, she has not considered family necessary for the growth of children. According to her, "Here also both things must be equally admitted and practised. There are many cases in which it would be a blessing for the baby to be separated from his parents."[46] This is particularly true in the case of broken families. Psychologists, criminologists and sociologists have admitted that in the case of disorganised and broken families it is better to keep the children away from family influence. Going a step further, The Mother points out that the only aim should be the spiritual growth of male and female and the children. Therefore, the marriage and family institutions should be shorn of all rigidity. As Bertrand Russell maintained in his famous work Principles of Social Reconstruction, these institutions should not be based upon authority but on creativity. The Mother has expressed this idea even more clearly when she said, "A minimum of rules. A maximum of freedom. All possibilities must have equal scope for manifestation, then humanity will progress more rapidly."[47] These words lay down the foundational principle of the future society cherished by The Mother.

Keeping the marriage and family institutions free and open however, does not mean that the parents have no responsibility in the education of their children. The Mother has rejected any employment of pressure upon the children in the family. She is absolutely against any imposition of the parental will upon the children. She asked, "What right have you to impose your will on the children, you who have brought them into the world without giving any serious thought to their problems or making the necessary preparations?"[48]

Thus, in keeping with her social philosophy, The Mother has asked the parents to treat children as expressions of Divine. It is a sacred responsibility of the parents to bring up children according to the rules of spirituality. This idea is a step further than that of Froebel in his Kindergarten system of education in which the teacher tends the child like a gardener. In the field of education, as in every other field of social life, the relations of parents and children, as that of the teachers and the students, are based upon the universal divine element among human beings. Thus in her social philosophy The Mother has admirably synthesised freedom with responsibility. If is significant to note that even in marriage institutions The Mother has held the husband responsible for providing sufficient opportunity for cultural progress of his wife as also of the children. To a disciple she wrote, "you say that you could not bring up your children properly because although you are well-educated and cultured you have no time to spare for them, and that your wife has time but she is uneducated, uncultured, good for nothing. Will you tell me who is responsible for her condition? For more than twenty-five years she has lived with you. What did you do in these twenty-five years to educate her or give her your 'culture' – absolutely nothing. Even the idea did not occur to you. You never thought that even if you had given her one hour daily for her education, it would have made a big difference in twenty-five years. For you she existed only as machine to look after your comforts and produce your children. You could not take her into your confidence, you could not do anything for her improvement, but there you stand with all your vanity, blaming her for being uneducated and uncultured."[49]

Educational Implications

The above explanation of The Mother's views concerning social institutions, particularly tie family and marriage, shows that both these institutions have been accepted to be usefully contributing to the spiritual progress of the members. Education, according to the Mother, is a lifelong process, so is spiritual advancement. Family and marriage are not ends in themselves. Like every other social institution, these are means for spiritual progress. Therefore, these should be based upon the principles of spiritual growth. In both these institutions the male has been held particularly responsible since modern family and marriage are male-dominated. However, The Mother is against all types of dominations in these institutions. In society as well as in social institutions including that of education, the aim is the seeking of divine. In other words. the aim is spiritual perfection, a total transformation, a final liberation. This however, has to be sought not only individually but also collectively since both the individuality and collectivity are equally necessary expressions of The Divine. Thus The Mother aims at not only individual liberation but also cosmic liberation. As Sri Aurobindo puts it, "Not only to seek and find the Divine in one-self, but to seek and find the Divine in all, not only to seek one's own individual liberation or perfection, but to seek the liberation and perfection of others is the complete law of the spiritual being."[50] These words laid down not only the basis of education but even the aims of education. Therefore The Mother has asked the teachers and parents to be friends, philosophers and guides in the educand's march to spiritual freedom. It goes without saying that this will provide a sound foundation for the realisation of kingdom of God upon earth.

References

1. *Conversations* (1971), 1-3.
2. *Message given by The Mother* on 9-2-1970.
3. *Sri Aurobindo and The Mother on the Future Society* (1972), p. 24.
4. Marx, K. & Engels, F., *Selected Works*, Vol. I (Moscow: Foreign Language Publishing House, 1955), p. 34.
5. *Sri Aurobindo and The Mother on The Future Society*, p. 24.
6. Marx, K. & Engels, F., *Das Capital*, Vol. I (1958), p. 764.
7. *Sri Aurobindo and The Mother on The Future Society*, p. 25.
8. *Ibid.*
9. Russell, B., *Authority and the Individual* (London: George Allen & Unwin Ltd.), p. 125.
10. Sri Aurobindo, *Mother India*, p. 929.

11. *Bulletin of Physical Education* (August, 1954), p. 15.
12. *C.W.M.*, Centenary Edn. (Pondicherry: Sri Aurobindo Ashram Trust, 1978), Vol. 12, p. 251.
13. *Ibid.*
14. *Ibid.*, p. 252.
15. *Ibid.*, p. 253.
16. *Ibid.*
17. *Ibid.*
18. *Ibid.*, p. 255.
19. *C.W.M.*, Vol. 14 (1980), p. 311.
20. *Ibid.*, p. 310.
21. *C.W.M.*, Vol. 2 (1978), p. 147.
22. *Ibid.*, p. 153
23. *Ibid.*, p. 156.
24. *Ibid.*
25. *Ibid.*, p. 164.
26. C.W.M., Vol. 14 (1980), p. 310.
27. *Ibid.*, pp. 310-311.
28. *C.W.M.*, Vol. 2, p. 155.
29. *Ibid.*, p. 147.
30. *Ibid.*, p. 146.
31. *Ibid.*
32. *C.W.M.*, Vol. 14, p. 313-
33. *Ibid.*
34. *Ibid.*
35. *Ibid.*, p. 312.
36. *Yajnavalkya*, I, 78, *Apastamba*, II, 5.11.12. etc.
37. *Mahabharata*, Adi; 74, 38.
38. *Manu*, II, 28.
39. *Ibid.*
40. *Manu*, IX, 138; *Mahabharata*, Adi, 74, 37; *Ramayana*, 107-12.
41. Mahabharata, Adi, 74, 40.
42. *C.W.M.* Vol. 14 (1980), p. 312.
43. *Ibid.*
44. *Ibid.*, p. 311.
45. *Ibid.*, p. 314.
46. *Ibid.*, p. 316.
47. *Ibid.*
48. *Ibid.*, p. 315.
49. *Ibid.*
50. *Sri Aurobindo and The Mother on Future Society*, p. 22.

7

Political and Economic Foundations of Education

Though The Mother was not very much concerned with, politics yet in keeping with her integral approach she has deliberated over some burning political problems such as war and violence, wealth and government, social and political progress and so on. Some of her views were expressed in answer to the questions of the disciples. Some of her views were only in the form of affirmations or negations in answer to the proclamations made by her representatives to the public.

Like anyone else in her times The Mother was shocked by the murderous consequences of the great war. However, in keeping with the tradition of religion and spirituality all over the world The Mother was an optimist so far as human destiny is concerned. Hie ancient Indian history of philosophy maintains that whatever may be present state of affairs, the forces of evil cannot be victorious over the forces of goods for a very long time. In consistency with Indian philosophy of history The Mother said, on 27th May 1940, "Don't worry about Hitler. No *asuric* force can stand eternally against the divine force and the hour of his defeat is bound to come."[1] She maintained that unless spiritual progress advances side by side with material, progress, the man cannot evolve to a better state., in her positive approach to scientific achievement she has not condemned the discovery of the atomic bomb but only insisted upon the need of inner progress. On 30 August 1945 she said, "The Atomic bomb is in itself the most wonderful nature. But what is to be regretted is that this material progress and mastery is not the result of and In keeping with a spiritual progress and mastery which alone has the power to contradict and counteract the terrible danger coming from these discoveries. We cannot and must not stop progress, but we must achieve it in an equilibrium between me inside and the outside."[2] As Rabindranath Tagore said. "Man's history is the history of his journey to the unknown in the quest of the realisation of his immortal self—his soul. Through the rise and fell of empire: through the building up of gigantic piles of wealth and the ruthless scattering of them upon the dust; through the creation of vast bodies of symbols that give shape to his dramas and aspirations, and the casting of them away like the playthings of an outworn infancy through the forging of his magic keys with which to unlock the mysteries of creation, and through his throwing away of the labour of ages to go back to his worship and work afresh in some new form: yes: through it all man is marching from epoch towards the fullest realization of his soul, — the soul which is greater than the things man accumulates, the deeds he accomplishes, the themes he builds, the soul whose onward course is never checked by death or dissolution."[3]

Non-Violence

It is a well-known fact that in her struggle for independence India followed the path of non-violence under the able guidance of her great sons like M.K. Gandhi and others. Explaining the importance of non-violence Gandhi said, "Without *Ahimsa* it is not possible to seek and find Truth. *Ahimsa* and Truth are so intertwined that it is practically impossible to disentangle and separate them. They are like the two sides of a coin, or rather of a smooth unstamped metallic disc. Who can say which is the obverse and which is the reverse?"[4] In a similar vein The Mother said, on 9 October 1951, "Violence is never a good way to make a cause triumph. How can anyone hope to obtain justice by injustice, harmony by hatred?"[5] According to both M.K. Gandhi and The Mother violence has no place in the spiritual world view. Advancing argument in support of his cult of non-violence Gandhi said, "The fact that there are so many men still alive in the world shows that it is based not on the force of arms but on the force of truth and love. Therefore, the greatest and most unimpeachable evidence of the success of this force is to be found in the fact that in spite of wars of the world, it lives on."[6] In tune with this spiritual world view The Mother said on 6 May 1971, "I disapprove totally of violence. Each act of violence is a step back on the path leading to the goal to which we aspire."[7] She pointed out that fear is always wrong. Nobody should fear any disaster to humanity in future. It is so since in the spiritual world-view it is the Divine who is ultimately responsible for whatever happens in the world. He alone is the basis of all safety. Therefore The Mother said on 26 May

1942. "In the Divine alone is their safety. Take refuge in Him and cast away all fear."[8] Again. "The best protection is an unshakable faith in the Divine Grace. Protection is active and can be effective only with faith on your side, absolute and constant. Let us give ourselves entirely and sincerely to the Divine and we shall enjoy His protection. Integral protection: that which can be given only by the Divine....Psychic protection: the protection resulting from surrender to the Divine. Physical protection is possible only with a total surrender to the Divine and the absence of all desires."[9]

Government and Politics

Contemporary Indian philosophers have supported what is known as Neo-Vedanta socialism. Sri Aurobindo, Swami Vivekananda, Rabindranath Tagore and M.K. Gandhi, all supported the political viewpoint which was at the same time the religious and spiritual viewpoint. They believed that the power of the state should be held at a minimum level so that the individual may get maximum freedom for spiritual progress. The best government, according to them, was self-government. Liberty, equality and fraternity were the ideal principles necessary for the foundation of society. In tune with this Neo-Vedanta socialism The Mother said, "One must be able to control oneself before one can hope to govern others: 1. To have complete control over oneself is the indispensable condition for controlling others. 2. To have no preferences, not to like one and to dislike the other — to be equal with everybody. 3. To be patient and enduring. Also to speak only what is quite indispensable and nothing more."[10]

As more and more power is concentrated in the hands of the state the opportunity for spiritual progress becomes less and less. Therefore, Gandhi was against any increase in the power of the state. He wanted to keep it subservient to the spiritual individuals. Pointing out his approach in this connection he said, "I look upon an increase in the power of the state with the greatest fear, because although while apparently doing good by minimising exploitation, it does the greatest harm to mankind by destroying individuality which lies at the root of all progress."[11] The best rule, according to Gandhi, was self-rule. Everything great comes from within. The spiritual progress of a society depends on individuals. Therefore, the individual should be given maximum freedom for evolving without interference. Therefore The Mother pleaded for the ancient Platonic ideal of the philosopher king. She observed that the wise men alone have a right to govern the world. As she said, "He only who has a perfect sense of true justice can claim the right to be obeyed."[12] On 17 September 1959 she said, "When I say that the "wise' should govern the world, I am not taking a political point of view but a spiritual one. The various forms of government can stay as they are; that is only of secondary importance. But whatever the social status of the men in power, they should receive their inspiration from those who have realised the Truth and have no other will than that of the Supreme."[13] Both M.K. Gandhi and The Mother asked for practice of truth in politics. M.K. Gandhi insisted upon truth as the ideal of political satyagrahi. He said, "There should be truth in thought, Truth in speech and Truth in action."[14] In more clear terms The Mother said on 4 October 1971, "Remain in politics and try to bring Truth into politics. It is a very sure way towards effective spirituality."[15] Thus like M.K. Gandhi The Mother wanted politics to be free from all intrigues. A disciple asked, "So far, we have considered 'Politics' as consisting of any movement, including intrigue and malpractice, to arrive at dominance either of oneself or of one's party over others. In this, one has to hold that one's own view or ideology is true and that of others is wrong. This politics we must completely avoid. Is it not so?' To this The Mother said, Yes'."[16]

Human Unity

According to Sri Aurobindo, "The whole process of Nature depends on a balancing and a constant tendency to harmony between two poles of life, the individual whom the whole or aggregate nourishes and the whole or aggregate which the individual helps to constitute. Human life forms no exception to the rule. Therefore the perfection of human life must involve the elaboration of an as yet unaccomplished harmony between these two poles of our existence, the individual and the social aggregate. The perfect society will be that which most entirely favours the perfection of the individual; the perfection of the individual will be incomplete if it does not help towards the perfect state of the social aggregate to which he belongs and eventually to that of the largest possible human aggregate, the whole of a united humanity."[17] Following the same integral politics The Mother said, in her message to World Union on 25 March, 1960, "The World is a unity — it has always been, and it is always so, even now it is so — it is not that it has not got the unity and the unity has to be brought in from, outside- and imposed upon it. Only the world is not conscious of its unity. It has to be made conscious. "[18] World peace can be established only by the establishment of human unity upon earth. Outlining the principle for all diplomacy between nations The Mother said on 15 April 1955, "If diplomacy could become the instrument of the Truth and the Divine Grace, instead of being based on duplicity and falsehood, a big step would be taken towards human unity and harmony."[19] Thus international relationships should be rather based on honesty, truth and sincerity. In the words of The Mother, "The earth will enjoy a lasting and living peace only when men understand that they must be truthful and sincere even in their international dealings. For the Government's honesty lies not only in saying what they are doing but also in doing what they say."[20]

According to The Mother world peace is possible only through human unity. That is the only sure way to avoid a future war on a global scale. Outlining her scheme about peace The Mother said on 24 April 1955, "It is only by the growth and establishment of the consciousness of human unity, that a true and lasting peace can be achieved upon earth. All means leading towards this goal, are welcome, although the external ones have a very limited effect; however; the most important, urgent and indispensable of all, is a transformation of the human consciousness itself, an enlightenment of and conversion in its working."[21] In the meanwhile The Mother suggests some exterior steps such as the acceptance of the principle of double nationality. She rejects the suspicion that double nationality will lead to an awkward position in the event of war between two countries. According to The Mother, if thoughtful human beings have perfect faith in. God and Divine purpose they should open the door for international communication without any fear of war. If a large number of people support peace, war becomes impossible. Therefore, in her message on May 1955 The Mother said. "Shake off all narrowness, selfishness, limitations, and wake up to the consciousness of Human Unity. This is the only way to achieve peace and harmony."[22] As Sri Aurobindo suggested, "Man must be sacred to man regardless of all distinctions of race, creed, colour, nationality, status, political or social advancement."[23] However, The Mother knew that the nations are as yet not prepared for such an opening. Therefore she suggested spiritual education for realising change of consciousness. To the question by a participant of First World Conference of the Sri Aurobindo Society, "How can human unity become one?"' The Mother replied, "By becoming conscious of its origin."[24] integral sociology bases all relationships upon the origin of human relationships *i.e.* God The entire cosmos is the self-expression of Divine. Since the plant nature and animal nature have not forgotten their instinct, they enjoy unity and harmony. But unfortunately with the growth of reason man has forgotten his original source. If human beings are made to remember that they are self-expressions of the Divine, much of the conflict, differences, divisions and resistances may be overcome. This consciousness of the origin however, requires a total change of consciousness.

In the philosophy of The Mother the two terms, total and integral, must be understood clearly. According to The Mother, "Total means vertically in all the states of being, from the most material, to the most subtle. Integral means horizontally in all the different and often contradictory parts which constitute the outer being, physical, vital and mental."[25] Therefore in man transformation must happen not only on the mind but also in the vital as well as the physical body. Similarly the outer being should also be transformed. Integral philosophy insists upon horizontal as well as vertical evolution. Integral evolution is necessary for man's victory over the present crisis. It is so since, as Sri Aurobindo pointed out, "At present mankind is undergoing an evolutionary crisis in which is concealed a choice of its destiny; for a stage has been reached in which the human mind has achieved in certain directions an enormous development while in others it stands arrested and bewildered and can no longer find its way."[26] Therefore in her message on February 1965 The Mother said, "If you want peace upon earth first establish peace in your heart. If you want union in the world, first unify the different parts of your own being."[27] It should be remembered here that integral philosophy believes in a parallelism between the individual and collectivity, part and whole. Within the human unity is national unity and within the national unity is individual unity. Therefore integral evolution should start with the individual and pass on to the nation before being established in humanity.

Educational Implications

Whereas Sri Aurobindo suggested religion of humanity as a possible solution to achieve human unity, The Mother points out to spiritual education. A member of First World Conference of Sri Aurobindo Society asked, "What is the way of making the consciousness of human unity grow in man" To this The Mother replied, "Spiritual education, that is to say an education which gives more importance to the growth of the spirit than to any religious or moral teaching or to the material so-called knowledge."[28] Spiritual education involves a radical change of consciousness, a new birth, a birth of supramental level. Not practical success but change of consciousness in the aim of spiritual education. Such an education will make an individual remember his origin and to become a fit instrument for the expression of Divine purpose upon earth. It is only after such an education is available to a growing number of people that the ideal of world unity may be realised.

Modernity *versus* Traditionalism

An important issue in sociology of education is the question of modernity versus traditionalism. Education, by consensus, must support modernity as against traditionalism, and The Mother is not an exception to this rule. Condemning all types of traditionalism, she said in her message on 13 December 1954, "Often we cling to that which was, afraid of losing the result of a previous experience, of giving up a vast and high consciousness and falling again into and inferior state. But we must always look forward and advance."[29] Explaining the meaning of modernization in reference to education A.R. Desai pointed out, the result of modernisation as, "emergence of a new cultural outlook characterised by emphasis on progress and improvement, on happiness and spontaneous expression of abilities and feelings, on the development of individuality as a value, and efficiency."[30] It is interesting to note that The Mother's scheme of education meets this criterion of modernisation of education. According to her, "The purpose of earthly life is progress. If you stop progressing you will die. Every moment that you spend without progressing is one step closer to your grave."[31] It may be remembered that modernisation involves a constant insistence upon progress. The Mother has asked the students and teachers to be constantly progressive. Life, according to her, is movement, efforts, marching forward. Learning is a constant progress and it should be lifelong. In her message on 11 September 1934, The Mother said, "One has always something to learn and a progress to make, and in each circumstance we can find the occasion of learning the lesson and making the progress."[32]

Progress means a readiness to change and sacrifice whatever is required to march ahead. Progress should be both on the individual as well as collective scale. It should be the necessary characteristic of every social institution. This requires absolute rejection of all conservatism. As The Mother said in her message on 7 November 1961, "Whatever is new will always meet an opposition from conservative people. If we yield to this opposition, the world will never advance one step."[33] Thus the educators and the educands, in the new integral education, must have a revolutionary spirit. They should themselves present examples to others. They should constantly aim at the goal. As The Mother said in her message on 7 April, 1952. "Never forget the goal. Never stop aspiring. Never halt in your progress, and you are sure to succeed."[34] Thus, education according to The Mother, continues from the cradle to the grave. No one is too old to learn. A life without progress is a dead light life. However, the aim is not success itself since this will bring vanity. Therefore The Mother has advised, "Success is a harder or deal to pass through than misfortune, it is in the hour of success that one must be especially vigilant to rise above oneself."[35] Forces of opposition attack as soon as a man succeeds in one direction. Similarly, relaxation spoils the game. Therefore one must keep a constant vigilance in the hour of success. Not success but transformation is the aim of spiritual education. This transformation requires the fulfilment of the following conditions:

1. Transformation should have a sanction from Divine.
2. There should be constant material growth.
3. Transformation should be total.
4. It should have physical plasticity.
5. Humility before the Divine is a necessary characteristic.
6. There should be supramental light in subconscient.
7. There should be psychic awakening in matter.

Economic Institutions

Sociological foundation includes economic institutions. The

Mother has written about wealth and government. Her views in this direction are comparable to that of Karl Marx and other illustrious thinkers. Traditional Indian social philosophy has maintained that all land belongs to Divine and therefore it should not be grabbed by a particular section of society. This view is against capitalism. In keeping with this ancient Indian ideal The Mother said, "It is to the Divine that all riches belong. It is the Divine who lends them to living beings, and it is to Him that they must naturally return."[36] According to her, money is only a means and never an end. Therefore she has insisted upon the ancient Indian ideal of Aprigrah. In her message on 6 January 1955 she said, "A day shall come when all the wealth of this world, freed at least from the enslavement to the anti-Divine forces, offers itself spontaneously and fully to the service of the Divine's work upon earth."[37] Therefore, money should be used in good work.

In keeping with the spiritual traditions of India The Mother has pointed out to the distinction and even opposition of the material and spiritual power, she has asked her disciples, "Never mix in your thought spiritual power and money because it leads straight to catastrophe."[38] Thus, like Sri Aurobindo, The Mother deplores the economic man. In tune with the Christ's theory that the rich will never get to heaven The Mother said, "Greed for money: the surest way to decrease one's conscience and to narrow one's nature."[39] Christ said, "Blessed are they who are poor for they shall be fulfilled." In tune with this Sermon on the Mount, The Mother said, "To the rich God gives money, but to the poor He gives Himself. All depends on the poor giving more value to the riches or to God."[40] Similar sentiments have been expressed by other contemporary Indian thinkers including R.N. Tagore, Swami Vivekananda and M.K. Gandhi. Swami Vivekananda said, "Rich men are merely the ornaments, the decorations of the country. It is the millions of poor lower-class people who are its life."[41] Like Karl Marx and M.K. Gandhi The Mother could foresee the inevitable fall of the capitalist. In her message on 12 March 1965 she said, "The financiers and businessmen have been offered the possibility to collaborate with the future, but most of them refuse, convinced that the power of money is stronger than that of the future,"[42] To quote similar statement of Swami Vivekananda, "The lower classes are gradually awakening to this fact and making a united front against this, determined to act their legitimate dues.

The masses of Europe and America have been the first to awaken and have already begun the fight. Signs of this awakening have shown themselves in India, too, as is evident from the number of strikes among the lower classes now-a-days. The upper classes will no longer be able to repress the lower, try the ever so much."[43] Thus the economic ideas of The Mother, like her political ideas are in keeping with her general philosophy of life.

References

1. C.W.M., Vol. 15 (1980), p. 47.
2. *Ibid.*, pp. 48-49.
3. Tagore, R.N., *A Message*, p. 78.
4. Gandhi, M.K., *From Yervada Mandir* (Ahmedabad: 1933), pp. 8-9.
5. *C.W.M.*, Vol. 15, p. 49.
6. Bose, *Selections from Gandhi*, p. 22.
7. *C.W.M.*, Vol. 15, p. 49.
8. *Ibid.*, p. 50.
9. *Ibid.*, p. 51.
10. *Ibid.*, pp. 58-59.
11. Quoted by Francis, W. Coker in *Recent Political Thought* (1934), p. 198.
12. *C.W.M.*, Vol. 15, p. 60.
13. *Ibid.*, p. 61.
14. Gandhi, M.K., *Yervada Mandir*, p. 2.
15. *C.W.M.*, Vol. 15, p. 61.
16. *Ibid.*, pp. 61-62.
17. Sri Aurobindo, *The Ideal of Human Unity* (Pondicherry: Sri Aurobindo Ashram, 1950), p. 8.
18. *C.W.M.*, Vol. 15, p. 68.
19. *Ibid.*, p. 64.
20. *Ibid.*
21. *Ibid.*
22. *Ibid.*, p. 65.
23. Sri Aurobindo, *The Ideal of Human Unity*, p. 364.
24. *C.W.M.*, vol. 15, p. 66.
25. *Ibid.*, p. 95.
26. Sri Aurobindo, *The Life Divine*, American Edition, p. 933.
27. *C.W.M.*, Vol. 15, p. 71.
28. *Ibid.*, p. 66.
29. *Ibid.*, p. 76.
30. Desai, A.R., 'Need for Revaluation of the Concept' in *Essays on Modernization of Underdeveloped Societies*, Vol. I (Bombay, Thacker & Co, 1971), pp. 462-63.

31. *C.W.M.*, Vol. 15, p. 82.
32. *Ibid.*, p. 82.
33. *Ibid.*, p. 84.
34. *Ibid.*, p. 86.
35. *Ibid.*, p. 88.
36. *Ibid.*, p. 53.
37. *Ibid.*
38. *Ibid.*, p. 55.
39. *Ibid*, p. 57.
40. *Ibid.*
41. Swami Vivekananda, *The Complete Works*, Vol. VI (1964), P. 354.
42. *C.W.M.*, Vol. 15, p. 57.
43. Swami Vivekananda, *The Complete Works*, Vol. VII (1964), p. 149.

8

Physical Education

Integral education is total education. Therefore, it is not only mental but also vital and physical. According to The Mother the aim and ideal of education is perfection. "To work for your perfection", she advised, "the first step is to become conscious of yourself, of the different parts of your being and their respective activities."[1] Thus man must understand his complex structure which includes body, vital sense organs and animal urges, mind and supramental levels. Those who fail to understand this complexity of nature and identify man with body or mind, cannot achieve perfection. A one-sided and distorted view of human nature leads to a distorted and one-sided philosophy of education. Modern developments in physiology, biology, psychology, sociology, anthropology and all other human sciences have unanimously agreed about the fact that man is no more a unity. He is a combination of several parts. Sigmond Freud calls them Id, Ego and Super ego. Sri Aurobindo has pointed cut to the physical, the vital, the mental and the supramental parts of the human beings. Therefore, Aristotle's definition of man as a rational being is no more a sufficient basis for outlining the aim of education. Hence The Mother has asked the teachers and the students to analyse their complex nature and to know the inner truth. Thus education requires internal as well as external progress. It requires a fourfold discipline, the discipline of the physical, the vital, the mental and the psychic being. Hence education must involve multi-sided methods.

According to The Mother, "As you pursue this labour of purification and unification, you must at the same time take great care to perfect the external and instrumental part of your being."[2] Thus The Mother supports the ancient Indian idea that the body is the eternal instrument for the realisation of all *Dharma*. Therefore physical education is a necessary part of what The Mother calls "The Science of Living". Explaining the four-fold perfection which is called education The Mother said, "Lastly, by means of a rational and discerning physical education, we must make our body strong and supple enough to become a fit instrument in the material world for the truth-force which wants to manifest through us."[3]

Meaning and Scope of Physical Education

Defining physical education The Mother said, "Physical education is meant to bring into the body, consciousness and control, discipline and mastery, all things necessary for a higher and better life."[4] In other words, physical education is the education for physical perfection. It leads to what is known as physical culture. Integral physical education aims at integral cultural evolution of the educand and the educator. Integral evolution requires evolution of the culture of the body, the vital, the mind and the psychic element. Therefore, evolution and education start with physical culture. Explaining the meaning of physical culture The Mother said, "Physical culture is the best way of developing the consciousness of the body, and the more the body is conscious, the more it is capable of receiving the divine forces that are at work to transform it and give birth to the new race."[5] Physical culture includes all sorts of exercises, sports and games. However, there is a difference between sports training and physical culture. The aim of the sports training is to compete for some games or competitions. Physical education, on the other hand, does not aim at winning some competitions but perfection of the body. Distinguishing between sports and physical education The Mother said, "Sports are all the games, competitions, tournaments, etc., all the things based on contests and ending in placings and prizes. Physical education means chiefly the combination of all exercises for the sake of the growth and upkeep of the body."[6]

However, sports form an important part of physical education. In her message to Athletics competition, 1964, The Mother said, on 24th August, 1964, "We are here to lay the foundations of a new world. All the virtues and skills required to succeed in athletics are exactly those the physical man must have to be fit for receiving and manifesting the new force." Therefore, in Sri Aurobindo Ashram, regular athletics competition is organised.

The scope of physical education also includes training in yoga. In ancient India, preliminary yogic practices formed an essential part of the syllabus. *Yuma, nivama, asans pranayama* were practised by the students. Practice of concentration was an essential training. Both education and yoga seek the same ultimate ideal of individual and social development. Where educational practices exhaust their means for this purpose, yoga takes up to lead man to perfection. Therefore, The Mother said, "Any well-planned and scientifically arranged programme of exercises practised with a yogic attitude will become yogic exercises and the person practising them will draw full benefit from the point of physical health and moral and spiritual uplift."[7] Thus *yoga* helps in the creation of a new Divine society upon earth, not only by bringing down the Supramental but also training the body and leading it to physical transformation. In her message to Competitions 1970 The Mother said on April 1, "The world is preparing for a new creation, let us help through physical education, by making our bodies stronger, more receptive and more plastic, on the way to physical transformation."[8] All the virtues and skills required for success in athletics are helpful for the growth of man's body to fit in the new society.

Value of Physical Education

Pointing out the need of physical development Aldous Huxley said, "Where the body is maladjusted and under strain, the mind's relations, sensory, emotional, intellectual, conative, with external reality are likely to be unsatisfactory."[9] Education aims at an ail round and total perfection of the individual and society. Hence physical culture should form an important part of the educational process. As Sri Aurobindo puts it, "If our seeking is for a total perfection of the being, the physical part of it cannot be left aside; for the body is the material basis, the body is the instrument which we have to use."[10] Hence The Mother maintained, "The Captains of Physical Education can be the nucleus of Physical education. They need not be many in number, but a good selection, first class people, true candidates for supremehood, ready to give themselves entirely, unreservedly to the big divine work."[11]

Physical culture aims at the perfection of the body, health, strength and fitness. Sports and games develop habits, capacities and qualities which are required in the individual and collective endeavours of man's life. Physical culture, besides keeping the body fit and strong, helps in the development of discipline, morale and character Different sports need different qualities and thus help in their development. But as Sri Aurobindo points out, "One development of the utmost value is the awakening of the essential and instinctive body consciousness which can see and do what is necessary without any indication from mental thought and which is equivalent in the body to swift insight in the mind and spontaneous and rapid decision in the will."[12] Collective marches and drill lead to the formation of a capacity for harmonious and right movements of the body. This results in an economy of physical effort and elimination of any waste of energy. It develops the sporting spirit. Games help develop the sense of discipline, obedience, order and habit of team-work. These qualities are helpful in the individual, national and international development of all kinds – physical, mental and spiritual. Summarising the value of physical education The Mother said on April 1, 1966 in her message to Competitions 1966, "We want to come in contact with the supreme consciousness, the universal consciousness, we want to bring it down in ourselves and to manifest it. But for that we must have a very solid base; our base is our physical being, our body. Therefore we have to build up a body solid, healthy, enduring, skillful, agile and strong, ready for everything. There is no better way to prepare the body than physical exercise: sports, athletics, gymnastics, and all games are the best means to develop and strengthen the body."[13]

Therefore, Sri Aurobindo Ashram Department of Physical Education was founded in May 1945. It organises the physical education programme for the students and teachers of the Centre of Education and for the members of the Ashram. Its activities are coordinated and supervised by a group of instructors called captains, who give training in Athletics (track and field events), aquatics, gymanstics, games, combative sports and asanas. The yearly schedule is divided into four seasons: during the first three, there is a period of training followed by competitions; at the end of the year, participants prepare an annual demonstration of physical culture which is presented on December 2nd at the Ashram Sports Ground, Facilities of the department include a library, gymnasium, playground, sportsground, swimming pool, judo hall and tennis courts. The Mother took active interest in the development of the physical education department and helped to shape its programme. For years she spent her late afternoon and evening hours with those who took part in the various physical activities. Explaining the aim of physical training The Mother said, "the aim in the training is to develop this power of concentrating the attention at will on whatever subject or activity one choose from the most spiritual to the most material, without losing anything of the fullness of the power, — for instance, in the physical field, transferring the use of the power from one game to another or one activity to another so as to succeed equally in all,"[14] Thus the Department of Physical Education aimed at the development of power of concentration among the educands. They were taught to renew their energies through sports and yogic discipline. Yogic science was utilised to put the education in relation to the energies accumulated in the terrestrial material world and to draw freely from this inexhaustible power. In other words, it was utilised to establish a harmonious relationship between the human being and material Nature. The child was taught correct judgment and control of desires and needs. Tournaments, competitions and athletic needs were organised to achieve the perfection of the body. It is so since The Mother maintained, "The body must learn to obey before it can manifest power; and physical education is the most thorough discipline for the body."[15] In her numerous messages and letters The Mother has explained various aspects of physical education. She has particularly given attention to physical education of woman.

Physical Education of Women

As an enlightened Western woman, well versed in modern science, The Mother deplored all distinctions made upon the basis of sex. She considered male and female having equal capacities and abilities in almost every aspect. Therefore, she asked the women not to be conscious of their body in particular. She asked, "For God's sake can't forget that you are a girl or a body and try to become a human being?"[16] She insisted upon becoming master of the body rather than its slave. To the question should a girl participate in her normal programme of physical education during her periods? She replied, "Certainly if she is accustomed to physical exercise, she must not stop because of that."[17] She asked for the development of an attitude of quiet forbearance among the educators and the educands. She pointed out that both the boys and girls can participate in all types of sports and games to increase their health and strength. She deplored the tendency among modern women to be physically feminine. She said, "Weakness and fragility may look attractive in the view of a perverted mind, but it is not the truth of Nature nor the truth of the Spirit. If you have ever looked at the photos of the women gymnasts you will know what perfectly beautiful bodies they have; and nobody can deny that they are muscular."[18] She pointed out that the practice of vigorous types of exercises does not bring any difficulties in childbirth if a girl wants to marry and have children after physical education. Outlining the ideal of physical education of woman she said, "A perfect harmony in the proportions, suppleness and strength, grace and force, plasticity and endurance, and above all, an excellent health, unvarying and unchanging, which is the result of a pure soul, a happy trust in life and an unshakable faith in the Divine Grace."[19]

In keeping with her general philosophy of life The Mother rejected all distinctions among human beings based upon sex. She prescribed almost similar exercises and sports competitions for boys and girls. She maintained that man and woman have to play their goals in new society according to their capacities and abilities without any distinction of sex. Outlining the general aim of physical education both for boys and girls, The Mother said, "Physical education has for its aim to develop all the possibilities of a human body, possibilities of harmony, strength, plasticity, cleverness, ability, endurance, and to increase the control over the functioning of the limbs and the organs, to make of the body a perfect instrument at the disposal of a conscious will. This programme is excellent for all human beings equally, and there is no point in wanting to adopt another one for girls."[20] The physical body is capable of progressive development. Transformation of the physical body infuses new spiritual consciousness even in the cells of the body. This creates marvellous results. To realise such results however, one must practise physical culture in a methodical and rational way. The Mother has analysed the nature of human body, its capacities and limitations, its diseases and deformities in details and guided in almost every aspect of physical development.

Foundation of Physical Education

According to The Mother, "All education of the body should begin at birth and continue throughout life. It is never too soon to begin nor too late to continue,"[21] Physical education is based upon three fundamental aspects:

1. "Control and discipline of the functioning of the body;
2. An integral, methodical and harmonious development of all the parts and movements of the body; and
3. Correction of any defects and deformities."[22]

Control and Discipline of the Functioning of the Body

This starts right from the very first days, even the first hours of the life of the child. This includes matters concerning food, sleep and evacuation, etc. In these fields the child must be taught to form good habits so that a lot of trouble and inconvenience may be avoided. These physical habits will be an asset for the rest of his life. This training however, requires a knowledge of the structure and functioning of the human body. The child should know the functioning of his internal organ so that he may be able to control them more and more. He should be taught correct positions, postures and movements. The diet should be controlled and balanced. With reference to food, The Mother has laid down the rule, "But it is very important to remember that the instinct of the body, so long as it remains intact, is more reliable than any theory."[23] Therefore, instead of depending upon the general theoretical knowledge one must pay more attention to the physical instinct of the child himself. Normally, the child instinctively knows his needs and how to fulfil them. Needs are different from desires. While the former must be fulfilled, the latter should be controlled. As The Mother maintained, "One must educate the child with care and teach him to distinguish his desires from his needs."[24] The child should be taught to eat according to the needs of his hunger. He must learn to observe hygiene and cleanliness. Food must be chosen according to the age and activities of the child.

Besides food another control and discipline of the functioning of the body is concerning cleanliness and observance of the principles of hygiene. Both the boys and girls should try to develop a well-built, robust, muscular, strong and well-balanced body. This requires regular exercises. The Mother has insisted upon methodical and regular exercises of all the parts of the body. She said, "In the general programme of the child's education, sports and outdoor games should be given a prominent place; that, more than all the medicines in the world, will assure the child good health."[25] Instead of using medicines and tonics the educand should be made to live in healthy environment with plenty of open sun and fresh air. This will do more good to his body than all the medicines of the world.

The child should have sufficient number of hours of sleep. The number of hours of course vary according to the age of the child. Supporting the age-old Indian wisdom about the value of early morning to rise and to sleep early, The Mother has pointed out, "The hours before midnight are the best for resting the nerves."[26] Besides sleep relaxation of muscles and nerves should be taught to everyone. The Mother however, deplores the tendency of the parents to use the child for household services. She said, "At the risk of going against many current ideas and ruffling many prejudices, I hold that it is not fair to demand service from a child, as if it were his duty to serve his parents. The contrary would be more true, and certainly it is natural that parents should serve their child or at least take great care of him."[27] However, the child should be allowed to do anything that he chooses freely to work from the family. This principle is very much different from the theory of teaching basic craft in M.K. Gandhi's scheme of Basic Education. In keeping with her aim of life and the general aim of physical education as beauty The Mother has said, "A young child should aspire for beauty, not for the sake of pleasing others or winning their admiration, but for the love of beauty itself, for beauty is the ideal which all physical life must realise.[28]

Attitude towards Food

In ancient Indian philosophy it was recommended that before starting eating food, some portion of it should be offered to God. Appreciating this attitude The Mother has written on different aspects of food in details. According to her, "With regard to the food that man takes, there are two factors that determine or prescribe it. First of all the real need of the body, that is to say, what the body actually requires for its maintenance, the elements to meet the chemical changes taking place in it, something quite material and very definite, *viz.*, the kind of food and the quantity. But usually this real need of the body is obscured and submerged under the demands of another kind of agency, almost altogether foreign to it, (1) vital desire and (2) mental notions."[29] Therefore, The Mother has asked for liberating the body from the slavery of the vital and the mental. A dominant tendency in Indian philosophy has been the rejection of body as low and earthly. The extra-terrestrial interpretation of liberation and the spiritual aim of life has led so many Indian saints, poets and religious savants to ignore if not despise the body as filth and worth rejection. On the one hand this led to a lot of mortification of the body and on the other hand ignorance about the ideal of physical beauty which was so much insisted upon by the Romans in the West. This is particularly due to the *Advaita Vedanta* metaphysics that *Brahman* alone is real, the world is unreal and the body has to be rejected. Against this age old dominant tendency The Mother insisted that the body is as much divine as any other element in the human being. This theme will be taken again in cur discussion about the physical body in this chapter It should be noted here that in her integral approach The Mother has rejected all claims of the vital and the mental over the body. This is a comical revolution in psychology. Till now the mind or the vital have ruled the body. The Mother, on the other hand, maintains that the vital or the mind have no right to dictate the body. According to her most of the ailments of the body are due to this slavery.

Advising the correct attitude towards eating The Mother said, "Eat at fixed, reasonably — calmly, quietly, composedly. Do not eat too much; for then you will have to concern yourself with digestion: that would be a disagreeable thing; it will make you lose time. Eat just what is necessary. You must give up all desire and attraction, all vital movement."[30] Distinguishing between the need and desire The Mother recommended that while needs should be fulfilled desires must be rejected. In the case of the body needs are real wants and require fulfilment. But desires concerning body are not physical but vital and therefore must be rejected. The body should refuse to be the slave of the vital and must insist upon its own natural and normal fulfilment which is the satisfaction of physical needs and not the desires. As The Mother said, "The all absorbing interest that men. without exception, even the most intellectual take in food, in its preparation and consumption should be replaced by an almost chemical knowledge of the needs of the body and a wholly scientific system of Austerity in the way of satisfying them."[31] Endorsing the ancient Indian idea of eating as offering to Divine The Mother wrote, "When one eats, one aspires that the food taken should not be for the sake of the little human ego but as an offering to the divine consciousness within oneself."[32]

In the history of man eating has been guided by vital and mental attachments and tastes. Integral philosophy grants freedom to each part of human being and therefore rejects the role of attachments and tastes. So many types of food are not useful to the body and are harmful to the vital and the mind. The Mother has asked to reject such intakes. About smoking, drinking and drugs she wrote, "One must strictly shun all excess, all vice, small or big, one must deny oneself the use of such slow poisons as tobacco, alcohol, etc. which men have the habit of developing into indispensable needs that gradually demolish their will and memory."[33] These are based upon human perversions. The animal being nearer to nature does not succumb to these things. Man has even less reason to succumb to them.

In integral psychology the lower follows the rule of the higher. It is not the body which governs, the supramental principle governs the mental, the vital and the physical. Therefore before seeking purification of the body one must seek the purification of the vital and the mind. Mortification of the body is wrong since it involves tyranny of the mind and the vital over the body. Therefore, The Mother said, "What I mean is this: do not try to be an angel in the body before you are already something of the kind in your mind and in your vital."[34] According to the principle of harmony, different parts of human being cannot evolve in isolation, if the body has to evolve the vital and mental evolve even before it. All these three remain on the same level and one of them cannot be pulled up for long leaving the other behind. The Mother has rejected mortification of the body in the form of excessive fasting. On the other hand, she has also decried excessive preoccupation with food. Thus pointing out to a golden mean between fasting and feasting, The Mother said. "However, instead of thinking all the while about food, how to get it and eat, if one were to take to fasting for the sake of freeing oneself from the bondage of food preoccupation, rising a little in the scale of consciousness, it would be a good thing. If you have the faith it will do you good, it will purify you, make you progress a little. In that way it is all right: it will not do any harm to your body excepting making it a little thinner. But if you fast and then continuously turn back to it and think of the food that you might have eaten or are likely to eat after the fasting, well, such fasting is worse than feasting."[35] As the Gita says, "*Yoga* is not for one who eats in excess nor for one who abstains from eating altogether.

Thus spiritual progress requires a detached and balanced attitude to food. As The Mother said, "It is not by abstaining from food that you can make a spiritual progress. It is by being free, free not only from all attachment, from all desire and preoccupation for food but even from all needs in respect of food, by being in a state in which these things are so foreign to the consciousness that they have no place there. It is then and as a natural and spontaneous consequence that one can fast usefully."[36] Thus what is important is liberation from the matters concerning body. This can be realised only by bringing the body in touch with supramental divine forces.

Sleep and Dream

Similar is the principle concerning sleep and dream. Here also, the effort should be done to follow nature and needs of the body. Progress can be made by letting the divine power work in these fields as well Laying down the principle about how to sleep, The Mother said, "When the sun sets, a kind of peace descends upon the earth and this peace is helpful for sleep. When the sun rises a vigorous energy descends upon the earth and this energy is helpful for work. When you go to bed late and get up late, you contradict the forces of Nature and that is not very wise."[37] The Mother has given the following directions for a better sleep:

1. Light food gives quiet sleep.
2. The most important thing is to keep the mind clear and quiet.
3. Meditation helps in concentration and rest.
4. Stretch and relax on the bed before sleeping.
5. Repeat a mantra or a word before going to sleep.
6. Ask the mind to wake up at the appointed hour.

According to The Mother, "Sleep is indispensable in the present state of the body. It is by a progressive control over the subconscient that the sleep can become more and more conscious."[38] Thus sleep has to be learnt by gradual experience and self-control.

Dream is a normal phenomena. Psychologists have been always concerned with it Most of the psychologists have explained it with reference to physical and psychological reasons. The Mother has looked to dream from the spiritual viewpoint. Therefore she has said, "We should therefore learn to recognise our dreams and, above all to distinguish, between them, for they vary greatly in their nature and quality."[39] According to The Mother dreams may be due to the following causes:

1. Physical circumstances such as health, digestion etc.
2. Vain expression of certain mental faculties.
3. Revenge of the inner being to be free for sometime.

Of the above-mentioned three types of dreams according to their causes the first is the least important, the second shows internal disorder and the third exhibits inner tendencies, tastes, impulses and desires. Dreams are forgotten because they do not happen in the said place. It is useful to note down one's dreams in order to know oneself. Conscious will can change the course of one's dream. Premonitory dreams, if rightly interpreted may give some idea about future. Somnambulism is a sigh of the fact that all the parts of man's being, including the most material, have an independent consciousness. It may be cured by putting a will upon the body before going to see. One must maintain a balance between sleep and rest.

Nature of The Physical Body

It has been already pointed out that education seeks four types of perfection. Beauty is the aim of physical perfection. Perfection of the physical however, requires a deep understanding of its nature. The Mother has explained the nature of the body and the physical in her numerous writings and messages. On 16 June 1941, she said, "In the physical the joy of being is the best expression of gratitude towards the Divine."[40] Thus the Divine expresses through the body. In her message on 29 May 1954 The Mother said, "The Physical being itself can be the seat of perfect existence, knowledge and bliss."[41] Knowledge in the body is secured by doing things. Endorsing the modern Western educational dictum of learning by doing The Mother said in her message on 23 June 1954, "For the body, to know means to be able to do. In fact the body knows only what it can do"[42] Peace in this sense is an indispensable condition for the progress of the body. This may be realised by knowing what God wills as the best condition of the body light in the physical cells is the first step towards purity. This purity can be realised by the conquest of desires. It, however, is a necessary condition to good health The physical cells of the body have a capacity of aspiration towards the divine. The physical prepares for transformation through the symptom of Ananda. The physical body may achieve divine Ananda by purification of all desires and repulsions and through perfect equality and surrender. Summing up the integral philosophy of the body The Mother said, "Integral even basis in the material: when all your material movements are organised, harmonised and co-ordinated and when all things find themselves in you their respective places and your entire material basis is thus prepared and becomes ready to receive the Light and the Power."[43] Thus, according to The Mother, the physical body may become a superhuman body by means of physical culture involving physical activities. Thus one of the goals of education as well as yoga is to make the body a fit vehicle for the expression of higher beauty and consciousness. As The Mother said, about the goals of Auroville, "The human body must be improved, perfected, and it must become a superhuman body capable of expressing a being higher than man. And this certainly cannot happen if we neglect it. It is by an enlightened physical culture and by using physical activities — the activities of the body — not for little personal needs and satisfactions, but to make the body more capable of expressing a higher beauty and consciousness. And for that, physical education has an important place, which should be given to it."[44]

Illness and Health

An important part of physical education is the training in the rules of health and the knowledge concerning the causes of illness and its remedies. Pointing out the importance of a healthy body The Mother said, "Do not forget that to succeed in our yoga one must have a strong and healthy body. For This, the body must do exercise, have an active and regular life, work physically, eat well and sleep well. It is in good health that the way towards transformation is found."[45] Good health expresses inner harmony. Therefore, one must try to attain good health and for that understand the principle concerning inner harmony.

Illness, on the other hand, is a result of disruption of this inner harmony. The Mother has extensively written about the nature and causes of illness. As has been already pointed out, according to The Mother's philosophy of education, this forms the third aspect of physical education. Explaining the nature of physical ailments in her message on 22 May 1957, The Mother said, "Physical ailments are always the sign of a resistance in the physical being; but with surrender to the Divine's will and a complete trust in the working of the Grace, they are bound to disappear soon."[46] The following are the most important causes of illness according to The Mother:

1. *Disequilibrium:* Disequilibrium is not always physical, it may be vital or mental. The physical disequilibrium again, may be functional or organic. According to The Mother the functional disequilibrium is cured more quickly than organic disequilibrium. Illness due to functional unbalance are cured much quicker.

2. *Resistance*: In her message on 22 May 1957, as has been already pointed out, The Mother maintained that resistance is also a cause of physical illness. This is internal disharmony. In her message on 1 October 1959 The Mother said, "An illness of the body is always the outer expression and translation of a disorder, a disharmony in the inner being; Unless this inner disorder is healed, the outer cure cannot be total and permanent."[47]

3. *Lack of Receptivity*: Maintenance of health requires a constant adjustment with the changing environment. This depends upon receptivity of the organism. Lack of receptivity, therefore, may be a cause of illness. As The Mother said, "Well, just a little lack of receptivity somewhere, something that is unable to receive the Force, that is completely shut up (when one looks at it, it becomes as it were a little dark spot somewhere, a small thing hard as a stone: the Force cannot enter into it, it refuses to receive — either it cannot or it does not want) and immediately that produces a great unbalance; and this thing that was moving upward, that was blooming so wonderfully finds itself sick, and sometimes while you were in the normal equilibrium in good health, everything going on well, you had nothing to complain."[48]

4. *Adverse Forces*: Adjustment with the environment is not always spontaneous since all round is therefore adverse forces working against the physical body. Pointing out to this cause of illness The Mother said, "All illnesses are attacks from adverse forces (that is what I call mischief) to test our endurance and try to break down our faith — we must answer to them by more endurance and more faith — thus they go away badly defeated and it makes a Victory for the Truth."[49]

5. *Fear*: The most important cause of illness is fear. Most of the troubles come from fear. This fear is subconscient in the 90% cases of illness. Therefore the patient does not understand it. Hence The Mother advises, "If you want to get cured there are two conditions. First you must be without fear, absolutely fearless, you understand, and secondly you must have a complete faith in the Divine protection. These two things are essential."[50]

6. *Black Magic*: According to The Mother black magic is not an illusion or a superstition. Therefore in some cases it may be causes of illness.

7. *Unknown Circumstances*: Disease is a complex phenomena. Therefore, one cannot always necessarily understand all the circumstances leading to illness. As The Mother pointed out, "And then if there is a group of such small entities, they may come into clash with one another, because among themselves they do not have a peaceful life: they come into clash with one another, they fight, they destroy, demolish each other. And that is the origin of microbes. They are forces of disintegration."[51]

8. *Worry*: While worry may not always initiate illness, it certainly exaggerates it. Therefore, The Mother has advised, "My advice is not to worry. The more you think of it, the more you concentrate upon it and, above all, the more you fear, the more you give a chance for the thing to grow."[52] The parents unnecessarily worry about the health of their children. This worry spoils the atmosphere and increases troubles of the parents as well as those of the children.

9. *Wrong Thinking*: Pointing out the close relationship between wrong thinking and illness The Mother said in her message in 1943, "In fact I can assure you that the pain in the stomach as well as many other discomforts are due 90% to wrong thinking and strong imaginations — I mean that the material basis for them is practically negligible."[53] Wrong thinking includes exaggeration, imagination and lack of confidence.

10. *Lack of Faith*: In the end the ultimate cause of illnesses is the lack of faith in God. This lack of faith is the real cause behind all worry, wrong thinking and physical, vital and mental fear. It is the real cause behind all wrong attitudes.

Remedies to Illness

The Mother has suggested the following remedies to cure

illness. These remedies, are obviously based upon the foregoing causes of illness. These remedies are as follows:

1. *Benevolence*: An attitude of benevolence towards oneself, others and life in general cures so many disturbances particularly those of the digestive system.

2. *Divine Peace*: The fundamental cure against all ill health is to bring down Divine Peace. To quote The Mother, "For your ill-health, do not forget to try to bring down the Divine Peace. Because no illness can resist the peace of the Lord, and even to remember and to try will give you some relief."[54]

3. *Faith:* According to The Mother, "It is generally when the body is convinced that it has been given the conditions under which it must be all right; it has taken the resolution that it must be all right and so is cured."[55] Faith is the only remedy against lack of faith, wrong thinking, worry and fear. Hence The Mother has advised, "Health: not to be preoccupied with it, but to leave it to the Divine."[56]

4. *Endurance:* According to The Mother, "Even the most acute physical pain, if it is faced calmly and quietly, diminishes and becomes bearable — even in agony, we can rely on the Divine and the Divine changes our agony into delight."[57] The doctors should teach the body to bear pain When the body has decided to bear the acuteness of pain disappears. Inner peace sometimes converts pain into pleasant sensations.

5. *Relaxation*: The Mother endorses the age old wisdom of a relaxed attitude to life. As she says, "The first thing to do then, by a force of will, is to relax this clenching as you do when your nerves are drawn, or a muscle is cramped; you must learn how to let got', you must be able to relax the tensions anywhere in the body."[58]

6. *The will to conquer:* In her message on 28 August 1966 The Mother wrote, "Do not love your ill health and the ill health will leave you."[59] Thus one must exercise his will to conquer illness. One must be not only detached but exercise the will to conquer. As The Mother said, "The body should reject illness as energetically as we reject falsehood in the mind."[60]

7. *Control of desires*: Wrong desires can be checked by means of control That is the only cure against unhealthy desires such as greed for good.

8. *Divine Grace*: In the integral philosophy of The Mother divine grace is the ultimate cure. It is the spiritual power of healing. It is the essence of all medicines. Even the physicians support it. It is the real force behind the curative power of the medicines. This divine grace is not only prescribed by religion but equally supported by medical science. The Mother said, "To medical knowledge and experience, and full faith in the Divine's grace and your healing capacity will have no limits."[61] Again, according to The Mother, "The chief role of the doctor is, by various means to induce the body to recover its trust in the Supreme Grace."[62]

9. *Tranquility*: According to The Mother, "Foreverything, to live the spiritual life, to cure illness, foreverything one must be tranquil."[63] This is the principle of harmony. This is again what has been called balance. This is the surest way to invoke divine influence. As The Mother said, "The best way is to call for the Divine presence of Truth and Harmony, to replace the vibrations of disorder and confusion."[64]

10. *Supramental Evolution*: In the end most of the causes of illness are due to the predominance of the material, the vital or the mental power. If one rises to supramental consciousness, all causes for illness will finally disappear. Such is the ideal of divine body envisaged by The Mother and Sri Aurobindo. As The Mother points out, "But once it is done and the consciousness becomes the supramental consciousness, then the action will no longer be determined by a mental choice or be subordinated, to the physical capacity; the whole body will be spontaneously and integrally the perfect expression of the inner truth; that is the ideal you have to move; but you must not have the illusion and belief that it will be a swift, miraculous, immediate, marvellous transformation without effort, with labour."[65] This alone can give absolute immunity from the action of all lower forces and the causes of illness.

The Ideal of Physical Education

Defining health, The Mother said, "Health is the outer expression of a deep harmony, one must be proud of it and not despise it."[66] A disciple questioned, "What is it that you call "the basis of equality in the external being'?" In reply The Mother said, "To be well balanced, to be able to absorb what one receives, one must be very quiet, very calm, one must have a solid basis, a good health. One must have a very solid basis. That is very important."[67] This health, the harmony, the equality and the balance is the achievement of the ideal of beauty, to the four types of perfection beauty is the ideal of physical education, since The Mother said, "It is through Beauty that the Divine manifests in the physical, in the mental through knowledge, in the vital through power, and in the psychic through Love."[68] Explaining the ideal of beauty in more details The Mother said, "Beauty interprets, expresses, manifests the Eternal. Its role is to put all manifested nature to contact with the Eternal through the perfection of form, through harmony and s. sense of the ideal which uplifts and leads towards something higher."[69] It may be remembered that thus beauty includes most of the foregoing remedies to illness. According to Sri Aurobindo "Beauty is Ananda taking form."[70] It is the way of the body to reach the divine. Beauty is an all pervading ideal since it includes the ideal of work, action, thoughts, sentiments and also that of the soul. Art is an expression of the beauty in external forms. Yoga itself requires a sense of beauty. The Mother has written in details about beauty and art. According to her, "Art is a living harmony and beauty that must be expressed in all the movements of existence. This manifestation of beauty and harmony is part of the Divine realisation upon earth, perhaps even its greatest part."[71] To quote Sri Aurobindo, "A complete and universal appreciation of beauty and the making entirely beautiful our whole life and being must surely be a necessary character of the perfect individual and the perfect society."[72] Beauty is the most important aspect of the physical world. Beauty is harmony. Unbalance is ugliness. All the diseases of the body are due to unbalance and the only remedy, according to The Mother, is the awakening of the sense of beauty in the body. As she puts it, "Here are a thousand reasons for this unbalance but only one remedy, to instill into the being this instinct, this sense of true beauty, a supreme beauty which will gradually act on the cells and make the body capable of expressing beauty."[73] Harmony and beauty of the mind and soul are the ideal of education. It is necessary to create likeness for beauty in the child. The most important disease in the present-day education, is the preference of toe vulgar, the crude against the harmonious. According to The Mother the ideal of making the life beautiful, noble, fine and harmonious is the aim of all education. It is even the aim of all life, individual as well as national. The truth of beauty however, cannot be realised or seized by the intellectual reason. It requires the help of a higher insight. This is explicit in the history of development of literary and artistic criticism. Pointing out the result of this development, The Mother has indicated to the evolution of man.

The sense of beauty may be incorporated in the child both through negative as well as positive methods. Ancient Indian philosophy of education has pointed out that character may be developed by both a positive as well as a negative approach. While the positive virtue or thought should be repeated again and again, the negative virtue or thought should be scrupulously avoided. Endorsing this ancient Indian method of education The Mother has pointed out both to the negative and positive approach to the creation of a sense of beauty. Explaining the negative method she said, "That is perfection in the negative method. It is quite elementary: never to notice the evil, never to speak of the evil that is in others, not to perpetuate the vibrations by observation, criticism, resistance on the bad fact. That is what Buddha taught: each time you mention an evil, you help in spreading it."[74] However, The Mother does not support the negative approach of Buddhism since the positive approach of Hinduism is equally valuable. Therefore, according to her the negative method is only the first step. "A second step is to be conscious positively of the supreme Good and the supreme Beauty which is behind all things, which supports all things, permits them to exist."[75] According to The Mother one should aim on getting rid of the worldly ugliness in order to create spiritual beauty and perfection. According to her unless human relationships are divinised, harmony cannot be maintained, similarly man and nature may be harmonised only, in the harmony of Divine. Synthesising the eastern as well as the western approach on this issue The Mother said, "Man is not the cause of external Nature, nor external Nature the cause of man, but both depend on the same one thing that is behind them and greater, and both are part of a perpetual and progressive movement of the material world to express it."[76]

References

1. *C.W.M.*, Vol. 12 (1978), p. 3.
2. *Ibid.*, p. 4.

3. *Ibid.*, p. 7.
4. *Ibid.*, p. 276.
5. *Ibid.*, p. 285.
6. *Ibid.*, p. 290.
7. *Ibid.*, p. 287.
8. *Ibid.*, pp. 280-281.
9. Huxley, A., *Ends and Means* (London: Chatto & Windus, 1951), p. 220.
10. Sri Aurobindo, *The Supramental Manifestation* (Pondicherry: Sri Aurobindo Ashram, 1952), p. 8.
11. *C.W.M.*, Vol. 12, pp. 273-274.
12. *Bulletin of Sri Aurobindo International Centre of Education*, Vol. XII, No. 1 (Feb. 1960), p. 94.
13. *C.W.M.*, Vol. 12, p. 278.
14. *Ibid.*, p. 261.
15. *Ibid.*, p. 280.
16. *Ibid.*, p. 292.
17. *Ibid.*, p. 295.
18. *Ibid.*, p. 297.
19. *Ibid.*, pp. 298-299.
20. *Ibid.*, p. 298.
21. *Ibid.*, p. 12
22. *Ibid.*
23. *Ibid.*, p. 13.
24. *Ibid.*
25. *Ibid.*, p. 15.
26. *Ibid.*, p. 16.
27. *Ibid.*
28. *Ibid.*
29. *Sri Aurobindo and The Mother on Food* (1973), p. 2.
30. *Ibid.*, p. 3.
31. *Ibid.*
32. *Bulletin of Physical Education* (August, 1966), p. 37.
33. *The Mother on Education* (1960), p. 105.
34. *Sri Aurobindo and The Mother on Food*, p. 11.
35. *Letters on Yoga*, Centenary Edition, Vol. 24, p. 1470.
36. *Sri Aurobindo and The Mother on Food*, p. 22.
37. *Bulletin of Physical Education* (November 1970), p. 65.
38. *C.W.M.*, Vol. 15 (1980), p. 141.
39. *Words of Long Ago* (1952), p. 33.
40. *C.W.M.*, Vol. 14 (1980), p. 383.
41. *Ibid.*, p. 384.
42. *Ibid.*

43. *Ibid.*, p. 386.
44. *C.W.M.*, Vol. 13 (1980), p. 344.
45. *C.W.M.* Vol. 15, p. 147.
46. *Ibid.*, p. 148.
47. *Ibid.*, p. 149.
48. *Sri Aurobindo and The Mother on Illness* (1977), pp. 8-9.
49. *The Mother, White Roses*, Part III (1968), p. 5.
50. *C.W.M*, Vol. 15, p. 152.
51. *Sri Aurobindo and The Mother on Illness*, Part I, p. 14.
52. *C.W.M.*, Vol. 15, p. 154.
53. *Ibid.*, pp. 155-156.
54. *White Roses*, Part I (1964), p. 75.
55. *Sri Aurobindo and The Mother on Illness*, Part I, p. 19.
56. *C.W.M.*, Vol. 15, p. 154.
57. *White Roses*, Part I (1964), p. 14.
58. *Sri Aurobindo and The Mother on Illness*, Part II (1973), p. 10.
59. *C.W.M.*, Vol. 15, p. 158.
60. *Ibid.*, p. 159.
61. *Ibid.*, pp. 167-168.
62. *Ibid.*, p. 167.
63. *Sri Aurobindo and The Mother on Illness*, Pan II p. 19.
64. *C.W.M.*, Vol. 15, p. 176.
65. *Sri Aurobindo and The Mother on Illness*, Part II, p. 24.
66. *Some Answers* (1964), p. 190.
67. *Bulletin of Physical Education* (August 1967), p. 49.
68. *Words of The Mother* (1949), p. 208.
69. *Bulletin of Physical Education* (November 1956), p. 65.
70. Sri Aurobindo, *The Future Poetry*, Centenary Edition, Vol. 9, p. 492.
71. *Conversations* (1949). p. 161.
72. Sri Aurobindo, *Social and Political Thought*, Sri Aurobindo Centenary Edition, Vol. 15, p. 128.
73: *Questions and Answers* (1972), p. 48.
74. *Bulletin of Physical Education* (February 1961), p. 85.
75. *Sri Aurobindo and The Mother on Beauty*, p. 21.
76. *Ibid.*, p. 28.

9

Vital Education

According to The Mother vital education is the most important part of the educational scheme since the human mind is most confused on this issue and also because it is very difficult to impart vital education. According to her the vital nature of man is a despotic tyrant. It holds power, energy, enthusiasm and dynamism. It is a tyrant master who can never be fully satisfied. Ancient Indian psychologists have repeatedly insisted that vital is the cause of all bondage and liberation may be achieved only of controlling the vital. Again, since liberation is the ideal of all education, therefore vital education is absolutely necessary. On the other hand, Western civilization has been busy in pleasing the vital. Westernisation and modernisation of the Bast has led of what Sri Aurobindo calls the Economic man, the modern barbarian in the garb of civilisation. Explaining the cause of this malady, The Mother said, "Two ideas which are very widespread, especially in the West, contribute towards making its domination more sovereign, One is that the chief aim of life is to be happy; the other that one is born with a certain character and that it is impossible to change it"[1]

Hedonism has insisted upon pleasure as the goal of life. Jeremy Bentham and J.S. Mill propounded the theory of utilitarianism in ethics. Ethical hedonism was supported by psychological hedonism. However, the basic idea was a childish deformation of the truth that existence is based upon delight of being. The Mother accepts the Hindu theory that delight is the essence of being and there would be no life without delight. However she points out, "But this delight of being, which is a quality of the Divine and therefore unconditioned, must not be confused with the pursuit of pleasure in life, which depends largely upon circumstances."[2] Therefore, the ideal to make one's life happy at any cost never found any place in Indian thinking. Neo-Vedanta insisted upon the realisation of liberation rather than securing personal happiness as the goal of life. This is in keeping with the ancient Indian ideal of liberation as the highest *purusartha*.

Like Sri Aurobindo The Mother steers clear of the extremes of hedonism and asceticism. She rejects the attitude of the ascetics that a rigorous discipline of the inconsistent is necessary. According to her, it is not by repression or suppression but by Divine grace that the vital may be conquered This however, does not mean that discipline is impossible. As The Mother said, "The transformation of character has in fact been realised by means of a clear-sighted discipline and perseverance so obstinate that nothing, not even the most persistent failures, can discourage it."[3] The edifice of what Swami Vivekananda called man making is built upon the foundation of 'know thyself.' Both ancient Indian and ancient Greek philosophy insisted upon starting man's education by the knowledge of man himself. The Upanisads prescribe introversion as a necessary starting point in all education. This introspection clearly shows bipolarity in human psychology. With psychoanalyst, The Mother accepts that human psychology runs into opposite poles. Therefore, there is a constant need of detachment and harmony of the opposites. Education encourages the process of harmony.

It has been accepted by most of the educationists that the child's development is governed by the influence of heredity and environment alike, MacIver and Page have said very correctly, "Every phenomena of life is the product of both. Each determine the character of the individual. Neither can ever be eliminated nor can ever be isolated."[4] Pointing out the opposite influences of the environment The Mother said, "In certain cases this education will encourage the movements that express the light, in others, on the contrary, those that express the shadow. If the circumstances and the environment are favourable, the light will grow at the expense of the shadow; otherwise the opposite will happen."[5] Experiments relating to heredity have proved that it is not the sole factor which determines development of the personality of human beings. And similarly, experiments conducted in the field of environment also indicate that it is not the only factor influencing personality, Therefore, The Mother rejects the claim of the environmentalist that the environment governs the man's development. According to her all education is a contradiction of environmentalism since education involves the role of reason in human life, as she puts it; "And in this way the individual's character will crystallise according to the whims of Nature and the determinisms of material and vital life, unless & higher element comes in time, a conscious will which, refusing to allow Nature to follow her whimsical ways, will replace them by a logical and clear-sighted discipline. This conscious will is what we mean by a rational method of education."[6] Therefore the child's education should begin as soon as he starts using his senses.

Aspects of Vital Education

According to The Mother, "This vital education has two principal aspects, very different in their aims and methods, but both equally important. The first concerns the development and use of the sense organs. The second the progressing awareness and control of the character, culminating in its transformation."[7] Thus vital education starts with the use of sense organs. In this the child has to be taught proper and correct use of every individual sense organ. On the other hand, he should also be checked from misusing or wrongly using any sense organ. After the sense education is achieved, character formation may start. According to the psychologists' character is the organisation of sentiments and each sentiment is the organisation of emotions. Again, according to modern educationists, the highest sentiment is the sentiment of self-regard. This is the master sentiment. According to The Mother, on the other hand, the highest sentiment is not the sentiment: of self-regard but the sentiment of regard for the Divine.

Education of the Senses

There has been a controversy about the number of senses provided to the human being. While, according to some ancient Indian thinkers, senses axe seven or twelve, most of the Indian psychologists have agreed that there are five sense organs only. However, it is a common knowledge that one or the other of these senses has been particularly developed in people-residing in different geographical circumstances. Education of the senses means the cultivation of the functioning as well, as discrimination, among the senses. The education of the senses never ceases in man's life. However, it starts in early childhood and the foundations are laid there. To start with the sense organs are taught concentration and discrimination.

The first response upwards the environment from a child is in the form of education. This sensation is received through some sense organ. Different sense organs receive different type of sensations. These sensations are closely interconnected.

Some spontaneous responses have been observed in an infant when he is stimulated internally or externally. Different sensations are gradually differentiated. The infant knows his environment only through sensations particularly those of vision, hearing, touch, taste and smell. The same organs must work properly if the child has to gain knowledge of the environment. Much of this is the result of maturity and development, but some learning is also helpful. This requires sense training.

The sense organs develop in the womb, therefore, a neonate has almost all the sense organs. In the embryonic period the embryo reacts to light. The infant cannot understand anything in his environment before experience. As he gathers experience he gradually learns to distinguish between different types of sensations. The just born infant is seen to react towards sound and taste. While he prefers sweet solutions, he dislikes different types of saline things. He cannot distinguish between smells, but he gradually learns to do so. He experiences the sensations of heat and cold, hunger and thirst, pain and pressure. He can express the feelings of pleasure and pain towards sensations. These feelings can be seen in his physical activities and facial expressions. In the beginning, the stimulus affects his total body, but gradually different sensations affect different sense organs. As the child achieves maturity and receives various types of sensations from the environment, he learns to react towards them. He begins to understand meanings of the gestures of his mother. He can distinguish between various persons. He recognizes different types of food. Thus gradually he learns to distinguish between various types of sensations and understands their meanings

The power of the sense organs of the child can be improved by means of training. Sense organs are the means of the child's knowledge of the environment. Sensations constitute perceptions. It is, therefore, necessary that the child should be presented with material involving different types of sensations. As things of different colours, forms and touch etc. are presented before the child he gradually learns to distinguish among them. In the absence of sense training the child's mental growth suffers. Sense training, therefore, occupies an important place in the early education of the child. He finds innumerable things to see, hear, smell touch and taste and teams to distinguish among them. This practice improves the efficiency of his sense organs. Thus the basic mode of sense training is the presentation of particular types of material before the child. The training of different sense organs, however, involves some specific items, A description of these is as follows:

(1) *Visual training* — As the infant is seven or nine days of age he is seen reacting differently to different colours. The blue colour gets maximum reaction, while the red colour gets the minimum. The girls are more impressed by colours than boys. Some boys are colour blind and they have no sensation of the red colour. The infant reacts to light within three hours of his birth. Intense light unfavourably affects the eyes.

For visual training the child is given objects of different colours and different forms. While he plays with them he learns to distinguish between different colours and forms. At the kindergarten stage the child learns the use of vision while playing with different types of balls. In the kindergarten method he is given woollen balls of different colours and forms by which he learns to distinguish between colours and forms. The flowers are also used for this purpose. In the Montessori system of education different types of toys are given to the child to play with. In advanced classes the children are shown different types of films, flowers, plants, animals and things. The child learns to distinguish among these and thus trains his vision.

(2) *Auditory training* – Immediately after few hours of birth the infant's ear reacts to sounds. This sense organ, however, is least developed at the time of birth. Some infants cannot hear anything even for several days. Normally, the infant begins to heat within one or two weeks of his birth. The auditory training starts right now. Different types of mechanical toys can be used to produce different types of sound and the child gradually learns to distinguish among them. He is very much interested in different types of musical instruments and loves to hear songs. These can be utilized for his auditory training. In kindergarten schools several types of musical instruments are utilised to train the child's sense of sounds. Similar is the procedure in Montessori schools. The child gradually learns to distinguish between the voices of different animals. Auditory training is necessary for the development of correct pronunciations of words.

(3) *Training of smell* — The just born infant distinguishes between different smells within few hours of birth. This sense organ acts all the time unless the person is unconscious. Smell is trained by means of providing different types of smells to the child.

(4) *Training of taste* — The just born infant has a developed capacity of taste, At the age of one week he is seen reading differently to different types of tastes. While he likes sweet tastes he rejects saline and bitter tastes. He can also distinguish between edible and non-edible things on the basis of smell. The sense of taste can be trained by providing the child with fruits and other edible things of different taste.

(5) *Training of touch* — The just born infant shows reactions towards heat and cold, touch and pressure. These reactions are observed in the whole body and yet some organs are more sensitive towards touch. For example, the infant's lips are found to be most sensitive. The sense of touch can be trained by providing different types of touch sensations to the child, such as heat and cold, pain and pressure etc. In Montessori schools the child is provided with pieces of muslin, silk and other types of cloth. He learns to distinguish between different types of touch through these.

Explaining the importance of education of sense Sri Aurobindo wrote, "It is only strengthening and sharpening these instruments to their utmost capacity that they can be made effective for the increased work which modern conditions require."[8] In the modern industrial and urban conditions the child has to deal with a wide variety of conditions of sensations around him. Therefore, his sense organs must be trained to note and observe correctly. Sensation and perception is the first response of an organism to the environment. Sense organs are the first and foremost equipment of education. Therefore, the most primary and early education starts with sense training. In fact, the sense training starts even before the child goes to school. It is the foundation of observation, judgement, imagination and all other mental processes. In the education of subjects like Botany, Astronomy, Geology, Zoology and Chemistry *viz.* the physical sciences, sense teaming is the most important.

Education of senses becomes important due to the tact that sense organs are sometimes uncertain modes of perception. As The Mother has said, "As a rule, everything is thought to be all right when judgements are based on a thorough technical knowledge and on a sufficient degree of impartiality. These judgements rely on sense-perception, which is normally considered incontrovertible. In fact, however, this mode of perception is in itself uncertain. The sense-organs are directly under the influence of the psychological state of the individual who uses them, and thus the sense-perceptions are altered, falsified, distorted in one way or another by the perceiver's feelings towards the thing perceived."[9]

Sense education forms a part of physical and vital education without it no progress towards harmony, beauty and health is possible. In the words of The Mother, "The senses should be capable of enduring everything without disgust or displeasure, but at the same time they must acquire and develop more and more the power of discerning the quality, origin and effect of the various vital vibrations in order to know whether they are favourable to harmony, beauty and good health or whether they are harmful to the balance and progress of the physical being and the vital."[10] The senses should be used as instruments to study the physical and vital worlds Sensations are the food of the vital. Just as for health it is necessary to choose proper food, similarly the choice of sensations and their control should be made for keeping the vital health growing and perfect.

According to The Mother, "As the capacity of understanding grows in the child, he should be taught, in the course of his education, to add artistic taste and refinement to power and precision. He should be shown, led to appreciate, taught to love beautiful lofty, healthy and noble things, whether in Nature or in human creation. This should be a true aesthetic culture, which will protect him from degrading influences."[11] Thus the education of the senses should lead to achievement of refinement in the use of the senses. The dividing line between civilisation and barbarism is the distinction between vulgarity and refinement. The aim of education of the senses is the achievement of this refinement. In the words of The Mother, "A methodical and enlightened cultivation of the senses can, little by little, eliminate from the child whatever is by contagion vulgar, common place and crude."[12] Thus the education of the senses lays the foundation of the other aspect of vital, education *viz.* the formation of character and its transformation, it is so since, as The Mother puts it, "For one who has developed a truly refined taste will, because of this very refinement, feel incapable of acting in a crude, brutal or vulgar manner. This refinement if it is sincere, brings to the being of a nobility and generosity which will spontaneously find expression in his behaviour and will protect him from many base and perverse movements."[13]

Goal of Vital Education

As has been already pointed out, The Mother's integral philosophy of education, aims at a four-fold liberation through a four-fold discipline. The vital liberation aims at the perfection of power through the *Tapasya* of power. The *Tapasya* of power is vital austerity, the austerity of sensations. The vital being is the seat of power. It is the source of enthusiasm. In it thought is transformed into will. It is the seat of desires and passions, violent impulses, violent reactions, revolt and depression. The Mother has analysed the nature of the vital in details as the foundation of the education of the vital. According to her, "In fact, the vital has three sources of subsistence. The one most easily accessible to it comes from below, from the physical energies through the sensations. The second is on its own plane, when it is sufficiently vast and receptive, by contact with the universal vital forces. The third, to which it usually opens only in a great aspiration for progress, comes to it from above by the inclusion and absorption of spiritual forces and inspiration."[14] Human beings strive towards these three sources of subsistence. This leads to most of the torments and misfortunes. Love is mistaken for vital communication among human beings, particularly the male and female.

According to The Mother, "It is by educating the vital, by making it more refined, more sensitive, more subtle and, one should almost say, more elegant, in the best sense of the word, that one can overcome its violence and brutality, which are m fact a form of crudity and ignorance, or lack of taste."[15]

Character and Its Transformation

This brings us to the second aspect of vital education which concerns the character and its transformation. Education has been defined as the process of character formation by the philosophers of education, Ancient and Modern, Eastern and Western. According to the psychologists, character formation is the aim of human development. This character formation however, has been generally realised through coercion, suppression, abstinence and asceticism. The medieval ages were notorious for brutality in the educational institutions. European educational institutions particularly specialised in all sorts of brutal punishment both oral and physical. Modern educationists have raised their voice against this sort of treatment to the educands. Modern pedagogy is paido-centric. Therefore it rejects all repression. According to The Mother the old method was easier and quicker but not enduring and effective. It eliminated the help and collaboration by the vital which is very much important in character formation.- The Mother agrees with Western thinkers like Bertrand Russell that vitality must be preserved in order to grow. According to her, "The child must be taught to observe, to note his reactions and impulses and their causes, to become a discerning witness of his desires, his movements of violence and passion, his instincts of possession and appropriation and domination and the background of vanity which supports them, together with their counterparts of weakness, discouragement, depression and despair."[16] In order to make this process useful the will for progress and perfection should grow along with the power of observation. The child is capable of having a will much earlier that it is usually believed. Therefore, The Mother maintains that will should be cultivated after achievement of skill in observation.

Thus the two-fold method of development of character is the development of taste and the development of will. Education of senses alone does not lead to refinement of taste. Emphasising the value of refinement of taste The Mother said, "Usually all education, all culture, all refinement of the senses and the being is one of the best ways of curing instincts, desires, passions. To eliminate these things does not cure them; to cultivate, intellectualise, refine them, this is the surest means of curing to give the greatest possible development for progress and growth, to acquire a certain sense of harmony and exactness of perception, this is a part of the culture of the being, of the education of the being."[17] The Mother rejects the dichotomous ideals of eating to live or living to eat. While the man of taste does not live to eat, he also does not eat only to live. All sort of greed should be removed from the consciousness. Taste requires raising the level of thought, feeling and sensation. In the integral psychology of development, every part of human being requires evolution. As The Mother explains it, "Education is certainly one of the best means of preparing the consciousness for a higher development. There are people with very crude and very simple natures, who can have great aspiration and attain a certain spiritual development, but the base will always be of an inferior quality, and as soon as they return to their ordinary consciousness they will find obstacles in it, because the stuff is too thin, there are not enough elements in their vital and material consciousness to enable them to bear the descent of a higher force."[18]

Taste literally means the reaction of the tongue. However, figuratively speaking, it includes all sort of refinements. The Mother has recommended development of the sense of beauty in the working of all the sense organs.

According to The Mother different methods may be adopted to improve will power among different educands. To quote her own words, "In order to awaken this will to surmount and conquer, different methods are appropriate in different cases; with certain individuals rational arguments are effective, for others their feelings and goodwill should be brought into play, with yet others the sense of dignity and self-respect. For all, the most powerful method is example constantly and sincerely shown."[19] After the resolution to will has been established in the educand, he should avoid all exceptions. Maximum efforts should be done to improve will power. Whatever has been decided to do must be done at every cost. If one gets failure he should proceed again immediately with renewed efforts. It is a psychological principle that practice makes a man perfect. Therefore, The Mother recommends sustained efforts. Thus the formation of character first requires knowledge of the vital, then improvement of will power and finally transformation of the vital.

Transformation of the Vital

In order to transform vital one must know its nature. According to The Mother there is a seat of creative vital force in body deep within behind the outer abdomen. According to her, "The vital is the seat of our power, energy, enthusiasm, effective dynamism. It needs a systematic education."[20] The vital centre is passionate and strong and therefore requires control. It always seeks novelty in the world. Its power of expression is useful in the worldly actions. However, according to the Mother, "To harmonise the vital is a psychological masterpiece. Happy is he who accomplishes it."[21] For this purpose the vital should be generous, strong, surrendered, consecrated, steadfast, stable, transparent, patient, progressive, governed by the presence, having candid simplicity, trust, joy, peace, silence, sincerity, light and finally spiritual awakening. Generosity in the vital gives it width. Strength in the vital shows its beauty and power. Consent of the vital makes it ever ready for action. Vital consecration makes it smile at life without wanting to draw attention to itself. By steadfast vitality it acquires integral consecration. Stability of the vital is an important result of its Divine conversion. For Divine conversion transparency is indispensable. So is vital patience. According to The Mother, "Vital progress: organisation around the Divine will and a progressive surrender to this Will."[22] This requires that the vital should be governed by Divine Presence and rendered peaceful and disciplined. The formative faculty in the vital is spontaneous but not always happy. It should be disciplined. Candid symplicity is one of the most difficult qualities for the vital to acquire. For this, trust in the divine is indispensable. Vital trust in the divine is full of courage and energy. Now the human being no longer fears anything. The reward of abolishing selfishness is found in the form of vital force in matter.

Ancient Indian philosophy of liberation has recommended desirelessness as an effective weapon for spiritual progress. Laying emphasis upon it, The Mother has recommended abolition of all desires. This results in peace in the vital. The Mother has recommended peace in the physical, the vital and the mental. Before arriving at the psychic or spiritual level this integral peace is a necessary condition for spiritual progress. This is a sound foundation for the realisation of perfection of the physical, the vital and the mental. Silence in the vital is a powerful help for inner peace. The Mother has also recommended silence in the mental. Again, sincerity in the vital is the sure road to spiritual realisation. Light in the vital is one of the first step in this long journey. By the spiritual awakening of the vital, it soars towards the heights in the hope of reaching it. To the statement, "I am disgusted with this world of battling, egos" by a disciple The Mother replied, "This is natural: the world of the human vital is an ugly one; it greatly needs to be changed."[23] Thus the first condition for any spiritual progress is the elimination of the egoistic vital reaction. The vital should be turned towards the Divine. Manifesting in life, the vital will is often a cause of greatest disorder. Therefore vital sensitivity must be controlled. It should be curbed and not allowed as justified and natural. Against the recommendation of the Western psychoanalysis for free expression of vital desires Indian psychologists have always insisted upon some sort of control through redirection of the vital towards the Divine.

Vital perturbations are caused by internal reasons. To eliminate them Indian psychologists have recommended yogic discipline, vigilance, self-detachment and a quiet but strict rejection. It should be noted here that The Mother has nowhere prescribed repression of the vital since it may lead to a lot of confusion and conflict. She has clearly directed, "As for the change in the vital, it will come by itself when you form the habit of remaining in your higher consciousness where all these petty things and movements are worthless."[24] The obscure vital can be changed into a luminous vital by the surrender of the vital and opening it to the divine light. Right attitude, self-confidence, quiet faith and trust in Divine grace led to the growth of consciousness resulting in transformation of the vital.

The Mother has given useful hints for transformation of the vital. One of such hints is the method of drawing upon the universal vital force. For this purpose first of all one must have faith in the existence of the universal vital force and the possibility of human contact with it. Education, according to The Mother, is a continuous process of expansion of consciousness. Contemporary scientists have accepted the hypothesis that the evolution of human consciousness is a sure testimony of the conscious nature of the universal force. If it is so then by expansion of human consciousness one may have direct contact with the total consciousness. In fact this is the real meaning of Brahman realisation and it has been explained in so many ways by the ancient Indian scriptures. Giving an example of contact with universal vital force The Mother has pointed out to the spontaneous activities of the children such as running, playing, jumping, shouting etc. Since this is spontaneously done the children come in contact with the universal vital force with the result that they are seldom tired. They spend much energy in these activities but by the contact with the universal force this loss is soon made up. It is hence that Indian psychologists have always recommended close contact with nature everywhere. Today the modern ecologists are also arriving at the same conclusion. Giving an example of a vital contact with the universal vital force, The Mother has written, "When one is in the countryside, when one walks under the trees and feels so close to Nature, to the trees, the sky, all the leaves, all the branches, all the herbs, when one feels a great friendship with these things and breathes that air which is so good, perfumed with all the plants, then one opens oneself, and by opening oneself communes with the universal forces. And for all things it is like that."[25] That is the reason why modern educators, particularly those connected with child education have recommended close touch with Nature. Extra curricular activities find an important place in modem education. Maria Montessori has rightly pointed out that the child learns naturally in natural circumstances. That is why Froebel called his system of education kindergarten, that is why modem infant education starts in nurseries. Just as a sapling is nourished, watched and grown in natural environment without any interference on die part of the gardener similarly the job of the teacher is to let the child come in intimate contact with Nature so that he may gather energy directly from the universal counterparts of the physical, the vital and the mental individual endowments. This is the secret behind the concept of harmony of the educand and Nature in Indian philosophy of education. Incidentally, The Mother's philosophy of education is a fine synthesis of ancient Indian and modern western philosophies of education.

References

1. *C.W.M.*, Centenary Edition, Vol. 12 (Pondicherry: Sri Aurobindo Ashram Trust, 1978), p. 18.
2. *Ibid.*
3. *Ibid.*, p. 19.
4. MacIver, RAJ. & Page, C.H., Society: *An Introductory Analysis* (New York: Macmillan & Co.), p. 95.
5. *C.W.M.*, Vol. 12, p. 19.
6. *Ibid.*, pp. 19-20.
7. *Ibid.*, p. 20.
8. *Sri Aurobindo Birth Centenary Library*, Vol. 17, p. 203.
9. *C.W.M.*, Vol. 12, p. 265.
10. *Ibid.*, p. 56.
11. *Ibid.*, p. 21.
12. *Ibid.*
13. *Ibid.*
14. *Ibid.*, p. 55.

15. *Ibid.*, p. 56.
16. *Ibid.*, p. 22.
17. *Ibid.*, Vol. 7 (1979), p. 58.
18. *Ibid.*, p. 59.
19. *Ibid.*, Vol. 12, p. 22.
20. *C.W.M.*, Vol. 14 (1980), p. 376.
21. *Ibid.*, p. 379.
22. *Ibid.*, p. 378.
23. *Ibid.*, pp. 379-380.
24. *Ibid.*, pp. 380-381.
25. *C.W.M.*, Vol. 7 (1979), pp. 138-139.

10

Mental Education

Commenting upon contemporary system of education The Mother has pointed out, "Of all lines of education, mental education is the most widely known and practised, yet except in a few rare cases there are gaps which make it something very incomplete and, in the end, quite insufficient"[1]. In her philosophy of mental education The Mother has tried to fill up these gaps and to provide a true mental education. Her philosophy of mental education, like her concept of physical education, is based upon her world view which is very much similar to that of Sri Aurobindo.

The ideals of education are drawn from the world view of the philosophers. The Mother's metaphysics postulates an integral reality. This integral reality manifests in individuality, commonality and essentiality. Thus, the individual, the collectivity and the total universe is the expression of the same Divine. Different philosophies of education are based upon different concepts of human nature. According to The Mother, as has been already pointed out, the human being is an organisation of the physical, the vital, the mental and the psychic aspects. These again are the components of the collectivity and the universe. Therefore, the aspects of individual nature have universal counterparts. Ancient Indian philosophy maintained that bondage is narrowness and limitation. Liberation, on the other hand, is freedom from this limitation. This was equally supported by Hindu and Buddhist philosophers. Therefore, both recommended liberation from individual physical, vital and mental limitations. In tune with this ancient Indian tradition The Mother held four-fold perfection as the goal of education This four-fold perfection results in four-fold liberation, the goal of life. The goal of mental education is knowledge which leads to mental liberation. Knowledge again, is the discipline (*Tapasya*) which leads to realisation of this goal. This is based upon an analysis of the nature of the mind. This has been done by The Mother in her numerous works.

The Nature of Human Mind

According to The Mother, the mind must learn to express only what is dictated by the Divine. In common human life however, the mind is driven by passions. The British philosopher David Hume remarked long ago, "Reason is and ought to be the slave of passions". The eminent psycho-analyst Sigmund Freud maintained that all human activities are covertly or overtly expression of sexual tendencies. William Mcdougall maintained that human activities are guided by instinctive propensities. The behaviourist psychologists refused to make any distinction between human and animal behaviour. Watson maintained that all behaviour may be explained by S-R formula. Thus the modern psychologists, in tune with empiricist western philosophers, maintained that human nature is essentially guided by animal passions. Not only this but they recommend that it should be so. Indian psychologists, on the other hand, always believed in the possibility of spiritual transformation of the human being. Hence the great distinction between Eastern and Western approach to education.

The Mother has analysed in details, the defects of common human mind. She pointed out, "In human beings, along with the growth of the mental activities grows the subtlety of self-deception. The more they are intellectual the more they are, in their self-deception, completely candid and insincere at the same time."[2] In his book *Mind Its Mysteries And Control* Swami Sivananda has pointed out the numerous ways of deception practised by the mind. The mind does not accept errors easily. Rationalisation is a common mental tendency.

Experts in abnormal psychology and the psychiatrists have pointed out to so many ways of self-deception, technically called mental mechanisms. These mental mechanisms never allow the human mind to know even the reality of individual life what to say of ultimate reality. Man's action is perverted by insincerity of the mind. The mind is ignorant as well as arrogant. The egoistic mind seeks to impose its principles upon his life and also upon the lives of the people around him. These are the whims of the mind. Mental fantasy is wild and disorderly. It lacks coordination. Mental imagination may be abundant, varied and charming but it always leads to falsehood. Persons guided by it live in falsehood and misery. Therefore, Confucius said, "Thought creates for itself its own suffering," Ugly thoughts lead to ugly feelings. Ugly feelings take away from divine. They are source of endless sorrow and suffering, Man is always surrounded by things about which he thinks. Average mind is full of doubts. It believes in falsehood. In the words of The Mother, "One of the chief functions of the physical mind is to doubt. If you listen to it, it will always find a thousand reasons for doubting. But you must know that the physical mind is working in ignorance and full of falsehood."[3] It is interesting to note that modern western philosophy starts with doubt. It is so because Descartes, the father of modern philosophy, equated philosophy with mathematics. Indian philosophers, on the other hand, have always looked beyond mind and therefore held doubt as a wrong condition. In tune with the ancient Indian philosophers and psychologists, The Mother pointed out that the physical mind is incapable of seeing correctly. The mental is always a limitation to the consciousness. It is often too much active. It cannot reach the complicated wisdom. It hampers the action of God's grace. It presents fanciful suggestions. It leads to consumptions called mental mechanism. It is lazy and seeks convenient answers which are not easily available.

According to The Mother, "In modern civilisation, men work on the surface. The mind is the surface of existence; they work on the surface and they try to find the Truth that is behind by studying more and more deeply. Whereas the true method is to enter into direct contact with the inner Truth, and impelled by that, guided by that, to make an outer construction which is not a seeking for the Truth, but a creation of the Truth; that is to say, the Truth-force realises itself outwardly through the human instrument,"[4] No human creation may be a complete realisation of mental constructions. Something is added, altered or diminished. This is attributed to chance, fortune, circumstances and all sorts of things. According to The Mother however, this modification is due to the fact that the results of happenings here are governed by Truth-force and not by the human physical, vital or the mental efforts.

The human mind is incapable of real knowledge and real creations. According to The Mother, "For the mind is an instrument of action and formation and not an instrument of knowledge; at each moment it is creating forms."[5] One can understand only what lie already knows in his own inner self. Attachment to the rule of the mind is m indication of human blindness The whole mental world is limited even if one never knows its limitations. Ninety nine per cent persons are governed by false mental constructions in their life. This is what ancient Indian seers have called bondage. Therefore it was prescribed that the mind must be controlled in order to achieve liberation. This is possible by purification, surrender and spiritualisation or mind. The Mother has given useful suggestions in this regard.

In her essay The Science of Living, The Mother wrote, "the mind is not an instrument of knowledge; it is incapable of finding knowledge, but it must be moved by knowledge. Knowledge belongs to a much higher domain than that of the human mind, far above the region of pure ideas. The mind has to be silent and attentive to receive knowledge from above and manifest it. For it is an instrument of formation, of organisation and action, and it is in these functions that it attains its full value and real usefulness."[6] The mind gives form to the thoughts. All the formation made by the mind appear to be coming from outside. Again, the mind is an instrument of organisation as well as disorder. Thus the following are the functions of the mind:

1. *Formation of thoughts* — This is the field of all knowledge in sciences and humanities. It also includes common sense world of thought.

2. *Organisation* — An important function of the mind is organisation of thought. This, however, is never perfectly achieved. As The Mother points out, "The mind is an instrument of organisation. On the outer plane, some people have an organised mind. They have organised their own ideas — note that this is not a very common occurrence! — their own thoughts. But if you look inside yourself, you will see that you have the most contradictory thoughts and if you have not taken care to organise them, they dwell side by side in your head, so to say, and create utter disorder."[7]

3. *Action* — Besides formation of thoughts and their organisation, the mind is an instrument of action. To quote The Mother, "The mind is also an instrument of action. The thoughts form plans. The mind forms a plan of action and with this formation of independent and active entities which mentioned earlier, it stirs the other parts of the being — the vital and physical — and impels them to action."[8] This has been supported by modern psychology. It has been admitted that mind is the seat of all urges, instincts,

tendencies and propensities. It is the seat of will. It has the faculties of reasoning, judging, comparing and decision-making. These are however, often governed by outside.

In action The Mother has recommended the ancient Socratic dialectical method in arriving at decisions. One may arrive at a synthesis only after passing through thesis and antithesis. As she puts it, "It is very necessary that one should consider everything from as many points of view as possible. There is an exercise in this connection which gives great suppleness and elevation to thought; it is as follows: A clearly formulated thesis is set; against it is opposed the antithesis, formulated with the same precision. Then by careful reflection, the problem must be widened or transcended until a synthesis is found which unites the two contraries in a larger, higher and more comprehensive idea."[9]

The Instrument of Knowledge

In her ideal of four-fold liberation The Mother has recommended mental liberation. This is mental perfection through the discipline of knowledge. Thus mental education aims at knowledge. In other words it aims at liberation. On the mental plane, this is mental control by the psychic power. The aim of education, according to ancient Indian thinkers, was described as Citta-*Vratti Nirodh*. Thus *Citta* is the instrument of education. Education is a process of the control of mind so that in the mind may dawn the realisation of the true self With Sri Aurobindo The Mother postulated mind or *antahkarana* as the instrument of education. *Antahkarana*, according to Sri Aurobindo and The Mother, consists of the following four layers.

(*i*) *Citta* — This is the reservoir of past memories and mental impressions. This has two aspects, passive and active, with passive and active memory, respectively. It is the latter which needs education and training.

(*ii*) *Manas* — This receives images of things through sensations of different sense-organs. It also directly receives mental images and forms mental impressions. These sensations and impressions supply material to thought. Thus the training of the sense organs and organs of activity is a prelude to all sound thinking and the first step in a proper education.

(*iii*) *Buddhi* — This is the proper instrument of thought. It systematises sensations, images and mental impressions. Its functions are of two types — (a) Functions and faculties of the right hand. These include judgment imagination, memory and observation. Its abilities are comprehensive, creative and synthetic. This part of the mind is the master of knowledge. It penetrates the soul. It grasps that which is elusive and uncertain. Its abilities act and manipulate in their own right; (b) Functions and faculties of the left hand. These are critical and analytic and include comparison and reasoning. The critical abilities are the component parts of the logical reason. They perform the functions of distinction, comparison, classification, generalization, deduction, inference and conclusion. This part of the mind follows the ascertained truths. It touches only the body of knowledge. Both the above-mentioned types of functions and abilities are essential for the working of human reason. Hence both require proper training and development in a sound system of education.

(iv) *Supra-normal faculties* — These comprise of the functions included in the working of psi-phenomena such as ESP (Extra-Sensory Perception) including telepathy and clairvoyance and PK (Psychokinesis) and the phenomena of genius. These, however, cannot be developed by instruction. The educator can only remove the impediments in their growth. He should see that they develop properly and without hindrances. It is to be noted here that The Mother has net only emphasised the importance of these supra-normal or (in modern parapsychological terminology) para-normal functions, she has also given hints for their control in her yogic writings.

The Mother is in favour of special education to each, suitable to his individuality She advises the educator to select the most perfect and rapid of mastering knowledge. The earliest permissible age for the commencement of any regular study, according to The Mother, is seven or eight. At this age, the child is fairly capable of concentration and can attend to a subject for a sufficiently long time. The complaint that the child cannot attend to a subject for long is applicable only to very young children and that is the argument given in favour of having so many subjects in the syllabi of early education. But the cause of inattention is either the young age of the educand or a wrong method of teaching based on harsh compulsion. This unnatural system should be substituted by a natural self-education.

Phases of Mental Education

According to The Mother, "A true mental education, which will prepare man for a higher life, has five principal phases. Normally, these phases follow one after another, but in exceptional individuals they may alternate or even proceed simultaneously. These five phases, in brief, are:

(1) Development of the power of concentration, the capacity of attention.

(2) Development of the capacities of expansion, widening, complexity and richness.

(3) Organisation of one's ideas around a central idea, a higher ideal or a supremely luminous idea that will serve as a guide in life.

(4) Thought-control, rejection of undesirable thoughts, to become able to think only what one wants and when one wants.

(5) Development of mental silence, perfect calm and a more and more total receptivity to inspirations coming from the higher regions of the being,"[10]

Development of Concentration

Most of the problems on the mental level are due to absence of concentration. Indian psychologists have always considered mental dissipation as the chief hindrance in mental control. This is *Viksipta Manas* which is constantly moving from this to that. Any spiritual progress requires control of this dissipation. For this purpose the mind should be quietened. As The Mother points out, "Quietness established in the mind the essential condition of its transformation."[11] This quietness is the opposite of fluctuation of thoughts. The capacity of concentration is given to every human being. The educator should help the child to become capable of a sustained effort of attention. According to The Mother, "All methods that can develop this faculty of attention from games to rewards are good and can all be utilised according to the need and the circumstances. But it is the psychological action that is most important and the sovereign, method is to arouse in the child an interest in what you want to teach him, a liking for work, a will to progress."[12] The quiet mind is however, not a silent mind. In order to make the mind completely silent, its activity should be stopped. Quiet mind leads to calm mind and the calm mind should lead to silent mind. Emphasizing the importance of silent mind, The Mother said in her message on 12 April, 1964, "But one thing is indispensable if they want a result: the mind must be silent. Then there is hope for the consciousness to be concentrated."[13] For this purpose the mind and consciousness must be distinguished as two things. The consciousness should be surrendered to Supreme Consciousness. This requires going beyond the mind.

Development of Capacities

Comenious based his educational system upon the dictum, "Children learn to do by doing." Froebel laid down the motto, "Children grow by doing." The Mother accepted this principle of learning through activities. She however, also emphasised what these philosophers have omitted, *i.e.* learning through passivity. The child should be taught to use his sense-organs and physical organs but at the same time he should also learn to make his mind passive and receptive.

Sri Aurobindo and The Mother have written extensively about the development of various mental capacities and suggested useful methods. According to The Mother, "The growth of the understanding should be stressed much more than that of memory,"[14] She endorses the general psychological principle that intelligent memory is more stable than rote memory. She is against all mechanical, burdensome and unintelligent, rote memory training. She agrees with Sri Aurobindo that memory training should involve noting of similarities and differences in things observed. According to Sri Aurobindo, "A Similar but different flower should be put in the hands and he should be encouraged to note it with the same care, but with the avowed object of noting the similarities and differences. By this practice daily the repeatedly memory will naturally be trained."[15]

The Mother has laid emphasis upon the importance of active interest in learning and study. For this purpose she has recommended arousal of healthy curiosity in the children by replying to their numerous questions. This encourages the interests of the children and attention becomes spontaneous. The children should be taught how to enjoy good reading material which is both instructive and attractive. This should be done by citing examples from everyday life. As The Mother has said, "The life of every day, of every moment, "the best school of all, varied, complex, full of unexpected experience, problems to be solved, clear and striking examples and obvious consequences."[16] In tune with modern western educationists The Mother laid emphasis upon constant development.

The ultimate ideal of the school is man-making. It prepares the educand to work first as a human being and then as a member of a nation and finally as an individual. The circles of moral responsibilities and loyalties proceed from wider to narrower and not *vice-versa.* The man has to develop first as a human being, then as a citizen and finally as an individual. Most of the present confusion of values is due to an inversion of this order. The Mother believes in three ultimate principles–individuality, commonality and essentiality. These, in other words, are the educand, the society and the humanity. Integral evolution, according to her, must include evolution of all these three elements. Thus the individuality and commonality should develop together. This is the purpose of the school. The school should treat all children as equal and provide sufficient scope for the development of their individual variations without insisting upon similarities. The colleges and universities should educate through their academic as well as social activities. Thus the college should have its bearing upon the community around it. The school cannot be isolated from society. It cannot give total education in isolation. Its teachings have to be practised in the society outside it. The university merely gives some materials to the educand which he may use.

An important mental faculty to be developed is the faculty of observation. The Mother has written extensively about the ways of developing the child's capacity of observation. According to her, "This faculty of observation can be developed by varied and spontaneous exercises, making use of every opportunity that presents itself to keep the child's thought wakeful, alert and prompt."[17] Observation is parallel to the tendency of thirsting for the wonderful. That which seems unrealisable fills man with the feeling of divinity. In order to encourage correct observation, all imagination must be eliminated and constant control should be exercised. Observation requires most meticulous sense for the exactness details. According to The Mother thirsting for the Wonderful and sincere observation should go together. To quote her words, "The two can be simultaneous and there is a moment when one has sufficient knowledge to perceive that they are the two aspects of the same thing and that is clairvoyance, higher discernment. Instead of a limited seeing and discernment, the discernment becomes altogether sincere, correct, exact, but it is vast, it includes a whole domain that does not yet belong to concrete Manifestation. From the point of view of education, it would be very important."[18] Thirsting for the wonderful and sincere observation are two polls of discernment. The two must go together. The educand must learn how to put together the knowledge upwards and the knowledge below. Thus The Mother recommends a combination of crude earthly and concrete observation with a vision of Divine.

According to The Mother, "In order to increase the suppleness and comprehensiveness of his mind, one should see not only that he studies many varied topics, but above all that a single subject is approached in various ways, so that the child understands in a practical manner that there are many ways of facing the same intellectual problem of considering it and solving it."[19] This will remove the rigidity of brain. It will make thinking richer and more supple. It will prepare the brain for a more complex and comprehensive synthesis. It will create the sense of relativity of mental thinking on the one hand and an aspiration for a truer source of knowledge on the other.

Organisation of Ideas

After development of the capacities of expansion, widening, complexity and richness, ideas should be organised around a central idea. In the education of the mind the central principle involved is the development from the most concrete to the most abstract. According to child psychology, the mental development succeeds physical and motor development. Sense training precedes mental training. Thus, first of all, the mind should be taught observation and then one should be told the names of the things. It is now that the ground is prepared for the training of the logical faculty. Here, again, The Mother lays emphasis upon practical training rather than theoretical study of books on logic. In the development of human mind, the highest achievement is the evolution of logical reasoning. Therefore, it is only in the fitness of things that The Mother lays so much emphasis on the training in logic. This involves training both in deductive and inductive reasoning. The educand should learn to deduce particular facts from the general premises. He should be equally good in generalising from the particular facts. Both these exercises must be done practically. "The student must be told to examine his defects himself. All this is possible only by creating a real interest in discovery of cause and effect. Gradually, the errors will be eliminated and the mind will master the use of logical reasoning in everyday life." As The Mother puts it, "To have a mind capable of progressing, of adapting itself to a new life, of opening itself to higher forces, it must be put through all kinds of gymnastics."[20] The purpose of all schooling is not imparting certain information but preparing the mind for better understanding and better comprehension. Therefore, the aim of learning agrees with the aim of gymnastics.

The capacity of organisation increases along with age. Organisation increases certitude and knowledge becomes stable. This provides the basis of a mental construction permitting the diverse and scattered and contradictory ideas to be organised in the brain. This organisation avoids chaos in thought. In order to resolve the contradictions The Mother has suggested, "All contradictions can be transformed into complements; but for that one must discover the higher ideas that will have the power to bring them harmoniously together."[21] This is the dialectical process of knowledge which has been already prescribed. The opposites of the theses and antitheses can be resolved by subsuming them under a higher synthesis. This leads to totality of thought. It requires a dynamic and constructive force. Therefore, The Mother has recommended that education should be based upon highest possible synthesis. The plan of education should be derived from the philosophy of education and the ideals of education should be derived from the ideals of life. Therefore, both the educand and the educator must evolve. As The Mother puts, "The higher and larger the central idea and the more universal it is, rising above time and space, the more numerous and the more complex will be the ideas, notions and thoughts which it will be able to organise and harmonise."[22]

Now, this organisation cannot be achieved all at once. It requires a constant progress, a constant enlargement and a constant reorganisation. As J. Krishnamurthy has rightly pointed out, one must constantly review his thoughts so that new ideas may be assimilated and old ideas evaluated in the light of new knowledge. Likewise The Mother advises. "The mind, if it is to keep its vigour and youth, must progress constantly, revise its notions in the light of new knowledge, enlarge its framework to include fresh notions and constantly reclassify and reorganise its thought, so each of them may find its true place in relation to the others and the whole remain harmonious and orderly."[23] The Mother has emphasised the importance of learning as well as creativity. According to her, learning is only one aspect of mental activity. Another very important mental activity is the constructive faculty. This has not been adequately studied by the educationists. It is the faculty of formation. The effort to discipline it faces many difficulties which are sometimes almost insurmountable.

Thought Control

In tune with the ancient Indian ideal of Citta-Vratti-Nirodh, emphasised by ancient Indian educationists, The Mother defined thought control as rejection of undesirable thoughts. Thought control is the most important aspect of self-education. No mental mastery is possible without it. According to The Mother, "The ideas that are accepted for translation into action should be strictly controlled and only those that agrees with the general trend of the central idea forming the basis of the mental synthesis should be permitted to express themselves in action."[24] Thus, every thought entering the mental consciousness should be examined with reference to the central idea. If it finds a logical place it will be admitted into the synthesis. If it is not coherent it will be rejected. This is mental purification. It should be done very regularly. It leads to gradual control of the mind over actions.

Mental control requires developing the faculty of reasoning. Reasoning provides a clear, precise, logical and objective view of things. It checks all the disturbances caused by impulses, feelings and desires. One must never allow his mind to judge things and men. In tune with the ancient Socratic dictum that the wise is he who knows his ignorance. The Mother said, "For people who exercises their intelligence, the more intelligence they are, the more do they grow aware that they know nothing at all and that with the mind one can know nothing."[25] The more one knows, the more one knows that he does not know. A certain amount of agnosticism, is the destiny of human knowledge. This was ably demonstrated in the history of philosophy from Descartes to Kant and Locke to David Hume. Kant, very ably demonstrated that metaphysics remains engrossed in antinomies and the mind cannot comprehend the noumenon. This again, was supported by the Jain theory of *syadvada*. Likewise The Mother points out, "One may think in a particular way, but one is never sure of anything — and never will be sure of anything. One can always say, "perhaps it is like that' or 'perhaps it is like this' and so on, indefinitely, because the mind is not an instrument of knowledge'."[26]

Development of Mental Silence

While the fourth phase of mental education is thought control, the fifth phase is the development of mental silence. Mental silence is characterised by perfect calm and a more and more total receptivity to the inspirations coming from the higher regions of the being. Pointing out the importance of mental silence The Mother wrote, "When one will have learnt to silence the mind at will and concentrate it in the receptive silence, then there will be no problem that one cannot solve, no mental difficulty to which a solution will not be found. Thought, while in agitation, becomes confused and impotent; in an attentive tranquillity, the light can manifest itself and open new horizons to man's capacity."[27] A quiet mind is the best way of learning. It is the essential condition for any progress. Again, it is the essential condition for transformation. It is not merely cessation of mental activity. It is shutting out all that comes from other minds. Therefore, The Mother has condemned unnecessary communication between human being. She has advocated control of speech. The educator should not talk unnecessarily. He should not brag about its achievement, nor should he time and again relate his personal biography. The Mother has even condemned unnecessary discussions in the form of so called academic seminars so much current in the modem educational system. These only fill up the mind with useless information and ideas. According to Sri Aurobindo and The Mother, the mind must be cleaned of all useless ideas, then alone one may rise above the mind. Silence of the mind gives power of understanding. A Sadhak asked now to get rid of the invasion of wrong suggestions. To this The Mother replied, "The only radical way is to concentrate and go beyond your mental silence and contemplation."[28]

Mental silence includes the silence of the heart. In her message on 8 January 1951, The Mother said, "In the silence of a simple and faithful heart one can understand the mystery of incarnation."[29] Thus a simple and faithful heart is a great boon. The heart must be full of an ardent aspiration. In depths of the heart is the great joy of the Divine Presence. This has been certified by mystics and religious saints. Divine grace is received in the heart, so also is received guidance and inspiration. The Divine speaks in the silence of the heart. Therefore, The Mother advised, "Experience goes far beyond the reasoning mind. Evidently, the reasoning mind finds it very difficult to reach the Divine, but a simple heart can enter into contact with him, almost without effort."[30] Therefore, The Mother has recommended knowledge through identity as a better means of knowledge than the dialectical method. Pure ideas can be comprehended only by knowledge through identity. In fact both Sri Aurobindo and The Mother ultimately label mental knowledge as ignorance, This is in keeping with ancient Indian concept of true knowledge. Ancient Indian philosophers maintained that reality can be comprehended only by knowledge through identity. To know is to be. Therefore The Mother said, "And knowledge can be obtained only by a total identification."[31] Hence mental knowledge remains only on the surface. It cannot help in realising the goal of liberation. Therefore it has been advised that the mind should be silenced.

In order to achieve mental silence The Mother suggests quiet review and synthesis of thought every day. It is only after this becomes habitual that the mind becomes concentrated and attentive. The intensity of concentration makes all thinking unnecessary. All mental vibration is stilled and total silence acquired. It is in this silence that the mind gets inspirations from above.

Again, according to The Mother, "Changing one's mental activity is certainly one way of resting; but the greatest possible rest is silence. And as far as the mental faculties are concerned a few minutes passed in the calm of silence are a more effective rest than hours of sleep,"[32] Thus, silence is the best type of mental rest. This rest provides attentive tranquility necessary for opening up new horizons to man's capacity.

References

1. *C.W.M.*, Vol. 12 (1978), p. 24.
2. *Ibid.*, Vol. 14 (1980), p. 364

3. *Ibid.*, p. 366.
4. *Ibid.*, Vol. 14, p. 369.
5. *Ibid.*, Vol. 3, p. 50.
6. *Ibid.*, Vol. 15, p. 320.
7. *Ibid.*, p. 331.
8. *Ibid.*, p. 333.
9. *Ibid.*, Vol. 4 (1972), p. 43.
10. *Ibid.*, Vol. 12 (1978), p. 24.
11. *Ibid.*, Vol. 14 (1980), p. 370.
12. *Ibid*, Vol. 12 p. 25.
13. *Ibid.*, Vol. 14 p. 371.
14. *Ibid.*, Vol. 12 (1978), p. 25.
15. *Sri Aurobindo and The Mother on Education*, Part II, p. 15.
16. *C.W.M.*, Vol. 12, p. 26.
17. *Ibid.*, p. 25.
18. *Bulletin of Physical Education* (April, 1963), p. 70.
19. *C.W.M.*, Vol. 12 (1978), p. 26.
20. *Ibid.*, Vol. 4 (1972), p. 203.
21. *Ibid.*, Vol. 12 (1978), p. 27.
22. *Ibid.*
23. *Ibid.*
24. *Ibid.*, p. 28.
25. *Ibid.*, Vol. 4 (1972), pp. 46-47.
26. *Ibid.*, p. 47.
27. *Bulletin of Physical Education* (November 1951), p. 33.
28. *C.W.M.*, Vol. 14 (1980), p. 372.
29. *Ibid.*, p. 373.
30. *Ibid.*, p. 374.
31. *Ibid.*, Vol. 4 (1972), p. 47,
32. *Ibid.*, Vol. 12 (1978), p. 29.

11

Moral Education

The aim of education is the complete development of the child, a development in which moral development occupies an important place. Man's greatest characteristic is his character. Swami Vivekananda has defined character as the sum total of an individual's instincts, the inclinations of his mind. Man is made by his thoughts. One finds that children develop characters according to the ideas presented to them during their growth. For this reason they should be initiated into the ideals of sacrifice, hard work and contemplation. Good thoughts lead to a sound determination and this in turn puts the man on the path to good life, and he is filled with strength of soul which inspire him to adhere to this path. In order to form character, it is necessary to pay attention to subtle and small things, for character is manifested through habits. Character can, therefore, only be improved by improving the habits of the individual. For this both determination and courage are required. Swami Vivekananda had said in a resonant voice that one must form one's character and express one's true nature, the enlightened pure element in oneself. One must also look for the same element in every other individual. In the words of Swami Vivekananda, "The work of ethics has been, and will be in the future, not the destruction of variation and the establishment of sameness in the external world... but to recognise the unity in spite of all these variations, to recognise the God within, ...and to recognise, the eternal, infinite essential purity of the soul in spite of everything to the contrary that appears on the surface."[1]

Value of Moral Education

According to The Mother, moral education is the education of the heart, without which no individual can be completely human. But this moral education cannot be imparted through lectures and textbooks because the basis of this education is proper feelings, proper conduct and the development of proper habits of thought, feeling and action. The task of education is to guide, direct and suggests to the child, without interfering with his activities in any way. Teachers should present the highest ideals but must also remember that moral education is imparted through imitation and setting examples rather than through discipline. In ancient India the child acquired moral education only by imitating his teacher. The modern teacher, therefore, must also have the highest ideals. In addition, moral education takes place through moral conversation and behaviour. Senior education should be required to read literature which encourages the purest emotions in them and inspires them to attempt at the highest ideals. In order to give moral training to the child, the latter should be acquainted with the means of distinguishing between the right and the wrong. The various emotions of the child are not to be suppressed but sublimated. M.K. Gandhi and Sri Aurobindo believed that development of character is the aim of education, for which, in their opinion also, moral education is essential, Swami Dayananda believed that education of any kind is impossible without the practice of abstinence. Dr. S. Radhakrishnan said that we must create the proper social order but we must also keep in mind that the individual does not become complete individual without the pleasure and beauty of the soul. This soul must be bringing with love, faith, and the willingness and ability to serve humanity.

Moral Philosophy

According to The Mother, "There are two things we must not confuse: certain necessities (which are purely necessities if one wants to succeed in completely controlling physical matter), and then moral notions. These are two very different things."[2] While the physical necessities are governed by the laws of nature and therefore need satisfaction, the moral notions, the theory of good and bad is a mental construction which is sometimes a hurdle in the spiritual development. Therefore, The Mother said, "And our whole moral notion of good and bad, we have thrown all that upon the creation with our deformed and perverted consciousness. It is we who have invented it. We are the deforming intermediary between the purity of the animal and the divine purity of the gods."[3] As F.H. Bradley aptly remarked, "It is a moral duty not to be moral, and this is the duty to be religious."[4] This phrase, while wrongly calling the religious urge the duty', rightly points out to man's aspiration for something higher than ethics, life seeks its absolutes.

Morality is essentially a matter of mental level. Kant rightly pointed out the persistent element of conflict in moral life. "Virtue, in fact, lives in the life of its antagonists,"[5] is the paradox of morality. To solve this paradox, one should transcend the moral level itself. It is then alone that the moral conflict is reconciled together with all other conflicts. Therefore, The Mother said, "Morality is something altogether artificial and arbitrary, and in most cases, among the best, it checks the true spiritual effort by a sort of moral satisfaction that one is on the right path and a true gentleman, that one does one's duty, fulfils all the moral requirements of life. Then one is so self-satisfied that one no longer moves or makes any progress."[6]

According to ancient Indian tradition, Meliorism is a bad philosophy. Science alone cannot make the world better nor can this be possible by religion. In fact, as man is not the creator, he does not have sufficient power to change the earth nature. Optimism must be based upon faith in the goodness of God. Ultimately, nature and man both are the products of God's will and therefore the Divine purpose will be fulfilled. This is the faith according to which morality is limited and relative. Man must rise above both good and evil. Therefore, The Mother has said, "He alone who is above likes and dislikes, desires and preferences can look at things with perfect impartiality, through senses that are in their functioning objective, like that of an extremely delicate and perfected machine, to which is added the clarity of a living consciousness."[7] Thus morality is transcended in a higher form of goodness. The spiritual vision includes ethics but also much more. Hence in her message on 14th August 1969 The Mother said, "For one who has fully realised that the world is nothing but the One Supreme in His manifestation, all human moral notions necessarily disappear to give way to a vision of the whole in which all values are changed — Oh, how greatly changed!"[8] Thus supramental change involves transvaluation of values. This transvaluation is the supramentalisation of mental values. The supramental vision changes the outlook towards the worldly evil. It leads to perfection. It leads to equilibrium. In it there is equality in quality and quantity. Pointing out the importance of the supramental vision of the Reality above moral viewpoint The Mother said, "The second step is to be positively conscious of the supreme Good and supreme Beauty behind all things, which sustains all things and enables them to exist. When you see Him, you are able to perceive Him behind this mask and this distortion; even this ugliness, this wickedness, this evil is a disguise of something which is essentially beautiful or good, luminous, pure."[9]

Thus air morality is relative. It is not Divine but human. It depends on the dichotomy of good and bad. It is governed by social and cultural circumstances. The moral notions philosophies have wrongly declared the relative moral to be absolute. Social anthropology teaches us those moral norms have been changing according to climates, times, epochs and countries. They are based upon desires. Therefore, they have no place in spiritual life which rejects desires altogether. According to ancient Indian tradition the goal is desirelessness above both good and bad desires. This viewpoint rejects morality as a mental construction not worthy of finding a place in spiritual vision. This is equally true of the individual as well as social morality. To quote The Mother, "The ordinary social notions distinguish between two classes of men, — the generous, the avaricious. The avaricious man is despised and blamed, while the generous man is considered unselfish and useful to society and praised for his virtue. But to the spiritual vision, they both stand on the same level; the generosity of the one, the avarice of the other are deformations of a higher truth, a great divine power."[10] According to The Mother, morality is not truth, since while morality is mental truth is spiritual, truth is above the mental notions. Therefore The Mother said, "At times moral notions also intermix and falsify the judgement but we must throw away from us all moral notions; for morality and Truth are very far from each other (if I am shocking anybody by saying this, I am sorry, but it is like that). It is only when you have conquered all attraction and all repulsion that you can have a correct judgement."[11]

Like M.K. Gandhi The Mother has held Truth in very high respect. According to her, "Efforts to reach the Truth should exist in every man of good will." As M.K. Gandhi said, "There should be truth in thought, truth in speech and truth in action."[13] Absolute truthfulness must govern spiritual life. All education aims at bringing the light of truth upon earth. This truth is the inner secret of man. It is the inner master and guide. It is the opposite of falsehood. Indian philosophy has always considered truth as stronger than falsehood. Supporting this ancient Indian optimism The Mother said in her message on 14th August 1971, "Truth is stronger than falsehood, there is an immortal Power that governs the world. Its decisions always prevail Join with it and you are sure of the final victory."[14] For those who are eager to get rid of falsehood The Mother asked to identify with Divine. Truth transcends the world. It opens the gates of true knowledge. Human truth is relative to time and space. Taken separately, it necessarily involves an element of falsehood, pointing out the Socratic truth as the rational truth The Mother said, "Intellectually, the Truth is the point where all the opposites meet and join to make a unity."[15] This is the philosophical truth, the truth, reached by the dialectical method. However, this is no more than mental opinion. Mental opinion is ultimately ignorance. Therefore, The Mother said, in her message on 24th October 1971, "Truth is above mind; it is in silence that one can enter into communication with it. To pray to the Divine and to surrender oneself entirely and in all sincerity to Him are the essential preliminary conditions."[16] Moral consciousness, as Immanual Kant pointed out, involves conflict It is based upon rational distinctions between right and wrong. Therefore, Indian philosophers have always considered moral consciousness as lower and spiritual consciousness transcending social rules and moral conscience. As The Mother Said, "There is a great difference between having a moral conscience and a consciousness which is the expression of truth. But I must say that it is infinitely more difficult to have a consciousness which expresses the truth than to have a moral conscience, because any fool who knows the social rules and follows them has a moral conscience, while to have a consciousness of truth one must not be an idiot — in any case, it's the first condition!"[17]

In her description of perfection as the goal, The Mother has explained virtues which she called psychological perfections. Therefore, one should never think that ethics has not been given its proper place in The Mother's integral education. In her detailed discussion of the qualities required on the way to perfection, the qualities of the educator and the educand, the necessity of discipline in educational institution and the need of overcoming the defects. The Mother has presented a positive moral philosophy. These have been collected in detail in volume 16 of the Collected Works.

The Moral Standard

An aspirant questioned, "What is my true destiny? What is

my true worth in this life?" To this The Mother said, "To serve the Divine."[18] As she explained in her message of 28th March 1970, "The true aim of life is to find the Divine's presence deep inside oneself and to surrender to It so that It takes the lead of the life, all the feelings and all the actions of the body. This gives a true and luminous aim to existence."[19] Thus life has a purpose. This teleological basis is the film foundation of the moral philosophy of The Mother. It rejects hedonism and utilitaranism. The British philosophers David Hume said, "Reason is and ought to be the slave of passions."[20] Thus man's solitary duty is the fulfilment or satisfaction of his passions. Reason helps him in this.

Hedonists proclaim that they are the followers of Socrates but they have interpreted his objective of life, bliss, as pleasure. Rejecting this hedonist standard The Mother said, "Happiness is not the aim of life. The aim of ordinary life is to carry out one's duty, the aim of, spiritual life is to realise the Divine."[21] In the history of ethics, hedonism was supported both by ancient and modem thinkers. Some of the more intelligent hedonists distinguish between sensuous and intellectual pleasures. Thus Epicurus supported intellectual pleasures as against the physical pleasure. Indian thinkers however, rejected even the intellectual pleasures as temporary and mundane. They always aimed at the eternal and immortal virtues. Explaining this viewpoint, The Mother said, "What is lasting, eternal and infinite, that indeed is worth having, worth conquering, worth possessing. It is divine Light, divine Love, divine Life — it is also Supreme Peace, Perfect Joy and All Mastery upon earth with the Complete Manifestation as the crowning."[22] This is in clear contrast to all sorts of hedonism and utilitarianism and even rationalism in ethics. It is based on the postulate that the Divine is always with man.

Indian philosophy always considered surrender to Divine as the best means of all progress and evolution. In her message of 11 August 1954 The Mother said, "The Divine Consciousness must be our only guide."[23] 'Phis has been supported by the Christian mystics, the Muslim Sufis and they seem of ancient Indian Upanisadic age. That is the confidence of human effort to progress. Explaining the meaning of Divine The Mother said in her message of 7 September 1952, "This is what we mean by 'Divine': all the knowledge we have to acquire, all the power we have to obtain, all the love we have to become, all the perfection we have to achieve, all the harmonious and progressive poise we have to manifest in the light and joy, all the new and unknown splendours that have to be realised."[24] Divine has also been called God. Explaining the meaning of the term God, The Mother said, in her message of 8 November 1969, "God is the perfection that we must aspire to realise."[25] This is the axiological explanation of the goal of life, found in almost all the Indian scriptures. Ancient Upanishads called God Saccidananda or the Existence, the Consciousness and the Bliss. It has also been called Satyam or the Truth, Sivam or the Good and Sundaram or the Beautiful. This is the real nature of man. To the question 'Who am I?,' The Mother replied, "The Divine under many disguises."[26] Therefore, there is no reason for any sort of pessimism, however great evil one may find in the world. Ramanuja recommended all sort of relationships with God. Indian Saints including Meera establish all sort of relationship with Divine. These were the relationships of friendship, closeness, intimacy. According to The Mother many types of relationships are possible with the Divine. These are: "The Lords and his Sakti, God and his devotees, The father and the child, The master and his disciple, The beloved and lover, The friend and co-worker, The child and his mother."[27] Intimacy with the Divine may be physical, vital, mental and psychic.

In her explanation of the path of yoga The Mother has explained her moral philosophy. In her message of 29 February 1952 she said, "Life is a perpetual choice between truth and falsehood, light and darkness, progress and regression, the ascent towards the heights or a fail into the abyss. It is for each one to choose freely."[28] Kant preached "Duty for the sake of Duty". The Mother, along with the Gita, accepts Duty for the sake of Good. She interprets the central teaching of the Gita in a way different from that of *Samskara*, Ramanuja and Tilak, etc. She strongly emphasises the value of Karma in life. There she agrees with Tilak. But she does not admit Karma as an end in itself. The ideal man of The Mother's moral philosophy works neither for himself nor for society, nor even for Duty itself but for God, as an instrument in His hand, It is a state higher than the ideal in Kantian ethics. Duty for 'Duty' is the highest principle and categorical imperative, so long as ethical being has not advanced from his mental level. But, as the man transcends mental level, his performance of works becomes an outgrowing from the soul. Thus The Mother presents an ethics of self-realisation. This standard as self-realisation synthesizes egoism with altruism, reason with sensibility, individual with society and even transcends this synthesis. Perfectionism or Eudaemonism is definitely an advance upon other theories, when it regards self-realisation as the end and includes social and individual, rational and sensible, egoistic and altruistic aspects in the total self. But while taking the rational self to be the highest, it falls short of the complete ideal. Reason, as Hegel has advocated, proceeds through a dialectical process. It cannot completely transform the infarctional. This fact has led to many anti-intellectual philosophers to revolt against the philosophy of "bloodless ballot of categories". Some extremists even subordinated reason to passion. Bradley retorted, "Metaphysics is the finding of bad reasons for what we believe on instinct."[29] Reason in Plato, Aristotle and even in Hegel, is certainly not intellectual, it is not the Spirit, since the spirit not only transcends but integrates. The spiritual self, as The Mother points out, is not only individual and social but above all transcendentals. This transcendental aspect of self has been missed by almost all the moralists. This self is more than Truth, Beauty and Goodness since it is Consciousness, Existence and Bliss. In it neither social nor individual, neither rational nor infarctional is subordinated to each other but integrated, transformed and spiritualised. Reason is not an end in itself. With infarctional, it also seeks its destiny.

Moral Virtues

The Mother has given a detailed analysis of moral virtues. The following virtues have been particularly emphasised:

1. *Tapasya* — According to The Mother, "A discipline imposed by the will for any spiritual end is *tapasya*"[30] *Tapasya* is physical, vital, and mental. The Mother is against asceticism. Maintaining an integral concept of *Tapasya* like that of Gautama the Buddha, The Mother has pointed out, "The true attitude is neither to be an ascetic nor to indulge in desire. The true attitude is to take in ail simplicity what I give, to be perfectly satisfied with it and neither to ask for more nor to refuse what is given."[31] The Mother's ethics, like her philosophy, is positive. It negates nothing but includes, integrates and fulfills all. And it is here that it has its superiority over other theories. The Mother's ethics is everywhere based on a sound psychology. It never preaches repression, far

from it, it preaches spontaneous growth. The really important thing in moral growth is sincerity and perpetual progress. Given this, the man can safely indulge in the enjoyments and thus weaken the passions, before they drop down like a ripe fruit. This is the Surest way of progress, since coercion and repression only lead to frustration and pathological symptoms. The real thing is the positive growth towards the realization of the divine self, for as the man advances in this path, the impediments automatically disappear in due course. In the old methods of yoga silence and solitude were insisted. The Mother however, supports the divine work in relation with the world. As she said, "Entire physical retirement is seldom healthy, although a temporary retirement is often helpful. But the main thing is the inner detachment and complete turning to the Divine."[32]

2. *Cheerfulness* — The Mother has supported the virtues of the cheerfulness. In her message of 29 October 1934 she said, "Keep a cheerful mind and a peaceful heart. Let nothing disturb your equanimity and make every day the necessary progress to advance with me steadily towards the goal."[33]

3. *Happiness* — Pointing out the value of happiness The Mother said in her message of 25 October 1934, "Happiness is as contagious as gloom — and nothing can be more useful than to pass on to people the contagion of a true and deep happiness."[34] Lasting happiness is possible only by the Divine grace. This is spiritual happiness. Spiritual happiness is permanent. It is good. It is Divine.

4. *Joy* — According to The Mother, "Once a man has tasted the joys of inner life nothing else will ever satisfy him."[35] This is the joy of spirituality. It is the joy of right attitude. It comes from surrender to Hie Divine. It is the joy of integral peace.

5. *Beatitude and Bliss* – In her message of 19 October 1954 The Mother wrote, "There is no greater bliss than that of being like a new born child in front of the Divine."[36]

6. *Hanxiony* — In tune with ancient Indian approach The Mother supports individual and collective harmony. According to her, "Integral harmony: harmony between things, harmony between people, harmony of circumstances and above all harmony of all aspiration directed towards the Supreme Truth."[37] Achievement of integral harmony is the ideal of all individual and social ethics.

7. *Goodwill* — The German philosophers Immanual Kant said, "There is nothing in the world, or even out of it, that can be called good without qualification, except a good will."[38] Good will is the one jewel which shines and glories in its own light. According to Kant, virtue is good will. Thus the ultimate end is the doing of duty for the sake of duty. Agreeing with Kant The Mother said, "Indeed, the good will hidden in all things reveals itself everywhere to the one who carries good will in his consciousness."[39] Good will is the basis of peace and harmony.

8. *Benevolence* — Indian moral philosophers have always held benevolence in great regard in the list of social virtues. Maintaining this tradition The Mother said, "A tireless benevolence, clear seeing and comprehensive, free from all personal reaction, is the best way to love God and serve Him upon earth."[40]

9. *Tolerance* — Moral philosophers all over the world hold tolerance as the basis of social ethics. This has been emphasised by almost all the contemporary Indian philosophers. M.K. Gandhi based his techniques of *Satyagraha* upon tolerance. The ideal of world unity, accepted by almost all the contemporary Indian philosophers, is based upon the ideal of tolerance. This tolerance makes the individualism balanced. As M.K. Gandhi pointed out, "I value individual freedom but you must not forget that man is essentially a social being. He has risen to the present status by learning to adjust his individualism. Individualism is the law of the beast of the jungle. We have learnt to strike the mean between individual freedom and social restraint for the sake of the wellbeing of the whole society of which one is a member."[41] The Mother however, prefers total understanding to tolerance. In her message of 9 August 1969 she said, "Tolerance is only the first step towards wisdom. The need to tolerate indicates the presence of preferences. He who lives in the Divine Consciousness regards all things with a perfect equanimity."[42]

10. *Freedom* — Defining liberty in her message of 28 March 1932 The Mother wrote, "Liberty is to depend only on the Divine."[43] Contemporary Indian philosophers have given a spiritual explanation of real freedom. As R.N. Tagore wrote, "Real freedom is of the mind and spirit. It can never come to us from outside. He only has freedom who ideally loves freedom himself and is glad to extend it to others. He who cares to have slaves must chain himself to them: he who builds walls to create exclusion for others builds

walls across his own freedom; he who distrusts freedom in others loses his moral right to it Sooner or later he is lured into the meshes of physical and moral servility."[44] Putting the ideal of spiritual freedom in more clear terms The Mother said in her message on 31 August 1966, "Freedom does not come from outer circumstances but from inner liberation. Find your soul, unite with it, let it govern your life and you will be free."[45]

11. *Truth* — Maintaining ancient Indian ethics M.K. Gandhi said, "There should be truth in thought, Truth in speech and Truth in action"[46] Identically The Mother said, "Absolute truthfulness must govern life if one wants to be close to Divine."[47] This is the inner truth.

12. *Control of Speech* — Indian spiritual tradition has insisted upon control of speech as a necessary practice for spiritual evolution. Maintaining this ancient Indian ideal The Mother said in her message on 5 March 1933, "Control over what one says is more important than complete silence. The best is to learn to say what is useful in the most exact and true way possible."[48] Thus one should never express anger, boasting, gossip, malice and criticism. No useless information may be gathered.

13. *Honesty* — Moral philosophers in East and West have insisted upon honesty in social relationships. The Mother recommends vital honesty, mental honesty and mental sincerity as essential conditions for integral honesty.

14. *Sincerity* — Sincerity is the key to spiritual evolution. It is the gate to Divinity. Defining it The Mother said in her message of 21 February 1930, "Sincerity means to lift all the movements of the being to the level of the highest consciousness and realisation already attained."[49] Insincerity leads to the path of ruin so also do pretentions and self-deceptions. Honesty towards oneself is required to eliminate self-deception.

15. *Aspiration* — This is a necessary condition for all spiritual progress. Explaining its real nature The Mother said in her message of 12 January 1934, "An aspiration which is not mixed with any interested and egoistic calculation"[50] is sincere aspiration.

16. *Confidence* — Moral progress requires absolute confidence. This confidence however, its not so much self-confidence as confidence in The Divine Grace. In her message of 13 August 1966, The Mother pointed out, "The best way of meeting difficulties is a quiet and calm confidence in the Grace."[51]

17. *Faith* — Confidence in Divine grace is faith. As The Mother puts it, "Faith-confidence in the Divine and the unshakable certitude of the Divine's Victory."[52] The great religions have believed in correlation of faith and grace. Faith brings Divine health. Trust in the Divine Grace and health is necessary to overcome worldly difficulties.

18. *Self-giving* — Self-sacrifice has been considered as the basis of social ethics everywhere. It maintains the equilibrium of the social and the individual. It has been equally emphasised by perfectionist moral philosophers as well as religious saints. Pointing out its value The Mother said, "Self-giving: by this the whole being gets progressively unified round the central psychic being."[53] Self-giving includes absolute devotion and surrender to divine. It means to will what the divine wills. It goes with Divine love which is more than human love. The Mother has insisted upon love for the divine as the only love worth aspiring.

19. *Love* — Following the ancient Indian spiritual tradition to transcend human love for Divine love The Mother said in her message of 4 December 1954, "There is a thirst for Love which no human relation can quench. It is only the Divine's love that can satisfy that thirst."[54] Love requires self-giving. It is devotion. Divine love has no trace for physical element of sex. It overcomes all evil. It brings peace and silence.

20. *Openness and Receptivity* — Defining the virtue of openness The Mother said, "Openness is the will to receive and to utilise for progress the force and influence, the constant aspiration to remain in touch with the Consciousness; the faith that the force and consciousness are always with you, around you, inside you and that you have only to let nothing stand in the way of your receiving them."[55] This openness leads to wideness, plasticity and receptivity — physical, vital and mental.

21. *Purity and Humility* — Defining purity The Mother said, "Purity is perfect sincerity and one cannot have it unless the being is entirely consecrated to the Divine."[56] Purity is integral, that of the whole being. It includes physical, vital and mental, individual as well as collective purity. It brings simplicity and humility. It involves gratitude and faithfulness.

22. *Will and Perseverance* — Western moral philosophers have based all ethics on the power of will Defining will The Mother

said, “Will: power of consciousness turned towards effectuation.”[57] This requires the resolution that nothing should stop development. It involves determination to get rid of all habits. It requires steady effort, persistence, perseverance, endurance and passions. The Mother recommends ancient Greek virtues of heroism and bravery, boldness, strength, force and power on the one hand and prudence and balance, enthusiasm and straightforwardness, nobility and refinement, on the other. All these virtues lead to moral elevation but they do not stop there.

Integral moral philosophy does not end at moral development. It leads to further conquests, on the religious and finally on the spiritual level. It includes not only physical, vital and mental virtues but virtues of the whole being. It does not depend purely on the human effort but calls for the Divine Grace. In fact, there is no dividing line between moral and religious education. It is so since integral is the only real and it is only through theoretical analysis that one distinguishes between the physical, the vital and mental, the individual and collective, the moral and religious. In reality the integral being keeps all these together as part of a single whole.

MEANS OF MORAL EDUCATION

Discipline and Freedom

The Mother has rightly said, “No big creation is possible without discipline.”[58] Defining discipline in terms of the highest principle Sri Aurobindo maintained that it is “to act according to a standard of truth or a rule or law of action or in obedience to a superior authority or to the highest principle discovered by the reason or intelligent will.”[59] Thus discipline is a controlled life. Its physical, vital and the mental sources are guided by spirituality. It is against unbridled indulgence in fancies, impulses and desires. It is obedience of the inner sense. Partly it is also obedience of authority.

Kinds of Discipline

Discipline, according to The Mother, is individual discipline, group discipline and finally discipline towards the divine. These distinctions have been made on the basis of the authority functioning imposition of discipline. Individual discipline is imposed by the individual oneself. Group discipline is imposed by the group or the majority or the leader in it. Discipline towards the Divine means, rigorous perusal of the dictates of the Divine. However, these three types of discipline are essentially the same since underlying the individual, group and the universe there is only one Divine principle. Sri Aurobindo maintains that the three aspects of reality *viz.* individuality, essentiality and commonality are in fact one.

Disciplinary Measures

The best way to impose discipline, according to Sri Aurobindo is the atmosphere and the example of the teacher. The following measures have been recommended by The Mother to inculcate discipline among the students:

1. Generally speaking, the discipline should start at the age of twelve.

2. The most important measure is the example of the teacher.

The teacher should be punctual, properly dressed, calm, methodical, orderly, sympathetic and courteous. He should himself present high examples of sincerity, honesty, straightforwardness, courage, disinterestedness, unselfishness, patience, endurance, perseverance, peace and self-control. He should first of all train his emotions and morals. He should have a respect for the child. Nothing should be imposed from outside but suggested by examples. Examples are the best for the personal guidance and to exercise influence upon the educands. In the words of The Mother, "It is through example that education becomes effective. To say good words, give wise advice to a child, has very little effect, if one does not show by one's living example the truth of what one teaches."[60]

The vibrations between the teacher and the taught should be favourable, there should be no use of force in discipline. According to The Mother before the age of seven years the child is not conscious of himself and does not know why and how to do things. During this period he should be trained to acquire traits of a human being. From the age of seven years to fourteen years of age, the child should be taught to choose what he wishes to be. At 14, he should be clear as to what he wants to do. After 14 years of age he should be left independent to pursue his course. He may be only advised now and then. There can be no definite rules for the guidance of the students in the process of discipline.

Discipline and Freedom

From the above discussion, it is clear that according to The Mother, freedom is the real discipline. This, however, is only spiritual freedom. In the realm of Spirit there is no chasm between discipline and freedom. Each one has to grow and expand according to his own principle. The inner voice in every educand is in fact the divine principle in him. Thus realisation of freedom is God realisation. As order is the prelude to liberty similarly discipline is a precondition for realisation of freedom.

Code of Conduct

This however does not mean that there is no code of conduct in The Mother's International School or Sri Aurobindo's International University. As the principal guide of both these institutions The Mother laid down code of conduct for the educands. She was against any outward limitation of the child's liberty but she insists that once the choice for joining the above-mentioned institutions has been made, there is no turning aside. She was against any use of compulsion or obligation. She, however, insisted upon taking judgement and following them. She advised the educands to arrive at rational decisions. She maintained that the class discipline must be followed. In her own words, "But if a student has decided to follow a class, it is an absolutely elementary discipline for him to follow it, he must go to the class regularly and behave decently there, otherwise he is quite unfit to go to school."[61] She was against any illusions about the abilities of the educands. She warned, "Do not mistake liberty for licence and freedom for bad manners. The thoughts must be pure and the aspiration ardent."[62] She laid down the following code of conduct for the students:

1. The good manners should be always observed.
2. Everyone should always speak the truth.
3. Truth in speech demands truth in acts too.
4. It is forbidden for children to fight at school, in the street, in the playground, and at home. "Always and everywhere it is forbidden for children to fight among themselves, for each time one gives a blow to someone it is to one's own soul that one gives it."[63]
5. The child should always remember:

   The necessity of an absolute sincerity.

The certitude of Truth's final victory.

The possibility of constant progress with the will to achieve.

Technique of Moral Education

For The Mother, as for Aldous Huxley, "A perfect education is one which trains up every human being to fit into the place he or she is to occupy in the social hierarchy, but without, in the process, destroying his or her individuality."[64] The Mother strongly emphasised the need of moral education in a sound system of education. This however, cannot be done by instructions through a fixed syllabus. These can improve the intellect but cannot lead to emotional integration. Moral text-books, like other books, may render moral thinking mechanical and artificial. Man's moral nature is composed of three things — emotions, sanskaras and svabhava. These are to be transformed if man has to become moral. Without this transformation, all outer changes at best touch the fringe and not the centre. Rigid discipline in educational institutions or at home leads to compulsions, repressions and fits of violence. "The essence of discipline is, thus, not forced subordination to the will of hated tyrants, but submission to the example of admired superiors."[65] Nothing persists unless it becomes a part of nature. This, however, does not indicate formal moral and religious education can be neglected. This negligence will influence personality and character. Wherever this is the system of education, there are bound to be complaints of indiscipline and lack of character and balance in the educated young men and women. The ancient Indian system of education in which the Gum was the living ideal before the disciples was far better than the modern Indian or European system of education. That system, however, cannot be brought back on account of many new problems, such as increase of population, urbanization, industrialization and complexity of modern culture. But it is not impossible to establish an educational system in which teachers may be friends, guides and helpers and not hired instructors or benevolent policemen. The only compulsion necessary for the educand is the compulsion of the inner situations of his self-development.

Moral training, according to The Mother, can be imparted by suggestion and not by command. As Swami Vivekananda puts it, "Like fire in a piece of flint, knowledge exists in the mind, suggestion is the friction which brings it out."[66] This suggestion has to be exercised by personal example, daily talks and the books read from day to day. Books provide a kind of satsang, the company of great souls. For the younger students, the examples of the past should be presented in an interesting style. For the elder students, ideas and activities of great men should be presented in a way that may arouse deeper emotions and higher aspirations. The text-books should avoid all sermons. Sermons do not change hearts. What is required is the noble example of the teachers themselves and freedom to the educand to express his moral impulses. The Indian Varna system presents a fine analysis of the different moral qualities required for the proper functioning of different persons in society. These qualities can be developed only when the young are given opportunity to train themselves in the Aryan tradition. Bad qualities, habits and sanskara of mind and body should be treated as curable diseases and removed through the cultivation of positive virtues and self-control.

The Ideal Teacher

As in the ancient Indian system of education, The Mother has assigned a very important place to the teacher. She has however not made him central as in the ancient Indian scheme. The central place, as in the Western systems of education, has been occupied by the educand. Her philosophy of education therefore, is paedo-centric. However, the teacher remains the philosopher and the guide. The Guru does not have absolute authority. He aims at turning the disciple's eye towards the beacon light of his own Godhead. In fact, the real teacher is within the educand. He is the God. He is the ultimate guide and yet the teacher plays an important role in arousing the educand towards God within. He has not to impose his opinions or demand passive surrender from the educand. He has to create an atmosphere so that the educand may grow freely. The mother accepts the role of a gardener for the teacher as maintained by many Western educational philosophers. The teacher acts as an aid, a means and a channel. His relationship with the educand is very close. In the ancient Indian tradition, The Mother emphasises an inner relationship between the educator and the educand. For this the teacher should develop certain innate qualities.

Describing as to who is a teacher, The Mother has laid down

the following qualifications, 'Teachers who do not possess a perfect calm, an unfailing endurance, an unshakable quietness, who are full of self-conceit will reach nowhere.

One must be a saint and a hero to become a good teacher.
One must be a great *Yogi* to become a good teacher.
One must have the perfect attitude in order to be able to exact from one's pupils a perfect attitude.
You cannot ask of a person what you do not do yourself.
It is a rale.
You must then look within you at the difference between what is and what should be, and this difference will give you the measure of your failure in the class."[67]

In brief the teacher should be an integral Yogi. He should be able to eliminate his ego, master his movements, develop an insight into human nature and to progress in impersonalisation. He should be absolutely disciplined and having an integrated personality. The most important thing in a teacher is not the knowledge but the attitude. An intellectual excellence is not sufficient without a development of other aspects of personality. The teacher should have the capacity to project himself to the educand so that he may have an understanding of the needs of the educand. The schools aim not only on the progress of the educand but also of the educator. In the words of The Mother, "The school must be an occasion of progress for the teacher as well as for the student. Each must have the freedom to develop himself freely. One never applies a method well unless one has discovered it oneself."[68] In practice, the central trait of the teacher is the inner calm. He should exercise influence not by scolding but by moral control. In the words of The Mother, "I must tell you that if a professor wants to be respected, he must be respectable."[69]

Personality Traits of The Teacher

In order to fulfil his role, the teacher should take it seriously and honestly. He should develop his personality more than the ordinary man so that he may be able to influence others. He should be a representative of Divine on earth. He should be in close touch with the divine consciousness. He should be a representative of the supreme knowledge, the supreme truth and the supreme law.

The Mother has prescribed the following personality traits for a true teacher:

1. Complete self-control not only to the extent of not showing any anger, but remaining absolutely quiet and undisturbed under all circumstances.

2. In the matter of self-confidence, he must also have the sense of the relativity of his importance.

Above all, he must have the knowledge. The teacher himself must always progress if he wants his students to progress. He must not remain satisfied either with what he is or with what he knows.

3. He must not have any sense of essential superiority over his students nor preference or attachment whatsoever for one or another.

4. He must know that all are equal spiritually and instead of mere tolerance he must have a global comprehension or understanding.

5. The business of both parent and teacher is to enable and to help the child to educate himself, to develop his own intellectual, moral, aesthetic and practical capacities and to grow freely as an organic being, not to be kneaded and pressured into form like an inert plastic material.

The Ideal Child[70]

The Mother has given the following description of an ideal child.

1. *Good tempered* — He does not become angry when things seems to go against him or decisions are not in his favour.

2. *Game* — Whatever he does he does it to the best of his capacity and keeps on doing in the face of almost certain failure.

3. *Truthful* — He never fears to say the truth whatever may be the consequences.

4. *Patient* — He does not get disheartened if he has to wait a long time to see the results of his effort.

5. *Enduring* — He never slackens his effort however long it has to last.

6. *Poised* — He keeps equanimity in success as well as in failure.

7. *Courageous* — He always goes on fighting for the final victory though he may meet with many defeats.

8. *Cheerful* — He knows how to smile and keep a happy heart in all circumstances.

9. *Modest* — He does not become conceited over his success, neither does he feel himself superior to his comrades.

10. *Generous* — He appreciates the merits of others and is always ready to help another to succeed.

11. *Courteous* — On the field he does jeer at errors: he does not cheer at the opponent's defeat; he treats them as guests, not enemies. In school he is considerate to the authorities, the fellow students, and the teachers. In life he is respected to others, he treats them as he would be treated.

12. *Obedient* — On the field he observes the rules of the game. In school he observes all the regulations. In life he respects the rules which help to promote harmony.

13. *Fair* — On the field he completes in a clean, hard though friendly way; he helps an injured opponent. In school he does not waste his time nor that of the teachers. He is always honest. In life he sees impartially both sides of a question.

Thus The Mother's integral education gives highest place to the children. They are considered as divine force, the leaders of the future gnostic race on the earth. All the hopes for man's future lie upon the proper development of the younger generation. There is no gap between the teacher and the taught, the Guru and the children. Integral education considers the inner relationship and rapport as the first conditions of all education. It is in this spirit that The Mother said to the children of the Ashram, "My Children, we are united towards the same goal and for the same accomplishment — for a work unique and new, that the divine Grace has given us to accomplish. I hope that more and more you will understand the exceptional importance of this work and that will sense in yourself the sublime joy that the accomplishment will give you. The divine force is with you — feel its presence more and more and be very careful never to betray it. Feel, wish, act, that you may be new beings for the realisation of a new world and for this my blessings shall be always with you."[71]

In order to impart institutional moral education The Mother prescribed a code of conduct both for the educators and educands. This code was based upon the fundamental postulates that Divine is present everywhere. Therefore, all our activities should be such as are approved by the Divine. Hence the children were forbidden to fight in school, street, playground or home. Pointing out what a child should always remember The Mother said in her message on 15-1-1963, "The necessity of an absolute sincerity. The certitude of Truth's final victory. The possibility of constant progress with the will to achieve."[72] This takes us to religious education which will be discussed in the following chapter.

References

1. The Complete Works of Swami Vivekananda, Vol. I. (1984), p. 436.
2. *C.W.M.*, Vol. 5 (1976), p. 349.
3. *Ibid.*, Vol. 15 (1980), pp. 368-369.
4. Bradley, F.H., *Appearance and Reality* (1951), p. 436.
5. Muirhead, J.M., *The Elements of Ethics* (1865), p. 137.
6. *C.W.M.*, Vol. 8. (1977), p. 143.
7. *Ibid.*, Vol. 4 (1972), p. 12.
8. *Ibid.*, Vol. 10 (1977), p. 245.
9. *Ibid.*, p. 72.
10. C.WM., Vol. 3 (1977), p. 119.
11. *Ibid.*, Vol. 4 (1972), p. 11.
12. *Ibid.*, Vol. 14 (1980), p. 204.
13. Gandhi, M.K., *Yervada Mandir,* p. 2.
14. *C.W.M.*, Vol. 14, p. 209.
15. *Ibid.*, p. 213.
16. *Ibid.*, p. 214.
17. *Ibid.*, Vol. 7 (1979), p. 126.
18. *Ibid.*, Vol. 14, p. 5
19. *Ibid.*, p. 5.
20. Hume, D., *Treatise on Human Nature*, Book B, Part IB, Section IB.
21. *C.W.M.*, Vol. 14, p. 7.
22. *Ibid.*, p. 8.
23. *Ibid.*, p. 11.
24. *Ibid.*, p. 17.
25. *Ibid.*
26. *Ibid.*, p. 18.
27. *Ibid.*, Vol. 14, p. 22.
28. *Ibid.*, p. 29.
29. Bradley, F.H., *Appearance and Reality*, Preface.
30. C.W.M, Vol. 14. p. 45.
31. *Ibid.*, p. 47.
32. *Ibid.*, p. 50.
33. *Ibid.*, p. 192.
34. *Ibid.*, p. 193.

35. *Ibid.*, p. 195.
36. *Ibid.*, p. 196.
37. *Ibid*, p. 197.
38. Kant, I., *Critique of Practical Keaton*
39. C.W.M., Vol. 14, p. 199-
40. *Ibid.*, p. 200.
41. Gandhi, M.K, *Harijan* (May 27, 1939), p. 144.
42. *C.W.M.*, Vol. 14, p. 201.
43. *Ibid.*, p. 202.
44. Tagore, R.N., *Creative Unity* (London: Macmillan, 1925), p. 136.
45. C.W.M, Vol. 14, p. 202.
46. Gandhi, M.K., *Yervada Mandir*, p. 2.
47. *C.W.M.*, Vol. 14, p. 204.
48. *Ibid.*, p. 218.
49. *Ibid.*, p. 67.
50. *Ibid.*, p. 75.
51. *Ibid.*, p. 85.
52. *Ibid.*, p. 82.
53. *Ibid.*, p. 106.
54. *Ibid.*, p. 127.
55. *Ibid.*, p. 151.
56. *Ibid.*, p. 156.
57. *Ibid.*, p. 167.
58. *Sri Aurobindo and The Mother on Education*, Part II, p. 26.
59. *Sri Aurobindo Birth Centenary Library*, Volume 23 (1970), p. 862.
60. *Sri Aurobindo and The Mother on Education*, Part II, p. 27.
61. *Ibid.*, Part III, p. 20.
62. *Ibid.*, p. 22.
63. *Ibid*, p. 27.
64. Huxley, A., *Proper Studies* (London: Chatto & Windus, 1928), p. 136.
65. Hughes, A.G., *Education and Democratic Ideal*, (London: Logman's Green & Co., 1951), p. 92.
66. Vivekananda, S., *The Complete Works*, Part I, 4th Ed., p. 26.
67. *Sri Aurobindo and The Mother on Education*, Part II, pp. 4-5.
68. *Ibid.*, p. 7.
69. *Ibid.*, p. 8.
70. *Ibid.*, Part II, pp, 28-29.
71. *Ibid.*, Part III, p. 22
72. *Ibid.*, p. 27.

12

Religious Education

The aim of contemporary education is not only the mental, physical and social development of the individual, but also his religious and moral development, which is why modern educationists have stressed the importance of religious education for the country. Swami Vivekananda said that religion is the basis of education although here he does not imply his own or someone else's religion. This comment also implies that the aim of religious education is not to propound the theories of any one particular religion but to create faith towards universally accepted religious values. The presence of religious faith helps the individual to face all kinds of adverse conditions with the belief that he can progress at least a little, irrespective of the darkness of the outlook. Hence religious faith helps man in his progress, raises him to a high level and also assists him in developing democratic qualities. Religion is the foundation of all moral character, because without religion man cannot have faith in truth, beauty and goodness. The freedom that we want to grant the child through education is not possible without religion. Besides, even culture has no meaning in the absence of religion which also acquaints us with the final goal of life. Without knowing this goal, education cannot progress. Religion is the basis of true humanitarianism.

It is evident from the foregoing comments that religion should be given its appropriate place in the curriculum for education. Swami Vivekananda has recommended that modern science should be used to awaken the educand's knowledge. History, geography and literature should be taught to the educand along with the teaching of religion which must be used to teach them the greatest truths. Sarvapalli Radhakrishnan also supported the teaching of religion at the various levels of education. He maintained that we would have to plan for a rational religion for our conflict ridden emerging humanity, a religion that does not ridicule man's soul filled with unrestrained individualism and hesitation born out of the conflict. We have to present a new philosophy of God with which we can fight against those doubting communities of men who are fighting against each other to establish their supremacy on men's souls. Rabindranath Tagore also expressed sympathy with this viewpoint in granting the greatest importance to humanitarian religion in education. Pointing to the basic humanitarian religion that is at the base of all religions Tagore maintained that these religions differ from each other in moral value, but each man is inspired by the same tendency. In these religions, man looks for his highest ideal, which he calls God. They try to discover it in some personality of human character Mahatma Gandhi has also attached the greatest significance to religious education, and he has advocated that educands should be acquainted with the basic elements of all religions. The Mother has considered religious education to be the most important aspect of education.

Importance of Religious Education

In her integral philosophy of education The Mother finds an important place for religious education, to be transcended and substituted only by psychic education. In the integral point of view, every part has its particular place in the whole beyond which it has to be transcended and substituted by a higher part. The evolution of the educand is not only horizontal but also vertical. In this vertical progress however, religious education is a necessary stage. As The Mother points out, "One can say that if this aspiration to the unknown and the higher found no expression, human existence would be very difficult. If there were not in the core of every being, the hope for something better, for some order, whatever it be, it would be difficult to find the necessary energy to continue to live."[1] Most of the ordinary human beings cannot do without religion. Thus, religion is a social need. In the words of The Mother, "In the life of societies it is necessity, for it serves as a corrective to collective egoism which, without this control, could take on excessive proportions."[2] The level of collective consciousness is always lower than the individual consciousness. Therefore, institutional religion too has its value. In fact, wherever there is some ideal, there is some religion. Thus every political or social idea is governed by some rudimentary ideal which may be called its religion. Thus, in order to harmonise the social life, religious education is necessary. However, religious education should not be the teaching of this or that particular religion. In fact, it is here that freedom is the guiding principle. It is so since different individuals practise even the same religion differently. As The Mother puts it, "Of course, when we speak of religion, if we mean the recognised religions, truly, everyone has his own religion, whether he knows it or not, even when he belongs to the great religions that have a name and a history. It is certain that even if one learns the dogmas by heart and complies with a prescribed ritual, everybody understands and acts in his own way, and only the name of the religion is the same, but this same religion is not the same for all the individuals who think they are practising it."[3]

Among different methods of human evolution, such as occultism, philosophy, religion and Yoga, the religious method is followed by those individuals who live almost exclusively in the physical consciousness. There are the ordinary people, the common human beings who live by faith or collective suggestion. They have not yet reached an inner development to adopt spiritual philosophy or occultism. Following the method of spiritual philosophy require a more complete mental development. It is their persons who are in need of a religious education. However, the ideal which they cherish shows the type of religion they have adopted. As The Mother puts it, "It can be said, of course, of individual as well as of groups, that their value is just in proportion to the value of their ideal, of their religion, that is to say, of the thing which they place at the summit of their existence."[4] Thus religious education has not been given a paramount place in The Mother's integral philosophy of education. In fact, it is not necessary foreveryone, certainly not for more intelligent and spiritual persons. Distinguishing between the religious teaching and spiritual teaching The Mother said in her message of 12 February 1972, "You must not confuse a religious teaching with a spiritual one. Religious teaching belongs to the past and halts progress. Spiritual teaching is the teaching of the future — it illumines the consciousness and prepares it for the future realisation. Spiritual teaching is above religions and strives towards a global Truth. It teaches us to enter into direct relations with the Divine."[5]

Nature of Religion

Defining the nature of religion, The Mother said, "It is the effort of man's higher mind to approach, as far as lies in its power, something beyond it, something to which humanity gives the name God or Spirit or Truth or Faith or Knowledge or the Infinite, some kind of Absolute, which the human mind cannot reach and yet tries to reach."[6] This definition places religion on the higher mental level. Hegelians, on the other hand while defining religion, emphasise the element of reason in it. As Professor McTaggart says, "Religion is clearly a state of mind.... It seems to me that it may best be described as an emotion resting on a conviction of harmony between ourselves and the universe at large."[7] Such a view presupposes a certain kind of rational knowledge as a necessary element in all religions, but many religious beings never philosophised, nor ever developed any kind of rational thinking. Love, which is the most potent instrument of religion, is neither knowledge nor cognition, but a psychic phenomenon. The confusion of psychic with mental or vital has been responsible for so many misunderstandings about the nature of religion. In a certain sense, revelation in religion, may be identified with the activity of pure reason, but the faith which impels man to God is not reason, pure or mixed, but inner psychic certainty of the divine destiny of man. Religion is not "the exaltation of the object released from the chains of mind,"[8] as Gentile conceived it; nor is it, "What the individual does with his own solitariness"[9] as Whitehead puts it. It is neither objective nor subjective but psychic, which includes both subjective and objective. Spirituality is the *raison d' etre* of all religions.

The Mother however, maintains that religion is essentially institutional in nature or it becomes that as based upon the collective mind. She agrees with A.N. Whitehead, and William James that religion starts as a personal man-God relationship. William James defined religion as, "The feelings, acts and experiences of individual men in their solitude so far as they apprehend themselves to stand in relation to whatever they may consider the divine."[10] This definition, though true in emphasising the divine element in religion, forgets the objective and communal aspect of it. Both Whitehead and James forget the aspect of salvation and freedom from limitations in which the man is lifted from his solitude into a Divine presence. The definition of religion as a flight of the alone to the alone'" represents the class of mystics who lay an exclusive emphasis on individual liberation. The spirit of the modern age, on the other hand, is more truly represented in The Mother's ideal of cosmic liberation* A union with Divine in all its integrity is not possible unless we feel unity with our fellow-beings. To be alone in the religious sense, should connote to be in the presence of the Divine, who is not exclusive of any person or group or interest, but is the end all and be all of all things.

According to The Mother, "Religion belongs to the higher mind of humanity."[12] Tracing its origin she said, "Religion may be divine in its ultimate origin; in its actual nature it is not divine but human."[13] Human nature is responsible for all the variety of elements involved in the origin of religion, The phenomenon called religion is extremely variegated, complex, intricate and full of paradoxes. As The Mother puts it, "In truth we should speak rather of religions than of religion; for the religions made by man are many."[14] It includes such facts as celebration, despair, ethical vigour, mystic retreat, social activism, monastic quietude, contemplation, animal sacrifice, rituals involving pain and terror, images of hope, symbols of fear, the affirmation of life and struggle against death, creative growth, unthinking superstitions, beliefs and dogmas about natural and supernatural etc. Therefore The Mother does not accept religion as purely divine or a spiritual phenomenon. As she says about Christian religion, "It was certainly not Jesus who made what is known as Christianity, but some learned and very clever men put their heads together and built it up into thing we see. There was nothing divine in the way in which it was formed, and there is nothing divine either in the way in which it functions."[15] Intellectual origin theories of religion believe that fundamentally it is the creation of man's mind. The emotive theories however, maintain that it is primarily an emotional response. As R.R. Marett argues, religion is not so much an intellectual endeavour as a set of profound emotional responses to various aspects of human existence. Accordingly, there are theories or views which consider emotional factor to be the essence of religion. According to these theories religion is based upon emotional elements. According to the celebrated psychologist Wilhem Wundt religion is simply projection of fear into the environment and according to Otto religion is identical with numinous feeling. Though Otto did not call this numinous feeling an emotion, other psychologists have identified religion with the sense of the mysterious, the uncanny, and the sacred, and termed it as numinous emotion. Therefore, religion primarily attracts emotional persons. As The Mother points out, "In all religions we find invariably a certain number of people who possess a great emotional capacity and are full of a real and ardent aspiration, but have a very simple mind and do not feel the need of approaching the Divine through knowledge. For such natures religion has a use and it is even necessary to them; for, through external forms, like the ceremonies of the Church, it offers a kind of support and help to their inner spiritual aspiration."[16]

However, The Mother does not agree that basically religion is infarctional. This view will not agree with the anti-religious statement of a Freud, a Russell and a Marx. Religion, according to Freud, restores the grandeur of the primeval father and makes possible the repetition of the emotions belonging to him."[17] It is an "Illusion" which will be shattered with the growth of knowledge. As The Mother points out, "The articles and dogmas of a religion are mind-made things and, if you cling to them and shut yourself up in a code of life made out for you, you do not know and cannot know the truth of the spirit that lies beyond all codes and dogmas, wide and large and free."[18] However, The Mother will not agree to Freud's tirade against all religion as such. Freud not only rejects a religion of totemism, naturalism and animal worship, but denounces all religion as such in unmistakable terms. He says, "The more the fruits of knowledge become accessible to man, the more widespread is the decline of religious belief, at first only of the obsolete and objectionable expressions of the same, then of its fundamental assumptions also."[19] Freud's conclusions about religion are based partly on the observation of what Sri Aurobindo calls "Religionism", as distinguished from true religion, and partly on the assumption of antagonism between religion and science. He wrote, "As you know, the struggle between scientific and religious Weltanschauung is not yet at an end; it is still going on under our eyes to-day."[20]

Disagreeing with the above-mentioned view The Mother would say, Taking it up in a serious and earnest spirit, you can try to find out what truth is there, what aspiration lies hidden in it, what divine inspiration has undergone transformation and deformation here by the human mind and a human organisation, and with an appropriate mental stand you can get religion even as it is to throw some light on your way and to lend some support to your spiritual endeavour."[21] The assumption of Freud has been questioned by even the Western scientists. However, irrelevant religion might appear to them, they do not think it opposed to science. Even Professor J.H. Leuba who condemns mystic experience as pathological, does not denounce the" value of religion in human life. In contrast to Freud's view, he says, "Religion and science would work hand in hand for the production of a better and happier, a diviner man."[22] This is the view widely prevalent at present, in spite of some agnostics and some materialist sceptics. Religion cannot be uprooted from human life, as it is instinctive, it can only change its form. As The Mother points out, "In the ordinary life, the individual whether he knows it or not, has always a religion, but the object of his religion is sometimes quite of an inferior order; the god he adores may be the god of success or the god of money, the god of power or simply a family god, a god of children, the god of the family, the god of the ancestors. Always there is a religion."[23]

But the denouncement of religion by Freud, Manx and others is not entirely baseless. The downwards curve of the evolution too has its reason and its lesson should be understood to avoid the repetition of failures. Thus, these anti-religious trends also have a certain truth at their back. The truth is not in their conclusion but in their premises. This revolt against religion has its justification in the fact that religions and their exponents have everywhere been too often a force of retardation, oppression and ignorance. Churches, cults and creeds have supported superstitions, aberrations, violence and crime and exploited them for their own benefit. As The Mother pointed out, "All religions have each the same story to tell. The occasion for its birth is the coming of a great Teacher of the world. He comes and reveals and is the incarnation of a Divine Truth. But men seize upon it, trade upon it, make an almost political organisation out of it the religion is equipped by them with a government and policy and laws, with its creeds and dogmas, its rules and regulations, its rites and ceremonies, all binding upon its adherents, all absolute and inviolable. Like the State, it too administers rewards to the loyal and assigns punishments for those that revolt or go astray, for the heretic and the renegade."[24] This however, does not warrant a total rejection of religion since, as The Mother points out, "Religion has been an impulse to the worst things and the best; if the fiercest wars have been waged and the most hideous persecutions carried on in its name, it has stimulated too, supreme heroism and self-sacrifice in its cause."[25]

In fact religion serves a social purpose. Religion has been rarely found in its pure form. Everywhere it was permeated with social and cultural ideals. A contrast between the secular and the religious is hardly possible, as even the secular life often expresses religious tendencies. The real contrast of the secular is with ecclesiastical. As The Mother pointed out, "In the life of the society it is a necessity, because it serves as a corrective to the collective egoism which would assume excessive proportions without this control."[26] In modern society social thinking plays a crucial role. A great deal of importance is attached to-day to the processes and conclusions of social thinking. All walks of modern life are influenced by and show the impact of social thinking. Earlier, it was believed that the religious, philosophical, psychological and physical thinking were independent processes uninfluenced by social thought. But today it is clear to everyone that no aspect of thinking is quite independent. There is mutual interaction between them; in particular, social thinking influences all of them profoundly. Earlier, religious thinking has a specific field and a particular approach and outlook. The central idea of religion in past was God. A belief in the supernatural power was the pivot around which all religious thinking revolved. The aim of religion was to discover the religion and complexion between terrestrial and celestial life and to find out the ways and means of achieving liberation. Besides this certain rituals also formed the important subject-matter of religion. The social dimensions of religion were all but ignored during these days. In modern times, with the realisation of the crucial importance of the social context under which all thinking takes place, the social aspect of religion has shot into prominence. Today the concern of religion is not only liberation and the life in heaven; but, more importantly, it is concerned with social welfare, social relations and social cohesion. All modern religions consider social welfare and the service of humanity as their prime concerns.

Pointing out the value of religion in a nation The Mother said, "All countries and all religions are built up out of a mass of traditions. In all of them you will meet saints and heroes and great and mighty personalities as well as small and wicked people. You will then perceive what a mockery it is to say, because I am brought up in this religion, therefore it is the only true religion; because I am born in this country, therefore it is the best of all countries'."[27]

Thus relativism and pluralism in religion is a direct corollary of its social nature. As William James pointed out, "Each of us must discover for himself the kind of religion and the amount of saintship which best comports with what he believes to be his powers and feels to be his truest mission and vocation."[28] Similarly, The Mother maintains "Things have an inner value and become real to you only when you have acquired them by the exercise of your free choice, not when they have been imposed upon you. If you want to be sure of your religion you must choose it."[29] Thus the value of religion is due to the individual cherishing it. All great religions have been born in this way. As The Mother pointed out, "In all religions we find invariably a certain number of people who possess a great emotional capacity and are full of a real and ardent aspiration, but have a very simple mind and do not feel the need of approaching the Divine through knowledge. For such natures religion has a use and it is every necessary to them; for, through external forms, like the ceremonies of the Church, it offers a kind of support and help to their inner spiritual aspiration."[30] Therefore it was correctly pointed out by J.H. Leuba, "For the psychologist who remains within the province of science, religious mysticism is a revelation not of God but of man."[31]

According to The Mother modern Christianity is not what was initially taught by Jesus Christ. Every great religion found today is based upon dogma and developed in the form of rigid institution. In the words of the Mother, "The first and principal article of these established and formal religions nins always, "Mine is the supreme, the only truth, all others are in falsehood or inferior. For without this fundamental dogma, established credal religions could not have existed."[32]? This, however, does not diminish the value of the Jesus Christ. To quote The Mother again, "And yet the excuse or occasion for the formation was undoubtedly some revelation from what one could call a Divine Being, a Being who came from elsewhere bringing down with him from a higher plane a certain knowledge and Truth for the earth. He came and suffered for his Truth; but very few understood what he said, few cared to find and hold to the truth for which he suffered."[33] Christ was great not because of religion but in spite of it. However, for the common man the institutional religion too has its value. It is only a great human being who may face the Truth. An ordinary person may breathe only in a mixture of truth and falsehood. The Mother shows a deep insight into the nature of the common man when she points out, "One who holds a particular faith or who has found out some truth, is disposed to think that he alone has found the Truth, whole an entire. This is human nature. A mixture of falsehood seems necessary for human beings to stand on their legs and move on their way. If the vision of the Truth were suddenly given to them they would be crushed under the weight."[34]

Thus, religion is utilitarian for the common man. In the words of William James, "We are supposed to gain even now, by our belief and lose by our non-belief, a certain vital good,"[35] According to The Mother the common man seeks safety, comfort, pleasure and amusement in religion. The urge for these values becomes a religion for them. It is by satisfying these values that religions have a hold upon the masses. Religions are valuable in proportion to the satisfaction which they offer to man. As The Mother points out, "It can be said of course, of individuals as well as of groups, that their value is just in proportion to the value of their ideal, of their religion, that is to say, of the thinking which they place at the summit of their existence."[36] As different persons seek different satisfactions in religion, therefore the same religion is interpreted differently by different followers. Therefore, The Mother said, "It is certain that even when one learns by heart the dogmas and follows a prescribed ritual, everyone understands in his own way and acts in his own way; the name only of the religion is the same, but this same religions is nbt the same for all individuals who believe in practising it."[37] For the psychologists, everywhere man seeks satisfaction of his desires, Only in religion, he fulfils them in what he calls Divine or God or some other supreme power. Nothing else is new in religion and hence no new categories are required to explain this particular type of human behaviour. As the psychologist J.H. Leuba points out, "To realise of the God of love is the mystic's method of securing the satisfaction of his essential wants."[38] Elsewhere he says, "God is not known, he is not understood, he is used."[39] Admitting this value of religion The Mother said, "People who carry in them a spiritual destiny and who are born to realise the Divine, to become conscious of Him and live Him will reach there necessarily, whatever the way followed. That is to say, even in religion there are people who have the spiritual experience and who find the Divine — not because of religion, generally, in spite of it — because they have the inner urge and this urge leads them to the goal in spite, of the obstacles and through them. Everything was good for them."[40]

Techniques of Religious Education

Techniques of religious education are based upon the aims of religious education, which are the following:

1. *Moral development*: James Ross has opined that without a religious education, the highest moral development of the educand is impossible because religion is the foundation of moral development and character. All the religions of the world have stressed the need for developing moral qualities, and for this reason religious education is essential for developing the educand's moral character.

2. *Refinement of human values*: One aim of religious education is to distinguish between the divine and the material, and to give a divine touch to human values. In this way, religious education refines human values and thus puts humanity on the path to higher ideals.

3. *Socialization*: Social service is recommended by every religion of the world. In the Gita people are advised to act with a view, not to personal gain, but to add to the prosperity of the humanity. By inspiring man to forget his own narrow interests and to think of humanity at large, religious education continues the process of socializing the individual.

4. *Development of democratic values*: Religious feeling relates man on one side with God and on the other with human beings, and by showing that the same God exists in every human being, it encourages the development of democratic qualities of liberty, fraternity and equality. In the absence of this sense of fraternity, equality has no meaning. It only remains a legal concept not reality.

5. *Cultural development*: Religion is an important part of culture, and for that reason religious education contributes to man's cultural development. In fact, cultural progress of a group is measured by its religious development. Sarvapalli Radhakrishnan has laid special stress on the contribution of religious education to the cultural development of the individual.

6. *Sense of respect for man*: Another objective of religious education is to induce a sense of respect for humanity in the educand. The basis of religion is the synthesizing element, and this is the basis also of education and culture.

7. *Proper attitude:* The aim of religious education is to achieve the total development of the child's personality and to induce in him the correct attitude to life and the universe.

The method and form of religious education is clarified by its objectives mentioned above. The question is how religious education can be imparted and what should be its subject matter. In this connection it is essential to remember the principle that religion is acquired, not taught, for it is not a subject to be learnt, but to be realized and translated into life. That is why Swami Vivekananda has suggested that religious education should be preceded by an account of the ideal of great men such as Rama, Krishna, Mahavira, etc. Religion means continued progress on the path to service and worship despite the greatest handicaps and obstacles. According to Swami Vivekananda, one example of this is the ideal of Hunuman. He has advised the young men of the country never to let weakness fall upon the mind. In such a situation they should think of Mahavir and Mother Goddess and they will find that this weakness vanishes immediately. Swami Vivekananda felt that the country needs a kind of religious education which achieves synthesis with science on the one side and teaches the lesson of patriotism, sacrifice and service, on the other.

According to the Mother, there is little to be gained by paying mere lip service to religious education unless religious education is actually transferred to real life and a tendency to worship, contemplation, self-control and abstinence does not grow. Spiritual development can be helped to a certain extent by worship, prayer, and the celebration of various religious festivals. The educand must be educated in his religious duties, prayer and contemplation, and in every school the educands must be initiated into the ideals of service to and living for God, humanity, the country and other countries. Religious education does not necessarily imply that the child should be forced to read all religious texts, as suggested by Mahatma Gandhi, Acharya Vinobha Bhave and other thinkers. This is also not necessary for religious tolerance. Study of different religions is not as important as actual application of the various principles of religion, and it is equally undesirable to foist any particular religious practice on every individual. Hence, the curriculum of religious education should centre around the basic elements of religion.

Syllabi of Religious Education

Religious education cannot be given by any fixed syllabi. Most of the great religions have their religious organisations which run institutions of religious education teaching their sacred books, rituals and dogmas. The syllabi of these institutions seldom include books concerning other religions. Due to exclusive concentration on the syllabi concerning their own religion these institutions produce only dogmatic and puritan individuals sometimes having a negative attitude towards other religion. The Mother condemns any such idea of a fixed syllabi concerning a particular religion for religious education.

Therefore the technique of religious education is not based upon reason alone or even primarily upon reason. This is so because, "Reason has indeed a part to play in relation to this highest field of our religious being and experience, but that part is quite secondary and subordinate. It cannot lay down the law for the religious life, it cannot determine in its own right the system of divine knowledge; it cannot school and lesson the divine love and delight; it cannot set bound to spiritual experience or lay its yoke upon the action of the spiritual man. Its sole legitimate sphere is to explain as best as it can, in its own language and to the rational and intellectual parts of man, the truths, the experience, the laws of our suprarational and spiritual existence."[41]

Limitation of Religious Education

According to The Mother, "Religion is always a limitation for the spirit."[42] Therefore, religious education is not the highest education. The highest education is psychic education. Even the ancient spiritual education has limitations characteristic of it. Therefore, The Mother has asked progressive persons to transcend religion. According to her, "There are persons who have necessarily to come out of religion if they do not want to be halted in their progress. But they who have practically no mental activity, who have no questions to ask, who have only an intense devotion in their heart an urge to give themselves to something that is infinitely greater for such, it does not matter whether they have a religion or have no religion. It is all the same. But if you are attached to form, you can never go any further."[43] Freedom is the criterion of the hierarchy in integral education. Vital education provides more freedom than physical education. Mental education provides more freedom than vital education, Religious education gives more freedom than moral education. But all these are limited to certain fixed rules or principles. Therefore in order to achieve perfect freedom one must rise above all these. According to The Mother the greatest plunder of religions is to institutionalise religious experience. They try to make the truth fixed by forms. Hence while the truth is pure in the beginning, it gradually becomes rigid and fossilized. Condemning what Sri Aurobindo calls religionism in the name of true religion The Mother has written, "That is why all religions, however fine they may behave always led men to the worst excesses. All crimes, all horrors that have been perpetuated in the name of religion are among the darkest spots in human history and simply because of this little original error: to what is true for an individual to be true for the mass or for the collectivity."[44]

Therefore The Mother advises to allow personal choice, variety, non-conformism and catholicity in religious education. True religion must be based upon personal experience. As Miss Evelyn Underhill puts it, "Not to know about but to be is the mark of real practitioner."[45] The religious progress depends upon God's grace. Otherwise religion degenerates into ceremonies and dogmas. In the last analysis The Mother has asked aspirants to be free from religion as such since according to her religion cannot make man universal. It shuts the door to all progress. This however, does not mean that The Mother is oblivious to the advantages of religious education. She admits, "If instead of looking only at the external forms of the great religions of humanity, the dogmas and intellectual conceptions, one took them in their spirit, in the principle which they represent, there would be no difficulty in unifying them. They are all but aspects of man's progress that complement each other quite well and should also unite with yet many others to form a more total and complete progress, a more perfect understanding of life, a more integral approach to the Divine."[46] Religion is a great intercessor between Spirit and Nature. It prepares man's mind and bodily existence for the advent of spiritual consciousness. It leads man to the point where the inner spiritual light begins to emerge. But it falls short of the complete realization. Religion is faith in the realization of God. This faith, however, is not actualised through religion, since it lacks psychicization, transformation and integration. This difficulty becomes more pronounced in the attempt of religion to realize this aim in masses. Religion cannot lead to the birth of the spiritual man, still less of a spiritual race. Therefore The Mother clearly says, "A new religion would not only be useless but harmful. A new life has to be created, a new consciousness has to be expressed, something which is beyond intellectual limitations and mental formulas It is a living truth that has to manifest."[47]

References

1. *Sri Aurobindo and The Mother on Religion*, p. 12.
2. *C.W.M.*, Vol. 9, (1977), p. 354.
3. *Ibid.*, 355.
4. Button of Physical Education (April 1959), p. 70
5. *C.W.M.*, Vol. 12, p. 120.
6. The Mother, *Conversations*, Ed. (1956), p. 114.
7. McTaggart, *Some Dogmas of Religion*, p. 3.
8. Gentile, G., *The Theory of Mind as Pure Act, Eng. Translation by H. Wildon.* Carr (Macmillan), p. 227.
9. Whitehead, A.N., *Religion in the Making*, p. 6.
10. James, W., *Varieties of Religious Experience*, p. 32.
11. Plotinus, *The New Platonists*, p. 103.
12. The Mother, *Conversations*, p. 114.
13. *Ibid.*
14. *Ibid.*
15. *Ibid.*
16. *Sri Aurobindo and The Mother on Religion* (1972), p. 5
17. Freud, S., *Moses and Monotheism*, p. 120.
18. Freud, S., *The Future of an Illusion*. p. 76.
19. *Ibid.*, p. 55.
20. Freud, S., *New Introductory Lectures on Psycho-Analysis*, p. 216.
21. *Sri Aurobindo and The Mother on Religion* (1972), p. 5.
22. Leuba, J.H., *The Psychology of Religious Mysticism*, p. 318.
23. *Ibid.*, p. 10,
24. *Sri Aurobindo and The Mother on Religion*, pp. 3-4.
25. *Ibid.*, p. 6.
26. Bulletin of Physical Education (April, 1959), p. 67.
27. *Sri Aurobindo and The Mother on Religion* (1972), pp 8-9.
28. James, W., *Varieties of Religious Experience*, p. 368.
29. *Sri Aurobindo and The Mother on Religion*, p. 369.
30. *Ibid.*, p. 5.

31. Leuba, J.H. The Psychology of Religious Mysticism, p. 316,
32. *Sri Aurobindo and The Mother on Religion,* p. 4.
33. *Ibid.*, p. 2.
34. *Ibid.*, p. 6.
35. James, W., The Will to Believe, p. 26.
36. *Sri Aurobindo and The Mother on Religion,* p. 11.
37. *Ibid.*
38. Leuba, J.H., The Psychology of Religious Mysticism, p. 120.
39. *Ibid.*, J.H. Monist (July 1901).
40. *Sri Aurobindo and The Mother on Religion,* p. 23.
41. *Sri Aurobindo and The Mother on Religion* (1972), p. 15.
42. *Ibid.*, p. 24.
43. Bulletin of Physical Education (April 1970), p. 59.
44. *Ibid.* (November 1958), p. 130.
45. Underhill, E., Mysticism, p. 86.
46. Bulletin of Physical Education (August 1957), p. 108.
47. *Sri Aurobindo and The Mother on Religion,* p. 30.

13

Psychic and Spiritual Education

The last but not the least valuable aspect of The Mother's integral education is the psychic or the spiritual education. It is here that she has presented the most original ideas hitherto unexplored by other philosophers of education. It is here that integral education goes further than contemporary system of education in East as well as West. It is here that sound foundation for a future scheme of education for mankind may be laid. Therefore it is necessary to explore this most important aspect of education.

The psychic is the most important part of the being. It is what has been called the soul in Indian literature. Ancient Indians believed that soul is a part of divine. *Ayamatma Brahman, Aham Brahma Asrni, Tat Twam Asi and Sarvam Khalividam Brahman*, all these *Mahavakyas* of the Upanisadic philosophy refer to soul as a part of Divine. While the physical, the vital and the mental were held to belong to the mundane, the soul was considered to be belonging to the transmundane field. Therefore, The Mother defined soul as "The soul is the Divine made individual without ceasing to be divine. In the soul the individual and the Divine are eternally one. Thus to find one's soul is to be united with the Divine. It can therefore be said that the role of the soul is to make of man a true being,"[1]

Different systems of Indian philosophy has defined soul in different ways. Each system has tried to advance arguments in its favour. However, in spite of all differences, the orthodox system of Indian philosophy have unanimously called soul as an eternal portion of the Supreme Divine. In fact most of the orthodox systems of Indian philosophy have supported the ancient Indian Upanisadic theory of soul with minor modifications and distinction of emphasis. According to the Upanisads, the individual self and the supreme self-reside in the same heart of the same body like darkness and light. The first has been called the *Jiva* while the second has been entitled the self. The *Jiva* suffers the consequences of his actions and feels pleasure and pain, but the self is beyond all these. Both are without beginning and end. The *Jiva* is ignorant and its pain and bondage are due to ignorance. By the knowledge of self, this ignorance is destroyed along with its pain and bondage. The self is one. Its knowledge destroys all dualism. Some Upanishads have not distinguished between Jiva and self, while in other the distinction is very clear. Self has been identified with God or Brahman, while Jiva has been taken as distinct from them.

Self has been defined as anandmaya. It is fall of bliss and without distinction of subject and object. It is infinite, transcendent and perfect. It is not a sheath of the self, but its essence. This self is the real essence of the Jim Le. Brahman. By its knowledge the bondage of the *Jiva* is loosened. This knowledge is attained through direct experience. In the Kaiho nisad this self has been called the Ultimate Reality, immortal, self-evident and self-enlightened. In the Parables of Yama-Nacikeia and Indra-Virocana, this self has been explained as the ultimate reality. In the words of Yajnavalkya, "The self is the ultimate knower, it is knower of all things, hence it cannot be known in the form of the object."[2] And yet it is not a mere nihi. Even after the setting of the sun and the moon and the extinction of fire, the soul shines in its own effulgence. According to the Kathopanisad, "It is by the shining of the self that everything else shines, it is by its light that all this is lighted."[3] In the words of the Mundaka Upanisads "The fire is its head, the moon and sun are its ears, the Vedas are its speech, the air is its breath, the universe is its heart. In fact it is the inner dweller, self of all Jivas"[4] Samkara has referred to a verse in which the self has been taken in various meanings.[5] According to this verse, the self means that which is present in all, which is subject and knower, which experiences and enlightens all objects, which is immortal and always the same.

The metaphysics of The Mother, as that of Sri Aurobindo, is based upon the philosophy of the Upanisads. Thus one finds much similarity in their views. According to The Mother, the entire universe is the playground of the Divine, However, this play is real and not an illusion as has been maintained by Advaita Vedanta. The universe is the play of Divine Consciousness Force. "In the Divine Consciousness the smallest things from below unite with the highest, the most sublime from above."[6] Thus, the whole universe is the manifestation of Divine. This manifestation, however, is different on different planes. According to The Mother, "On the physical plane the Divine expresses himself through beauty, on the mental plane through knowledge, on the vital plane through power and on the psychic plane through love. When we rise high enough, we discover that these four aspects unite with each other in a single consciousness, full of love, luminous, powerful, beautiful, containing all, pervading all."[7]

The world, according to the Upanisads, is the manifestation of Brahman. Just as the spider creates the web and then takes it back inside it, similarly the Brahman creates the world and then takes it back inside Him. He does not create it out of some matter, before creation. Before creation there was only one soul. He determined that He would create the world and He created the universe.[8] He created the subtle and the gross, the formless and with forms, Ether was born out of self, the air originated in ether, fire came out of air, the water was born in fire, the earth originated in water and finally from the earth came out the plants, etc.[9] In her message on 14 November 1954, The Mother said, "Upon this world of illusion, this sombre nightmare, the Divine has bestowed His sublime Reality, and each atom of matter contains something of His Eternity."[10] Thus the world was in Brahman in the unmanifested form. He manifested it. He created the names and forms and the objects. He created the distinctions, lire world originates in Brahman, is sustained through Him, and culminates in Him. Brahman is the cause of the names and forms of the physical world. Space, time, Nature, etc., are the coverings of Brahman. Brahman is everywhere, just as the plants are born in the earth, hairs come out of body or the web comes out of the body of the spider, similarly, the world comes out of the Brahman and returns into it. Water, earth, air, fire and ether, etc., the pranas, the organs and mind, all originate from Brahman. The rivers, oceans, mountains, plants, human beings, gods, animals, birds, the four Vedas and Kartnas, etc., all have their origin in Brahman. Therefore, all these have to fulfil the Divine purpose. As The Mother puts it, "These souls are emanated by the Lord to do His work in the world and each one comes upon earth with a special purpose, for a special action and with a special destiny, carrying in itself its own law which is imperative for itself alone and cannot be a general law."[11]

The soul is eternal and universal. It transmigrates. It is the same everywhere without distinctions. In her message on 23 September 1941, The Mother said almost in tune with the ancient Indian Upanisadic philosophy, "When one speaks to the soul of a man, one always speaks to the same soul, whatever may be the differences of body, race or culture."[12] Action on soul requires its consciousness. By evolution the soul becomes an individualised being. The mind, the life and the body must become and live what the soul knows and is. Therefore, the soul must be obeyed under all circumstances. In the human being the soul is the psychic being. According to The Mother, "Psychic centre, luminous and calm, it is made to govern the human being."[13] The power of expression of the psychic being is shown in the governance of the total man. Its power organises the activities of the Nature and makes them progress. Under its influence all the activity of the human being becomes balanced. It compels the physical to turn towards the Divine. Therefore, in her message on 25 September, 1934 The Mother said, "Live in the consciousness of the psychic centre; thus your will will express the Divine's will alone and your transformed being will then be able to receive and manifest the Divine Love."[14] The *Brhadaranyaka Upanisad*, along with Isa and its cognate Upanisads, has explained the identification of *Atman* and *Brahman*, of the individual spirit and the universal spirit, of the self and the Absolute. Thus in the third stage, the enquirer sees no difference between the self and the Absolute. In the *Isa Upanisad*, it has been proclaimed that if must be regarded as verily Brahman, that the Atman is infinite in its nature, that the Atman derives its being from Brahman and that if we subtract the infinite of the Atman from the infinite of the Brahman, the residuum is infinite. In the *Brhadaranyaka Upanisad*, it has been said that one must identify the self with the Absolute. In the *Chandogya Upanisad* the same doctrine is proclaimed where the self comes also to be 'projectively' identified with the Absolute.

According to The Mother a human being is made of many different parts and it takes time and conscious efforts to harmonise and unify all these parts. Lack of unification is the cause of all human problems. An easy and pleasure-seeking life cannot satisfy the soul, the psychic being. Explaining the cause of internal conflict The Mother said in her message on 29 October I960. "If is because an individual is not made all of one piece, but of many different entities which sometimes even contradict each other; some want the spiritual life, others are attached to the things of this world. It is a long and difficult work to reconcile all these parts and unify them."[15] This harmony is achieved through the psychic being. The psychic inspiration alone is true. The psychic being maintains internal democracy. All the suffering is in the mind, the vital and the physical. The psychic being never suffers. However, in her message on 5 April 1972, The Mother points out, "To find the psychic one must conquer the desires of the vital and silence the mind and then make a sincere submission to the Divine of whom the psychic is the instrument in man."[16]

The Mother has not only explained the nature of the psychic being but also pointed out its location in the heart region. The psychic is never depressed. It is the source of constant happiness. It is naturally pure. It is calm. Its peace is spontaneous and knows no difficulty. Its prayer is fervent. Its offering is the spontaneous attitude in relation to the Divine. Its generosity gives for the joy of giving. Its perfection is that of total being. "The psychic being is formed by the inner Truth and organised around it,"[17]

According to The Mother, "In various times and places many methods have been prescribed for attaining this perception [of the psychic presence in us] and ultimately achieving this identification [with it]. Some methods are psychological, some religious, some even mechanical. In reality, everyone has to find the one which suits him best, and if one has an ardent and steadfast aspiration, a persistent and dynamic will, one is sure to meet, in one way or another — outwardly through reading and study, inwardly through concentration, meditation, revelation and experience — the help one needs to reach the goal."[18] Religious methods of pointing out the psychic being have been adopted by the great religions. Psychological methods act upon the thoughts, feeling and action. These are far more effective than mechanical methods which are based on purely mechanical means.

The Mother has pointed out to the play of psychic force in the world through various examples. According to her, psychic relationships may be found among human beings and animals. She said, "If the master is really a good one and the animal faithful, there is an exchange of psychic and vital forces, and exchange which becomes for the animal something wonderful, giving it an intense joy."[19] The play of psychic being may be clearly observed among children since they are natural and pure. The goodwill among human being is a sure sign of the presence of psychic force. The sense of immortality, the urge to grow and to evolve is due to the presence of psychic element in man. Thus the psychic leads to a high, wide, generous and disinterested life. To quote The Mother, "What is psychic in the being is always pure, by its very definition, for it is that part of the being which is in contact with the Divine and expresses the truth of the being. But this may be like a spark in the darkness of the being or it may be a being of light, conscious, fully formed and independent. There are all the gradations between the two."[20] It is the psychic will which wants the being to be identified with the Divine. For this purpose it creates all sort of circumstances. The psychic light is the best remedy against all sort of fears. The equality of the psychic being is a psychological equality as different from material equality and body and the mental poise of the mind. The psychic harmony alone is the solid basis for achieving permanent harmony. There is no psychic being in the atom, there is only a possibility. This possibility, however, becomes an actuality on the human plane. The progress of the psychic being consists in individualisation. According to The Mother, "The aim of the psychic being is to form an individual being, individualised, 'personalised' around the divine centre. Normally, all the experiences of the external life (unless one does yoga and becomes conscious) pass without organising the inner being, while the psychic being organises, these experiences serially."[21]

Value of Psychic Education

Our description of The Mother's concept of psychic being so far must have clarified the value of psychic education. Explaining it The Mother said, "The three lines of education — physical, vital and mental — deal with that and could be defined as the means of building up the personality, raising the individual out of the amorphous subconscious, mass and making him a well-defined self-conscious entity. With psychic education we come to the problem of the true motive of existence, the purpose of life on earth, the discovery to which this life must lead and the result of that discovery: the consecration of the individual to his eternal principle."[22] The aim of modern education is the character building, development of human personality and betterment of his abilities. All these are essentially the result of psychic education. It is the psychic education which makes a person real individual. As The Mother puts it, "One could say, for example, that the creation of an individual being is the result of the projection, in time and space, of one of the countless possibilities latent in the supreme origin of all manifestation which, through the medium of the one and universal consciousness, takes concrete form in the law or the truth of an individual and so, by a progressive development, becomes his soul or psychic being.'"[23]

Self-realisation gives much strength. The Mundaka Upanisad has compared the strength preceding and succeeding self-realisation, when it says, "Though the individual self and the worldly self-lives together on the same truth, yet he was attached and miserable due to his worldly attachment. But once he is related with the Ultimate Reality, the source of all power, all his miseries disappear and he shares in the infinite strength of the world-soul."[24] Therefore The mother said, "Obviously there is only one solution: to become conscious of one's soul. And this completes the aphorism: unless one is conscious of one's soul does not have true knowledge. Therefore the first effort must be to find the soul within, to unite with it and allow it to govern one's life."[25] The mystic realisation results in the disappearance of all doubts and illusions. All problems are solved after self-realisation. According to the Mundaka Upanisad, "All the knots of his heart are opened, all his doubts are removed and the effects of his kamias are destroyed."[26] Therefore, The Mother said, "Men believe that doubt is a sign of superiority, whereas it is really a sign of inferiority. Scepticism and doubt are two of the greatest obstacles to progress; they add presumptuousness to ignorance."[27]

The voice of the soul is hidden in the noise of the vital and the mental. It is because the soul does not impose itself. It does riot compel you to listen. It is without violence. Therefore concentration, perseverance and persistence are required to hear the voice of the soul. Hence the mind should be quietened. The aspirant should be humble. As The Mother puts it, "One of the things which would make humanity progress most would be for it to respect what it does not know, to acknowledge willingly that it does not and is therefore unable to judge."[28]

Thus, self-realisation results in the satisfaction of all desires. In the words of *Chandogya Upanisad*, "One who finds the self after its search, he attains all the universe and all his desires are fulfilled."[29] Thus, after self-realisation one achieves satisfaction of all the physical desires, disappearance of all doubts, attainment of infinite power, realisation of absolute bliss, disappearance of all fear and the fulfilment of all desires. Self-realisation is the ultimate end according to the Upanisads, because self is the real essence of man. Self is in all and self is Brahman. Therefore self realisation leads to immortality. Explaining the nature of immortality The Mother said, "Immortality is a life without beginning or end, without birth or death, which is altogether independent of the body. It is the life of the Self, the essential being of each individual, and it is not separate from the universal Self. And this essential being has a sense of oneness with the universal Self; it is in fact a personified, individualised expression of the universal Self and has neither beginning nor end, neither life nor death, it exists eternally and that is what is immortal. When we are fully conscious of this Self we participate in its eternal life, and we therefore become immortal."[30] Annihilation of ego through knowledge and the realisation of the real nature of Brahman by identity cause the disappearance of bondage. The knowledge of Brahman implies being Brahman. This is to see Brahman everywhere and to see oneself in all. It is to see self in all. In it there is the unity and identity of the Jiva and God. In it there is no fear of merit and demerit, attachment and aversion, pleasure and pain, etc. It is the indescribable, eternal peace. It is self-play, self-enjoyment, absolute freedom and bliss. It is without dualism and pluralism. It is a unity. It is the ultimate self-consciousness, self-consciousness, selfless will and attributeless consciousness, and the stage of indescribable bliss. Therefore The Mother said, "Each time that the soul takes birth in a new body it comes with the intention of having a new experience which will help it to develop and to perfect its personality. This is how the psychic being is formed from life to life and becomes a completely conscious and independent personality which, once it has arrived at the summit of its development, is free to choose not only the time of its incarnation, but the place, the purpose and the work to be accomplished."[31]

Aim of Psychic Education

Pointing out the aim of psychic education that cannot be realised by other forms of education discussed so far, The Mother wrote, "In most cases the presence acts, so to say, from behind the veil, unrecognised and unknown; but in some, it is perceptible and its action recognisable and even, in a very few, the presence becomes tangible and its action fully effective. These go forward in life with an assurance and a certitude all their own; they are masters of their destiny. It is for the purpose of obtaining this mastery and becoming conscious of the psychic presence that psychic education should be practised."[32] Such a psychic education depends less upon instruction and more upon inner realisation, inner development and exercise of personal will. It requires a great determination, a strong will and untiring perseverance. It is almost similar to the conditions laid down by Samkara for a student of *Vedanta*.

Steps and Means of Psychic Education

Pointing out the steps in psychic education The Mother said, "The starting-point is to seek in yourself that which is independent of the body and the circumstances of life, which is not born of the mental formation that you have been given, the language you speak, the habits and customs of the environment in which you live, the country where you are born or the age to which you belong. You must find, in the depths of your being that which carries in it a sense of universality, limitless expansion, unbroken continuity."[33] The Upanisads have maintained that the knower of Brahman becomes Brahman. Moksa means seeing the self in all. It is the status of identity with Brahman. The Brahman's knowledge culminates in a stage where there is no difference between the knower, known and knowledge. From the transcendental standpoint, the self, the Brahman and the liberation are the same. The self is Brahman. it is eternally liberated. Liberation is the annihilation of the worldly names and forms, since really speaking the transcendental self has no relation with the universe. As it has been said in the Brhadaranyaka Upanisad, "This purusa is non-attached." Liberation means the identity of Brahman and the self. The identity is not imposition of Brahman on self. Summing up the value of psychic realisation The Mother said, "All help you to go beyond the barriers of your egoism, the wall of your external personality, the impotence of your reactions and incapacity of your will."[34] The following means should be followed for achieving psychic realisation.[35]

1. *Absence of reaction*: Abstain from all mental opinion and reactions.

2. *Burning desire for progress*: Be only a burning fire of progress and renounce all personal seeking for comfort, satisfaction and enjoyment.

3. *Niskama*: The Mother has instructed, "Try to take pleasure in all you do, but never do anything for the sake of pleasure."

4. *Perfect kama*: The Mother said, "Never get excited, nervous or agitated. Remain perfectly calm in the face of all circumstances. And yet be always alert to discover what progress you still have to make and lose no time in making it."

5. *Deeper and Cosmic-vision*: The Mother advised never to take physical happenings at their face value. They are always a clumsy attempt to express something else, the true thing which escape our superficial understanding.

6. *No complaints:* The Mother instructed, "Never complain of the behaviour of anyone, unless you have to power to change in his nature what makes him act in this way; and if you have the power, change him instead of complaining."

7. *Never forget the goal:* The Mother has asked for concentration and divine aspiration in every activity. In tune with the ancient Indian prescription, The Mother prescribed that before eating, sleeping or speaking one must remember the Divine and offer all activity to the divine. As she puts it, "To sum up, never forget the purpose and goal of your life. The will for the great discovery should be always there above you, above what you do and what you are, like a huge bird of light dominating all the movements of your being."[36] This can be done through every part of the being since, according to The Mother, one may realise the psychic being through each part of the consciousness. As she said, "One can find the psychic through each part of the consciousness: you can find a psychic behind the physical ... you can enter into contact with the psychic directly through the physical consciousness, directly through the vital consciousness, directly through the mental consciousness."[37]

Spiritual Education

Distinguishing between the psychic and the spiritual consciousness The Mother wrote, "So one can say that the psychic life is immortal life, endless time, limitless space, of forms. The spiritual consciousness, on the other hand, means to live the infinite and the eternal, to be projected beyond any creation, beyond time and space. To become conscious of your psychic being and to live a psychic life you must abolish all egoism; but to live a spiritual life you must no longer have an ego."[38] Psychic education and spiritual education are generally included in yogic discipline. According to the Mother however, the aims of the two are very different. The aim of psychic education is a higher realisation upon earth, the manifestation of the psychic being, the supramental being, the gnostic being, not only the gnosting individual but also the gnostic race. The aim of spiritual education in India however, has been liberation in the sense of escape from the cycle of rebirth. It is an escape from all earthly manifestation. It is a return to the unmanifest. Explaining such a spiritual education, The Mother has pointed out that it has been interpreted differently by different spiritual systems. To quote her words, "Those who have a religious tendency will call it God and their spiritual effort will be towards identification with the transcendent God beyond all forms, as opposed to the immanent God dwelling in each form. Others will call it the Absolute, the Supreme Origin, others *Nirvana*; yet others, who view the world as an unreal illusion, will name it the only Reality and to those who regard all manifestation as falsehood it will be the sole Truth."[39] In Indian philosophical system philosophers like Ramanuja, Madhva and Nimbarka have called God as the goal of spiritual evolution. Sankaracharya, on the other hand, called Him Absolute, Gautama, the Buddha, called it *Nirvana*. The *Advaita Vedanta* called the world Maya, an unreal illusion. According to Sankaracharya, the world is *maya*. Samkara has used different analogies to explain the nature of the world. Of these the most important are those of the rope and the snake, of the city of Gandhara, of the dream, the foam, the *Maya* of the *Alat Cakra*, the seeing of double moon, of the illusory elephant and the jugglery, etc. These analogies have been used to point out that the Brahman is the only reality and whatever is different from *Brahman* is unreal. According to the logic of the Advaita philosophy, *Brahman* cannot be one and many, Being and Becoming at the same time. As Samkara points out, if both were true, the worldly men would not be caught in the mire of untruth. Nor can it he said that liberation is attained by knowledge and in that condition the knowledge of one should not surpass the knowledge of many. Commenting on Samkara's theory of the world as *maya* and the Absolute as unmanifested, The Mother said, in her message of 27 January 1970, "The Lord laughed when this man, who thought himself so wise, complied with conventions, wrote useless words and gave an example of overactivity in order to preach inaction."[40]

In tradition with the ancient Indian spiritual practices The Mother has pointed out to the effective means of realising the spiritual idea of extra-terrestrial liberation. These are as follows:

1. *Total self-diving:* According to The Mother, this is the most effective starting point. It brings immediate joy. It leads to perfection. It leads to an experience of bliss, in comparable with any other experience.

2. *Aspiration for identification*: Identification of self and God has always been considered as the most effective method of achieving liberation. The Upanisads have insisted upon this identity through various Mahavakyas such as, Tat-Twam-Asi etc. Similarly, Gita has preached for total surrender as the ultimate means of achieving liberation. This is the traditional mystic method which is not only confined to India or East but also has been utilised by mystics of the West, the religious devotees all over the world. It is what Sufis called 'fana.' Christian mystics called it identification with God. The Buddhists called it attributeless Samaddhi. According to The Mother identification is a natural result of self-surrender. It leads to a total fusion of the individual with the Universal. According to The Mother, "There is an essential difference between this identification and the identification with the psychic being. The latter can be made more and more lasting and, in certain cases, it becomes permanent and never leaves the person who has realised it, whatever his outer activities may be. In other words, the. identification is no longer realised only in meditation and concentration, but its effects are felt at every moment of one's life, in sleep as well as in waking."[41] This is what Indian philosophers have called Jivan Mukti, liberation while living, as distinguished from Videh Mukti or liberation after death. Indian philosophers did not always insist upon the latter vanity of liberation but maintained the value of the former type of liberation. Therefore, it is wrong to call Indian philosophy other worldly. However, due to the influence of Advaita Vedanta, there has been an emphasis upon extra-terrestrial ideal of liberation. The Mother

has raised her voice against this form of spiritualism. She has asked for a new interpretation of ancient Indian scriptures, the Upanisads and the Gita. The interpretation of Gita as emphasising upon extra-terrestrial goal of liberation is no more relevant to modem times. According to The Mother, "Perhaps this was true a thousand years ago or even five hundred years ago, but now it is a stupidity."[42] Indian philosophy, today requires a reinterpretation in the light of modern problems. As The Mother puts it, "If you arrive at the conception of the world as the expression of the Divine in all His complexity, then the necessity for complexity and diversity has to be recognised, and it becomes impossible for you to want to make others think and feel as you do."[43]

In his commentary on *Brahman Sutra*, Samkara has given an elaborate description of the nature of liberation. Liberation or Moksa is the transcendental truth, immutable, eternal, all pervading like the space, devoid of all activity, eternally contented, partless of the future. This disembodied state is liberation. The liberated self regains his real form m the *Advaita Brahman Siddhi.* Moksa is said to be the liberation of the self from ignorance. According to Chitsukhacharya, liberation is the attainment of incessant bliss. It is eternal. The self is eternally liberated. Hence, nothing new is gained in liberation since otherwise it shall be non-eternal. Commenting and criticising such a view of liberation as absolutely unmodern The Mother wrote, "But a liberation that leaves the world as it is and in no way affects the conditions of life from which others suffer, cannot satisfy those who refuse to enjoy a boon which they are the only ones, or almost the only ones, to possess, those who dream of a world more worthy of the splendours that lie hidden behind its apparent disorder and widespread misery. They dream of sharing with others the wonders they have discovered in their inner exploration. And the means to do so is within their reach, now that they have arrive at the summit of their ascent."[44] These words echo the consciousness of the modern man the modem thinker, who not only seeks his own liberation but world peace, world unity and an establishment of the kingdom of God upon earth not only for himself but foreveryone.

However, The Mother has analysed the ancient Indian concept of soul in details. According to her, "Soul, the word for soul in French, 'ame,' comes from a word which means to animate". It is what gives life to the body. If you didn't have it you would be inert matter, something like stones or plants, not altogether inert, but vegetative."[45] This soul is useful in everyday life but not sufficient in the pursuit of Divine. It may be remembered here that what has been called soul in the above statement of The Mother is called Jiva in the orthodox systems of Indian philosophy. The Jiva however, is not the Atman. However, the two have been often confused with the result that extra-terrestrial goal of liberation was generally insisted. According to The Mother our goal is not Nirvana, it is almost the opposite. To quote her own words, "But for us who want to realise almost the very opposite, that is, who, after having identified ourselves with the supreme Reality, want to make It descend into life and transform the world, if we offer to this Reality instruments which are refined, rich, developed, fully conscious, the work of transformation will be more effective."[46] Equality of soul is a means as well as a goal but not the consummation of knowledge. In time with the ancient Indian concept of soul, The Mother accepts soul as witness. To the question what is the witness soul, she replied, "It is the soul entering into a state in which it observes without acting. A witness is one who looks at what is done, but does act himself. So when the soul is in a state in which it does not participate in the action, does not act through Nature, simply draws back and observes, it becomes the witness soul."[47] The soul incarnated in a body has to struggle to find its true path and discover its own self fully.

The Mother has distinguished between religious teaching and spiritual teaching, in her message on 12 February 1972, she said, "You must not confuse a religious teaching with a spiritual one. Religious teaching belongs to the past and halts progress. Spiritual teaching is the teaching of the future — it illumines the consciousness and prepares it for the future realisation. Spiritual teaching is above religions and strives towards a global Truth. It teaches us to enter into direct relations with the Divine."[48] Thus, in the gradation of refinement, spiritual education is higher than religious education. However, as has been already pointed out, integral education aims at beginning the Divine upon earth and therefore favours psychic education as more desirable than spiritual education. This is an improvement upon the ancient Indian philosophy of education.

In the history of human knowledge occult knowledge has been developed parallel to spiritual knowledge. The occult science is a kind of chemistry applied to the play of forces and the structure of the worlds. According to The Mother, "In another of its aspects, occult science is, for the individual seeker, like the discovery and exploration of unknown countries whose laws and customs one often learns at one's own cost."[49] Therefore, the occult should be pursued only under the expert supervision of an accomplished teacher. Defining the occult science The Mother said, "Occult science could thus be defined as a concrete objectification, in the world of forms, of what spiritual disciplines teach from the purely psychological point of view. The two should complement each other for the perfection of self-development and integral action."[50] Without spiritual discipline occult is a dangerous instrument. On the other hand, spiritual knowledge is not concretised in the absence of occult science. Therefore, The Mother has recommended the combination of both the occult science and the spiritual knowledge for achieving the goal of supramental education.

Supramental Education

Thus the integral philosophy of education aims at supramental education. This is education for future about which Sri Aurobindo has written in great details. As he said, I know with absolute certitude that the supramental is a truth and that its advent is in the very nature of things inevitable."[51] Realisation of supramental education depends on two conditions, firstly, the individuals have to be transformed, spiritualised and divinised. This is the ideal and purpose of education for future, secondly, the society should also be transformed, spiritualised and divinised. It is then alone that the gnostic society will be firmly established. The characteristics of the individuals of future society lay down the goals which education for future seeks to achieve, of these characteristics the most important is spirituality. In spirituality no part of man is allowed to remain on the lower level. The animal in man will be totally transformed. The society, on the other hand, will be governed by the subjective ideal of life, the ideal of the soul, the inner being. Education will seek to realise this twin purpose in psychology, philosophy, arts, poetry, painting, sculpture, music, ethics, politics, economics etc. This will lead to unexpected departures in research everywhere. Through education the supramental will first dawn among selected persons. The future education aims at the creation of some supramental individuals so that once it is established upon earth, it spreads everywhere.

Thus, future education will progress through psychic education since, as the Mother points out, "The psychic inspiration alone is true. All that comes from the vital and the mind is necessarily mixed with egoism and in arbitrary. One should not act in reaction to outer contact, but with an immutable vision of love and goodwill. Everything else is a mixture which can only have confused and mixed results, and perpetuate the disorder."[52] The awakening of the psychic power will lead to the change in the course of things and the birth of a new world. As against the ancient Indian ideal of individual liberation, The Mother favours Buddha's ideal of liberation of all the living being from the suffering, ignorance and death. This requires an integral transformation. To quote The Mother, "We want an integral transformation, the transformation of the body and all its activities. But there is an absolutely indispensable first step that must be accomplished before anything else can be undertaken: the transformation of the consciousness."[53] This requires aspiration, the will to realise and receptivity. After its realisation the consciousness becomes almost the reverse of the ordinary consciousness. Thus integral education of The Mother aims at a Copemican revolution in education since the consciousness of the educand will almost be reversed. This reversal however, will be sudden as it is in the case of psychological insight. Pointing out this revolutionary nature of integral education as against the present system of education. The Mother said, "In contrast with the types of education we have mentioned previously, which progress from below upwards by an ascending movement of the various parts of the being, the supramental education will progress from downwards, its influence spreading from one state of being to another until at last the physical is reached."[54] Change in physical body will be the last result of supramental education and not its first symptom. Concluding the nature of supramental education and its result The Mother wrote, "To sum up, one can say that the supramental education will result no longer in a progressive formation of human nature and an increasing development of its latent faculties, but in a transformation of the nature itself, a transfiguration of the being in its entirety, a new ascent of the species above and beyond man towards superman, leading in the end to the appearance of a divine race upon earth."[55]

References

1. *C.W.M.*, Vol. 14 (1900), p. 351.

2. *Brhadaranyaka Upanisad*, IV, 3.6.
3. *Katha Upanisad*, II, 2, 15.
4. *Mundaka Upanisad*, II, 1.4.
5. *Katha Upanisad*, II, 1.1.
6. *C.W.M.*, Vol. 15 (1980), p. 4
7. *Ibid.*, p. 6.
8. *Aitereya Upanisad*, I, 1.
9. *Taittraya Upanisad*, II, 1, 6, 7.
10. *C.W.M.*, Vol. 15, p. 8.
11. *C.W.M.*, Vol. 14, p. 351.
12. *Ibid.*, p. 352.
13. *Ibid.*, p. 353.
14. *Ibid.*, p. 354.
15. *Ibid.*, p. 356.
16. *Ibid.*, p. 358.
17. *C.W.M.*, Vol. 15 (1980), p. 323.
18. *Ibid.*, p. 324.
19. *C.W.M.*, Vol. 5, p. 241.
20. *Ibid.*, p. 394.
21. *Ibid.*
22. *C.W.M.*, Vol. 12 (1978), p. 30.
23. *Ibid.*, p. 31.
24. *Mundaka Upanisad*, III, 1.2.
25. *C.W.M.*, Vol. 10 (1977), p. 23.
26. *Mundaka Upanisad*, ii, 2-8.
27. *C.W.M.*, Vol. 10, p. 27.
28. *Ibid.*
29. *Chandogya Upanisad*, VIII, 7.1
30. *C.W.M.*, Vol. 10, p. 28.
31. *Ibid*, p. 29.
32. *C.W.M.*, Vol. 12, p. 32.
33. *Ibid*, pp. 32-33.
34. *Ibid.*, p. 33.
35. *Ibid.*, pp. 33-34.
36. *Ibid.*, pp. 34-35.
37. *C.W.M.*, Vol. 7, p. 74.
38. *C.W.M.*, Vol. 12, pp. 35-36.
39. *Ibid.*, p. 36.
40. *C.W.M.*, Vol. 10 (1977), pp. 302-303.
41. *C.W.M.*, Vol. 12, pp. 36-37.
42. *C.W.M.*, Vol. 10 (1977), p. 105.
43. *Ibid.*, p. 106

44. *C.W.M.*, Vol.12, p. 37.
45. C.W.M., Vol. 8, (1977) p. 304.
46. *Ibid.*, p. 366.
47. *Ibid*, p. 103.
48. *C.W.M.*, Vol. 12, p. 120.
49. *Ibid.*, p. 91.
50. *Ibid.*
51. *Sri Aurobindo and The Mother on Super mind* (Pondicherry: Sri Aurobindo Society, 1973), p. 26.
52. *C.W.M.*, Vol. 12, p. 337.
53. *Ibid.*, p. 80.
54. *Ibid.*, p. 38.
55. *Ibid.*

14

Concluding Remarks

The single most important contribution made by The Mother to contemporary philosophy of education is the clarification of the integral approach to education The integral approach is characteristic of most of the contemporary Indian philosophers' thinking. As Sri Aurobindo pointed out, "The work of philosophy is to arrange the date given by the various means of knowledge excluding none, the one supreme and universal reality."[1] Similar quotations may be found in the philosophical works of Sarvapalli Radhakrishnan, Swami Vivekananda, Sri Ramakrishna, Rabindranath Tagore, M.K. Gandhi, Bhagwandas and other notable Indian philosophers of education. This integral approach is characteristic of Indian philosophy right from the beginning. According to ancient Indian Vedanta everything and every being is the expression of one reality and man's aim is to realise the same. Perfection, as interpreted by ancient Indian Philosophy, has always being an integral ideal Ancient Indian psychology was integral. It aimed at multisided development of human personality. Its four-fold axiology included fulfilment of natural duties, economic advancement, satisfaction of human tendencies and finally liberation. In keeping with this ancient Indian ideal The Mother aims at four-fold liberation leading to a four-fold perfection through a four-fold discipline. The aim of education, according to her is the integral development of the educand. The education and the educand, together with the multisided school, formed the integral pattern of education. In this integral scheme the educand, the educator and the school each has been given its suitable place. None has been devalued. While the ancient education was teacher-centred, modern education is child-centred. In the integral scheme of education neither the educator nor the educand may have the sole importance but both are united in a common bond. The Mother has recommended spiritual rapport between the teacher and the taught as the most important basis of education. Among the contemporary Indian philosophers of education, Swami Dayananda, Annie Bezant and

Madan Mohan Malviya have laid emphasis upon the ancient model while thinkers like Rabindranath Tagore and Sarvapalli Radhakrishnan had laid emphasis upon international values. All these however, stand for an integral scheme of education, including different teaching methods, different subjects, different needs of the educator and the educand and fulfilment of different aims of education. All these show a synthetic approach. Everyone is against one-sidedness in education. The integral approach however, has been most comprehensively explained and consistently adhered by The Mother.

Integral Approach in Education

The Mother supported a five-fold system of education which aims at the development of the educand's physical, vital, mental, spiritual and psychic beings. According to her, the physical education should aim at physical beauty and harmony. The vital education seeks vital perfection and power of the vital. The mental education aims at mental perfection through knowledge. But the acme of education is the psychic education realised through love. This integral approach to education has been supported by almost all the contemporary Indian philosophers of education. Contemporary Indian philosophers have laid emphasis upon the integral principle within man. The reason for prescribing liberation as the aim of education in ancient India was the spiritual explanation of human nature. Man, according to Indian view, is neither solely biological nor purely social. He cannot be defined either as a rational or a social animal. He is the expression of Divine in the individual form. Therefore his only aim is to realise and practise his divine nature. In Sri Aurobindo's philosophy of education, one finds a detailed explanation of the spiritual nature of man. The Mother has everywhere laid emphasis upon the divine element in the child. This explanation of human nature has been equally accepted by Swami Dayananda, Swami Vivekananda, M.K. Gandhi, Rabindranath Tagore, Annie Besant and S. Radhakrishnan.

Integral Foundation of Education

The metaphysical background of The Mother's philosophy of education is the ancient Indian idealistic metaphysics. Interpreting the ultimate reality according to Indian philosophy, S. Radhakrishnan said, "It is the basis and background of our being, the universality that cannot be reduced to this or that formula."[2] The self, the God and Brahman are all names of the one universal spirit in different aspects. Against Samkara and with Sri Aurobindo, M.K. Gandhi, R.N. Tagore and Bhagwandas The Mother interpreted the world as the real play and evolution of Spirit. Matter, life and mind are the manifestation of the spirit in the world. While the world is the descent, man is the ascent of the Divine. Therefore, evolution and involution are the creative processes of the same one Spirit. As Bhagwandas puts it, "The words 'evolution' and 'involution' embody, with instinctive correctness, the idea that these processes are forth and back, circling and cycling in a spiral."[3]

Integral Axiology

Ancient India philosophy supports the following values or aims of life:

1. *Spirituality*: The aim of life according to Indian philosophy is spirituality. This however, is not the negation of material and vital aims but its fulfilment.
2. *Evolution*: Indian philosophy is evolutionary. The Varnasram system was based upon evolution of man and the ideal of purusartha was achieved through different asramas.
3. *Multidimensional*: As against Unidimensional approach the characteristic approach of Indian philosophy of life is multidimensional.
4. *Integral aim*: Indian philosophy recommends truth, good and beauty; existence, consciousness and bliss as aims of life.

All the above characteristics of Indian philosophy may be found in the aim of life defined by The Mother. She however, distinguished between spiritual and psychic and rightly rejected the other-worldly aims of life. The psychic aims at the realisation of the kingdom of God upon earth. The Mother rejected the goal of Individual liberation and with Sri Aurobindo supported the ideal of cosmic liberation agreeable to consciousness of modern man. In education, she supports evolutionary, multidimensional and integral approach not only to the aims and ideals but also to the means of education.

Body Beautiful

The Mother has made a signal contribution to physical education by her clarification of the aims and means of physical culture. She has given details of physical education for males and females, children and adults. She has defined the aims and means of vital education. She has explained knowledge as wisdom and therefore recommends progress to supramental level. As Radhakrishnan said, "The deepest things of life are known only through intuitive apprehension."[4] In the words of Bhagwandas, "It is the immediate cognition or rather awareness of the self by the self, eternal self-consciousness."[5] These are however only hints to the levels above mind. The Mother has however, explained details of the supramental and also provided detailed instructions concerning means to reach that level.

Moral Development

Like other contemporary Indian philosophers The Mother has insisted upon moral development of the educand. She agrees with education's goal as man-making interpreted by Swami Vivekananda. She has appreciated the value of discipline. According to her, "No big creation is possible without discipline." 'She prescribed detailed disciplinary measures for the educands. Of these the most important were as follows:

1. Discipline should start at the age of 12 and not earlier. The Mother agrees with the psycho-analyst Sigmund Freud and others that rigid discipline at an early age thwarts the natural development. When freedom is the aim of education, the child should be allowed to grow naturally.

2. According to The Mother, "It is through example that education becomes effective. To say good words, give wise advice to a child has very little effect, if one does not show by one's living example the truth of what one teaches."[7] Before the age of seven year the child does not know why and how to do things. During this period he should be trained to acquire physical and vital development. From the age of seven years to 14 years he may be allowed to choose what he wants to become. At 14 years of age however, he must be clear about his aim. After fourteen years of age he may be left free to follow his own course of action. The Mother recommended a code of conduct at The Mother's International School and at Sri Aurobindo's International University. She condemned all compulsions and physical punishments. She advised the teachers to help the educands to arrive at rational decisions and to follow them. She maintained that class discipline must be

observed. She said, "But if a student has decided to follow a class, it is an absolutely elementary discipline for him to follow it, he must go to the class regularly and behave decently there: otherwise he is quite unfit to go to school."[8] She was against any illusions about the abilities of the educands. She warned, "Do not mistake liberty for licence and freedom for bad manners. The thought must be pure and the aspiration ardent."[9] She laid down the following code of behaviour for the students:

1. The good manners should be always observed.
2. Everyone should always speak the truth.
3. Truth in speech demands truth in acts too.
4. It is forbidden for children to right at school in the street, in the playground and at home. "Always and everywhere it is forbidden for children to fight among themselves, for each time one gives a blow to someone, it is to one's own soul that one gives it"[10]
5. The child should always remember:
   The necessity of an absolute sincerity.
   The certitude of Truth's final victory.
   The possibility of constant progress with the will to achieve.[11]

Secular Education

The Mother's philosophy of religion is secular. Therefore her views about religious education are most in keeping with the modem secular spirit. It may be remembered here that no other contemporary Indian philosophers of education raised his finger against the evils of religious education and its limitations. This is particularly important. In view of the fact that the present day secular India is facing the rise of religious communalism with political motives almost everywhere in the country. M.K. Gandhi synthesised religion with politics hoping that the marriage of such contradictory elements will be useful for the country. He pleaded for toleration and catholicity. He said. "I believe Hinduism to be a religion of truth but Islam and Christianity also are religions of truth. From your standpoint Christianity is tame; Hinduism from my point."[12] The essence of all religions is one; only their approaches are different."[13] Thus according to Gandhi, religions differ only in non-essentials while in essentials they agree. He points out to the essential unity of all religions. Just as God is one though His names are different, religions have been derived from the God. In his Essential Unity of All Religions Bhagwandas has summarised points of agreements of world religions. In his Eastern Religions and Western Thought Radhakrishnan searches the heart of each great religion to discover the intuitive basis from which it springs and thus finds out their unity in integral intuition. In the words of Rabindranath Tagore, "Those religions differ in details and often in their moral significance, but they have a common tendency. In them men seek their own supreme value which they call divine, in some personality anthropomorphic in character."[14] In contrast to all these contemporary Indian philosophers, The Mother rejects the claim of religious education to the highest pedestal. Accepting its limited value for average human being, she called it an obstacle in the way of spiritual life. She downright rejected the claim of institutional religion for spiritual uplift of mankind. According to her, religious saints were not great due to religion but in spite of it. She accepted the value of religion for the ordinary man in society but pointed out that at the present stage of humanity it is better to transcend religion. Pointing out the reason for such an advice she said, "The strength and greatness of religion is adjudged by men according to the number of those that follow it, although the real greatness is not there. The greatness of spiritual truth is not in numbers."[15] She distinguished between religion and yoga and recommended yoga for the ascent of man. She pointed out that "Religion is always a limitation for the spirit."[16] In her vision of the kingdom of God on earth religion has no place. Stating this very clearly she said, "Religion and yoga do not lie on the same plane of being and spiritual life can exist in all its purity only when it is free from all mental dogma."[17] Therefore, she concluded, "In the supramental creation there will no more be religions. All life will be the expression, the flowering in forms of the Divine Unity manifesting in the world."[18]

Contemporary Indian philosophers of education were wedded to ancient Indian spiritual thought which never favoured religions as the technique of human evolution. It is strange and unfortunate that they laid so much importance upon religion. The Mother's views in this connection are more in keeping with the ancient Indian spirit and also the spiritual tradition everywhere in the world. It provides a better system of education for building up a secular and spiritual society.

Synthesis of Nationalism and Internationalism

Like Sri Aurobindo The Mother synthesised nationalism and internationalism in her philosophy of education. Her plan of education is generally meant for the entire humanity. She, however, held India in great regard in the community of nations. Pointing out the destiny of this great country, she maintained that it is, "To teach to the world that matter is false and impotent unless it becomes the manifestation of the Spirit.[19] Therefore she agreed with Sri Aurobindo's plan for national education. Yet more than Sri Aurobindo, she was conscious of the contrast between the East and West she admitted that, "The first aim then will be to help individuals to become conscious of the fundamental genius of the nation to which they belong and at the same time to put them in contact with the modes of living of other nations so that they may know and respect equally the true spirit of all the countries upon earth."[20] Therefore, she recommended the meeting of East and West, in the field of modern education. She said, "India has or rather had the knowledge of the Spirit, but she neglected matter and suffered for it. The West has the knowledge of matter but rejected the Spirit and suffers badly for it. An integral education which could, with some variations, be adapted to all the nations of the world, must bring back the legitimate authority of the Spirit over a matter fully developed and utilised."[21] In the system of world education, India may contribute her share by advocating and propagating Yoga as education. Therefore The Mother said, "I would like them (the Government) to recognise Yoga as education, not so much for ourselves, but it will be good for the country."[22]

Humanist Education

In spite of so much emphasis upon spiritualism and Yoga The Mother's philosophy of education finds a place for the current humanist trend in education. The humanist trend in education lays emphasis upon secular, rational and scientific approach to education. It emphasises humanist ideals and aims.

The individual as well as society have to realise humanist values. The highest value, according to humanism, is the human individual as an end in himself. The aim of education is to realise maximum and all-round perfection of human individual and to enable him to solve his problems in individual and social life. The humanist approach lays emphasis upon the value of humanist culture in every society. In the words of Lamont, "A humanist society will invest in education and general cultural activity sums proportionate to what present-day governments allocate to armaments and war. Particularly will schools and colleges, universities and research institutes, with their perennial budget difficulties, benefit from vastly enlarged financial resources. At long last educational institutions will be able to construct adequate physical plans and employ full teaching staff at generous salaries."[23] This description very much suits the educational plan of Sri Aurobindo International University. With humanism The Mother insisted upon these worldly goals of education, need of social service and a multisided wide based curriculum. Education, according to her, includes the physical, the vital, the mental, the psychic and the spiritual education. Therefore the curriculum must be five-fold according to these five types of education. Of these the education of the mind involves the most detailed curriculum. It requires different curriculum for the development of the different powers of the mind such as observation, memory, judgement, comparison, contrast, analogy, reasoning and imagination, etc. Sense training requires curriculum involving all the five senses.

Multisided Curriculum

Curriculum should be based on human nature since nothing may be taught or imposed upon the educand from outside. In the words of The Mother, "Fundamentally the only thing you must do assiduously is to teach them to know themselves, and to choose their own destiny, the way they want to follow."[24] Therefore, the curriculum should be planned according to the individual differences. It should be multisided and find a place for science and humanities. The Mother would agree with the humanist Lamont, when he said, "There need be no opposition between science and the humanities, from both of which the humanist draws inspiration, and no concentration upon one of them to the exclusion of the other."[25] The curriculum should particularly provide for the genius as well as the backward children. The aim of the curriculum is the actualisation of the potentialities of the educand. Therefore, the curriculum should provide for difference of age, personalities, abilities and endowments.

The Integral School

As the organiser of the day-to-day activities of Sri Aurobindo

International University and other educational institutions connected to it The Mother immaculately planned about all the aspects of her integral system of education. In the integral school, according to her, four types of rules are required to carry on various activities:[26] There are: (1) Rooms of silence, (2) Rooms of collaboration, (3) Rooms of consultation, and (4) Lecture room. The school should treat all children as equal and provide for not only teaching activities but also play discovery, innovation and multifarious development of the power of body, the mind and spirit of the educand. Thus The Mother provides a blueprint for an integral school, an integral college and integral university. She agrees with the humanist that the school management should be democratic. In her educational system the educators and the educands should participate in all the aspects of education such as management, formulation of curriculum, teaching methods, extracurricular activities etc. Education in a democratic set up is the surest ground for developing a democratic society. Going a step further where fraternity becomes natural, The Mother suggests a system of education where not equality but liberty and fraternity are the cardinal virtues. Like Sri Aurobindo, she recommends early education through the mother tongue. She, however, equally emphasises the need of training in English and other international languages.

Free Progress Systems

The free progress system of education supported by The Mother is characterised by the following features:[27]

1. The structure is oriented towards individual needs, interest and abilities.
2. The aspiration, experience of freedom, self-education and experimentation relating inner needs with the curricular provisions, discovering the higher lines of life and the art to encompass.
3. Each student is free to study any subject he chooses at any given time under a sympathetic guidance.
4. Promotion of individual endeavour.
5. Weekly announcement of timetable and lectures to be delivered.
6. Promotion of discussion between teachers and taught and between taught and taught.
7. Projects are announced in each subject and the students select according to their choice.

Sincerity is the fundamental requirement at all the stages and in all the aspects of integral education. To quote The Mother, "The whole question is to know whether the students go to school to increase their knowledge and to learn that which is necessary to know for living well or whether they go to school to pretend and to have good marks of which they can be proud, which is futile. Before the Eternal Consciousness a drop of sincerity has more value than an ocean of pretension and hypocrisy."[28] Therefore the teacher should always keep his eye upon the interest of the child since every subject, science, mathematics and history may serve as a vehicle of the growth of the child. It was asked: "How can mathematics, history or science help me in finding These?" To this The Mother replied, "They can help in several ways:

1. For being capable of receiving and bearing the light of the truth, the mind ought to be fortified, enlarged and made supple. These studies are a very good means to achieve it.

2. The sciences, if you study them deep enough, will teach you the unreality of the appearances and thus lead you to the spiritual.

3. The study of all the aspects and movements of physical Nature will put you in contact with the Universal Mother, and thus you will be nearer me."[29]

Paido-Centric Teaching Methods

Sri Aurobindo and The Mother gave particular attention to the methods of teaching children. In this connection the following suggestions are offered:[30]

1. The teachers should have sufficient documentation of what they know. They should be able to answer all questions.

2. They should have at least the knowledge if not the experience of true intellectual and intuitive attitude. This knowledge can be attained through mental silence.

3. He is the best teacher who has the capacity and not only knowledge of the different fields of evolution.

4. Thus the professors must be sincere in discipline and experience. They should not be propagandists.

5. To start with, "The children, as soon as they have the capacity to think (it begins at 7 years but towards 14 years it is very clear) should be given small indications at 7 and a complete explanation

at 14, of how to do it, and that it is the unique method to enter into relation with the profounds, that all the rest is a mental approximation, more or less inapt of something that can be known directly."[31]

Teaching very Small Children

About the teaching of very small children, The Mother has laid down the following principles for the teachers:[32]

> Never to deceive oneself.
>
> Never to be angry.
>
> Always to be understanding.
>
> Never try to impose on them.
>
> Never scold but always try to understand.

With Rousseau The Mother believed that the child is naturally good but gradually corrupted by bad environment. In an adverse environment the child loses all contact with the self in him. Therefore, The Mother has insisted that the most necessary thing to be taught to the child is to follow the inner psychic consciousness. As she said, "That is why I insist on that and I saw that from the very earliest age children must be taught that there is a reality within themselves, within the earth, within the universe and that he himself, the earth and the universe, exist only as a function of this truth and if it did not exist, he would not last, even the short time he lasts and that everything would dissolve as soon as it is created."[33]

This however, does not require philosophical explanations. The child is not prepared for mental understanding of the self. He should be made to realise the inner consciousness. His education therefore, should be by projects and play way methods. The child responds to the psychic vibrations. He is most impressed by affection and feelings. Therefore, integral education rules out all harsh treatment, scolding or being angry towards the children. One must have sufficient patience with them. The habits for cleanliness and hygiene should start very early. This however, does not require creating fear of illness in the child. The Mother has warned, "Fear is the worst incentive to education and the surest way of attracting what is feared."[34] This warning is timely not only for early education but for secondary and university education in our country.

With Sri Aurobindo The Mother favours successive teaching as against simultaneous teaching of several subjects to children.

Pointing out the distinction between the two approaches Sri Aurobindo observed, "The old system was to teach one or two subjects well and thoroughly and then proceed to others and certainly it was a more rational system than the modern. If it did not impart so much varied information, it built up a deeper, nobler and more real culture."[35] Thus different subjects should be studied one by one. The same principle is applicable to the teaching of text books. Each chapter should be studied thoroughly and in succession. In the words of The Mother, "One should leave a chapter when it has been fully grasped then only take up the next one and so on. If a chapter is finished, it is finished: and if it is not finished it is not finished."[36]

Co-education

The integral system of education favours co-educational institutions. Pointing out the irrationality of sex distinctions in education The Mother said, "What we claim is this, that in similar conditions, with the same education and the same possibilities, there is no reason to make a categorical distinction, final and imperative between what we call men and women. For us human beings are the expression of a single soul."[37] The Mother laid emphasis upon equality of sexes. She lamented that women were subjugated to man in India leading to degeneration of society. She rejected the ancient psychological dictum that male and female should avoid each other's company. She did not accept Dayananda's prescription that boys and girls should have entirely separate educational institutions. Maintaining the opposite view, in tune with modern western psychological and social thinking, The Mother said, "There is no impossibility of friendship between man and woman pure of this element (sex), such friendship can exist and have always existed. All that is needed is that the lower vital should not look in it through the back door or be permitted to enter."[38] Therefore, no distinctions are made between boys and girls in The Mother's International School or Sri Aurobindo International University at Pondicherry. The most unique feature of the education at these two institutions is the prescription of physical exercises both for boys and girls. Clarifying this policy The Mother said, "In all cases, as well as for boys as for girls, the exercises must be graded according to the strength and capacity of each one. If a weak student tries at once to do hard and heavy exercises, he may suffer for his foolishness. But with a wise and progressive training girls as well as boys can participate in all kinds of sports, increase their strength and health."[39] According to Sri Aurobindo both men and women are equally capable to evolve towards perfection to reach the gnostic age.

Self-evaluation and Examination

Rejecting the so-called mental tests, The Mother said, "I find tests an obsolete and ineffective way of knowing if the students are intelligent, willing and attentive. A silly, mechanical mind can very well answer a test if the memory is good and these are certainly not the qualities required for a man of the future."[40] She not only rejected the mental test but also suggested alternatives. "To know if a student is good, needs, if the tests are abolished, a little more inner contact and psychological knowledge for the teacher. But our teachers are expected to do *Yoga*, so this ought not to be difficult for them."[41]

To meet the purpose of spontaneous evaluation as against the essay type examinations, Sri Aurobindo's International Centre of Education, Pondicherry, has evolved. "Free Progress system", based upon subjective evaluation by the teachers. Progress records were to be filled by the students while the teachers had to note their comments. Clarifying this system of evaluation, The Mother told the teachers, "At the end of the year you will give notes to the students, not based on written test-papers, but on their behaviour, their concentration, their regularity, their promptness to understand and their openness of intelligence."[42]

Critical Evaluation

Philosophical knowledge is characterised both by criticism as well as construction. F.H. Bradley said, "To think is to judge, and to criticise is to use a criterion of reality."[43] Thus all criticism follows from some philosophical presuppositions. Consistency is the only virtue required in a philosophical theory. Different philosophical presuppositions lead to different philosophical theories. Therefore external criticism from different philosophical presuppositions is not warranted. This has been appreciably shown in *Syadvad* in Jain epistemology. Different blind persons touching different parts of the elephant's body claim that their own experience gives a correct picture of the elephant. One who has eyes to see, knows that everyone of them is true so far as his own experience is concerned but Everyone is mistaken to consider his own one-sided experience as the total experience. Catholicism and understanding of the opposite viewpoint are cardinal virtues in any philosophical understanding. Among the followers of Indian philosophical systems, the *Sastrartha* usually became meaningless since none could comprehend reality in its totality. Man is destined to be limited in his comprehension of reality and still more in its expression in the limited linguistic forms. Therefore no spoken or written word or theory may claim to comprehend the *entire* reality. In this sense F.H. Bradley was correct in pointing out that, "Metaphysics is the finding of bad reasons for what we believe upon instinct, but to find these reasons is no less an instinct."[44]

Then what should the philosopher do in order to arrive at a valid criticism. No philosophical theory should be criticised from a different viewpoint though at the same time no philosopher should claim his personal viewpoint to be the repository of the total truth. One must *first* clarify the presuppositions in a philosophical theory and then proceed to find out as to how these presuppositions have been consistently followed by the philosopher in working out the details of his philosophical theory. *This* is known as internal criticism and certainly every philosopher worth the name will agree about its validity. Self-contradiction is the sin forbidden in any intellectual discussion. Consistency is the minimum virtue for any effort at intellectual communication. Whatever may be the methods to know the reality once it is known, its intellectual presentation should adhere to the settled principles of grammar and language. All philosophy aims at communication and not enjoyment of reality. Its test is consistency and logical validity and not the personal satisfaction of the philosopher. This is particularly true in the case of philosophy of education. It is true that every great teacher has his own philosophy of education but if it is presented as a philosophical theory for the guidance of others it must have the virtues of consistency and non-contradiction. This is the solid bed rock for any valid criticism.

The Mother's philosophy of education is based upon her philosophical presupposition that total truth is integral. While totality shows the vertical, integrality shows the horizontal dimensions of the truth. This is equally true about the theory of reality. Undoubtedly, it gives us a wide and therefore a wider spectrum of the philosophical problems involved in education. Undoubtedly, it may help us in finding out a more comprehensive solution of the problems in philosophy of education, such as the problems of curriculum, teaching methods, school administration, discipline, evaluation etc. Philosophers of education today agree that an integral approach to the problems of education is necessary. This justifies the superiority of The Mother's philosophy of education over rival theories. But this again is the basis of our criticism of her theory.

Ascetic Male-female Relationship

A philosopher's theory is often conditioned and limited by his own experience in life however great he may be. With all homage to the spiritual height of the experiences of The Mother, she did not have that intimate experience of marriage and family which is the bed rock of the life of the more ordinary mortals. Therefore, if a common student of the philosophy of the education finds her injunctions about male female relationships as lacking in warmth and intimacy it only shows that a philosophy of education cannot be based upon isolated experiences of great men and great women however high they may be. Philosophy of education serves a humble purpose. It cannot aim at converting a child into an instrument of God's action upon the earth. In order to be practical, and that is the only criterion of its validity, it should confine its efforts for an all-round development of child's personality.

Utopian Sociology

The sociological foundations of education of The Mother's philosophy of education sound rather utopian. Her dream of a race of gnostic being, however lofty it may be, is not the dream of an ordinary human being. Great persons, including M.K. Gandhi and Sri Aurobindo, commit the mistake of applying their personal experiences to the ordinary human being and imposing their own aims and ideals upon him. In education, the child has not to follow the great men, still less the teachers, but his own propensities, his own inclinations, know thyself and be thyself are nowhere more truer as they are in the field of education. The Mother's high sounding aims and ideals suffer from psycho-centric predicament. They suffer from a perfectionist's bias. They lack human warmth and intimacy. Her speculation of future society is shorn of all human warmth and intimacy which are immensely valuable to the ordinary mortals, in fact, so far as social theory is concerned, particularly in the field of education, the philosopher should be guided by the experiences of the ordinary mortals, rather than guiding them by his own personal experiences. Modern pedagogy is paido-centric. It is a precise inversion of the ancient system of teacher-centred education both in East and West. Our contemporary philosophers of education including M.K. Gandhi, Sri Aurobindo and The Mother have missed this Copernican revolution in the modern theory of education by making the educand central to the whole scheme.

Moral Purism

It is here that contemporary Western philosophers of education present more practical schemes. It is a strange paradox of human life that aiming too high has the risk of falling too low. Unfortunately, Indian philosophers of education have tried to divinise human being and the danger is that their system may even fail to humanise males and females Modern psychological, sociological and humanist trend in education suggests a more down to earth scheme. In theory, The Mother has agreed to the ideal of liberation while living but before achieving liberation one must be able to live and a sound integral philosophy of education should be able to develop every aspect of the educand. Communication among human beings, particularly male and female, has been no less satisfying, no less elevating than man-God relationships. Therefore too much emphasis on psychic and spiritual aims and ideals makes the philosophy of education of The Mother less integral and less practical.

The Mother has called the goal of education as liberation and the methods as austerities. These aims and means, whatever may be their implications, suffer from asceticism and moral purism. While these may appeal to some few persons it is difficult to understand how they may be applied to the child education which The Mother herself values so much.

In keeping with her integral approach in education The Mother has presented a synthesis of the Western and Indian aims and ideals of education. She rejected the extra-terrestrial interpretation of the ancient Indian ideal of education as liberation. On the other hand, she presented a theory of four-fold liberation while living which may be achieved through the four-fold austerity. Such an interpretation of the idea of liberation may be agreeable to the modern man. Liberation here is tantamount of expression and evolution which is acceptable to modern educationists as the aim of education. This four-fold ideal of education supplies a wider, more complex, more total and integral aim of education. It is based upon an integral theory of reality and an integral theory of knowledge and truth in the philosophy of The Mother. It is justified by the differences found among types of men and the levels of consciousness and mind. True to her integral approach The Mother presented the concept of integral men and an integral personality theory. Her concept of five psychological perfections directly follows from her integral psychology.

Second Class Status to Marriage

But the weakest spot in The Mother's philosophy of education is its sociological foundation particularly her views about marriage and family. Though as a western woman she has raised her voice for women liberation and demanded her equality with man in very forceful terms, her views about marriage and family may not be agreeable to the modern man. Allowing the value of marriage for the common males and females The Mother has given a second class status to the institution of marriage. This is in keeping with the tradition of ancient Indian philosophy as well as the views of contemporary Indian philosophers including M.K. Gandhi, R.N. Tagore and others, it is unfortunate that *Grihastha Asrama* is the foundation of the social fabric Indian philosophers, ancient as well as modern, could not appreciate the mutual fulfilment of the male-female relationships in very clear terms The Mother deplores all love and communication between male and female as second grade. This is in keeping with the spiritual traditions everywhere in accepting human love to human being only as a means to man's love to God. While the religious and spiritual significance of such a view may be justified both by tradition and logic, it cannot be a sound basis for education. An important aim of education in a society is to provide better adjustment between males and females. A philosophy which gives a second-grade status to marriage and family accepts them, only as necessary evils, cannot evolve mutual love among boys and girls and cannot encourage them to find integral, satisfaction in mutual communication. On the other hand, it rather increases guilt consciousness, a necessary bye-product of the traditional Indian ideal of *Brahmacarya.* One cannot challenge the value of celibacy in the growing period upto 25 years of age but then by making it a cardinal virtue, a value in every stage of development, Indian philosophers have failed to provide a sound philosophical foundation for the institution of marriage and family. The philosopher of education has no conflict with the spiritual man or the spiritual savant, he only wants to point that their scope is very much outside the field of education. However, high may be religion and spirituality, the goal of the education is more mundane. It is to make a man evolve in totality and integrity. It is left to the human individual to rise as much as he likes, but the goal of the teacher is only to create an atmosphere for the healthy growth of male-female relationships and these certainly include sex and marriage. Finally, if the foundations of marriage institutions are shaky, the foundations of family institutions cannot be solid. If the children are denied proper attention and if the father and mother do not have sufficient intercommunication, the psychological development of the children cannot be adequate. Psychologists have amply pointed out the pathological and even positively disintegrating effect of strict sanitary training, moral purism, asceticism and even idealism upon the development of the children. The Mother has herself admitted that the child learns by imitation of the parents. If the parents do not have sufficient communication among themselves not on spiritual but on physical, vital, and mental levels the development of the children on these levels is bound to suffer.

Pointer to Future Philosophy of Education

In spite of the above critical evaluation of The Mother's philosophy of education it may be appreciated as pointer to the direction to which future education may be directed. So many thinkers have admitted that if man has not to fall below the present cultural level, he must make progress in psychic and spiritual evolution. Ancient wisdom of East and West as depicted in the philosophy of education of India and Greece rightly pointed out the value of spiritual advancement in human life. As the primitive age could not imagine the present cultural level of the human beings, so the modern man cannot appreciate the evolution of the gnostic being and the gnostic race. Though no conclusive arguments may be given to prove that supramental evolution is possible, the hypothesis is worth trial. If it has failed repeatedly, it does not mean that it is impossible. Even if it is the most difficult the game is worth the candle. In this sense The Mother's philosophy of education has made a solid contribution to the treasure of philosophies of education.

References

1. Aurobindo, S., The Renaissance in India (1951), p. 72.
2. Radhakrishnan, S., *An Idealistic View of Life* (London: George Allen & Unwin, 1961), p. 205,
3. Bhagwandas, *The Science of the Self*, p. 44.
4. Radhakrishnan, S., *An Idealistic View of Life* (1961), p. 142.
5. Bhagwandas, *The Science of the Self*, p. 44.
6. *Sri Aurobindo and the Mother on Education*, Part II, p. 26.
7. *Ibid.*, p. 27.
8. *Ibid.*, p. 20.
9. *Ibid.*, p. 22.
10. *Ibid.*, p. 27.
11. *Ibid.*, p. 22.
12. Gandhi, M.K. in C.S. Shukla's *Conversations of Gandhiji*, p. 30.
13. *Ibid.*
14. Tagore, R.N., *The Religion of Man* (London: Macmillan, 1931), p. 63-
15. The Mother, *Conversations* (1956), p. 125.
16. *Bulletin of Physical Education* (April, 1970), p. 58.
17. *Sri Aurobindo and The Mother on Religion*, p. 31.
18. *Ibid.*, p. 32.
19. *Ibid.*, Part I, p. 6.
20. *Ibid.*, p. 28.
21. *Ibid.*, p. 4.
22. *Ibid.*
23. Lamont, C., *The Philosophy of Humanism*, p. 228.
24. *Sri Aurobindo and The Mother on Education*, Part II, p. 1.
25. Lamont, C., *The Philosophy of Humanism*, p. 228.
26. Joshi, K., *Navchetana* (Pondicherry: Mother's International School, 1977), pp. 5-7.
27. *Ibid.*
28. *Answer Given by The Mother on* 17.12. 66.
29. *Ibid.*
30. *Sri Aurobindo and The Mother on Education*, Part III, pp. 19-21,
31. *Ibid.*, p. 20.
32. *Ibid.*, p. 21.

33. *Ibid.*, p. 23.
34. *Ibid.*, p. 26.
35. *Sri Aurobindo Birth Centenary Library* (1972), Vol. 17, p. 213.
36. *Sri Aurobindo and the Mother on Education,* Part II, p. 17.
37. *Sri Aurobindo and The Mother on Women* (1978), p. 17.
38. *Sri Aurobindo Birth Centenary library* (1970), Vol. 23, p. 817.
39. *The Mother on Women* (1978), p. 58.
40. *Sri Aurobindo and The Mother on Education*, Part II, p, 30.
41. *Ibid.*, p. 31.
42. *Ibid.*
43. Bradley, F.H., *Appearance and Reality*, 2nd Ed., 9th Imp. p. 120,
44. *Ibid.*, p. 1.

Bibliography

Works of The Mother

(*Published by Sri Aurobindo Society*)

About Savitri — Comments by The Mother, Paintings by Huta Book I, Canto I (1972).

Burning Brazier, 2nd Imprint (1974).

Conversations — Answers to Questions put to Her, 10th Imp. (1973).

Flowers And Their Messages, 2nd Edition (1979).

The Golden Vision (1980).

Health and Healing in Yoga. (1979).

Ideal Child for Children of All Ages (1979).

Letters to My Little Smile — The Mother's letters to Vasudha (1977).

The Mother's call to Youth (1978).

The Mother on Sri Aurobindo (English-Sanskrit), (1972).

The Mother on Herself (1977).

Mother's Light, 2nd Imp. (1978).

Prayers and Meditations (Selected), 4th Imp. (1971).

Prayers and Meditations — With 8 photos (1975).

Prayers and Meditations (Complete) (1979).

Questions and Answers (1956, 1973).

Questions and Answers (1957-1958, 1973).

The Supreme Discovery, 5th Imp. (1979).

Seeds of Light, Pocket Edition (1979).

Tales of All Times, 6th Enlarged Edition (1980).

White Roses

Words of Long Ago, 3rd Imp. (1974).

Words of The Mother (1977).

The Collected Works of The Mother (16 Volumes).

Centenary Booklet Library

Illness—Part I & II, *Evolution, Meditation, Sleep and Dream Occultism, Truth, Prayer and Mantra, Science, Education* — Parts I, II & III,

Aspiration, Surrender and Grace, Religion, Food, Work, Democracy and Socialism, Yoga, The Future Society, Money, Gods and the Divine, Avatarhood, Helping Humanity, Beauty, Transformation, Happiness and Peace, On Themselves — Parts I & II, The Aim of Life — Parts I & II, *Death, Rebirth, Human Unity, Art — Parts I & II, India, Gita, Veda-Upanishads Tantra,Planes and Parts of Being* — Parts I & II, *Nature, Self-perfection* — Parts I, II, III & IV, *Fate and Free-Will, Love* — Parts I & II. *super mind.*

General

Sri Aurobindo and The Mother on Collective Yoga (1974).

Sri Aurobindo and The Mother on Education, 6th Imp. (1978).

Sri Aurobindo and The Mother on Love Pavitra, 2nd Enlarged Ed. (1973).

Sri Aurobindo, The Mother, Their Manifestation and Symbols (1978).

Descent: Some Glimpses of The Mother (1979).

Glimpses of The Mother's Life I — Nilima Das (1978).

Glimpses of The Mother's Life II — Nilima Das (1980).

Auroville

The Mother on Auroville (1977).

Matrimandir — Huta (1974).

Auroville, The City of The Future.

Today and Tomorrow

Journals

Sri Aurobindo Archives and Research — Bi-annual.

All India Magazine — Monthly.

The Advent — Quarterly.

Mother India — Monthly.

World Union — Quarterly.

The Bulletin of Sri Aurobindo International Centre of Education — Quarterly.

Other works

Aurobindo, *S.,A System of National Education* (Calcutta: Arya Publishing House, 1949).

Aurobindo, S., *Essays on The Gita* (New York: The Sri Aurobindo Library Inc., 1950).

——, *The Ideal of Human Unity* (Pondicherry: Sri Aurobindo Ashram, Library Inc., 1950).

——, *The Life Divine* (Complete) (New York: The Sri Aurobindo Library Inc., 1951).

——, *Social and Political Thought* (Pondicherry: Sri Aurobindo Birth Centenary Library, 1970).

——, *The Renaissance in India* (Pondicherry: Sri Aurobindo Ashram, 1951).

Altekar, A.S., *Education in Ancient India* (Banaras: The Indian Book Shop, 1934).

Blanshard & others, *Philosophy in American Education* (New York Harper & Bros, 1945).

Bradley, F.H., *Appearance and Reality*, 2nd Edn. (London: Oxford University Press, 1951).

Cole, G.D.H., *Essays in Social Theory* (London: Macmillan, 1950).

Das, Bhagwan, The Science of the Self.

Devi, Indira, The Glory That is The Mother (1979).

Desai, A.R., (Ed), Essays on Modernisation of Underdeveloped Societies (1971).

Dowett, N.C., *The Psychology for Future Education* (Pondicherry: Sri Aurobindo Ashram, 1977).

Durkheim, E., Education and Sociology.

Francis, W.C., *Recent Political Thought*, 4th Imp. (Calcutta: The World Press Pvt. Ltd., 1971).

Freud, S., *New Introductory Lectures on Psycho-analysis* (London: The Hogarth Press Ltd., 1949).

——, Moses and Monotheism.

——, *The Future of an Illusion* (London: The Hogarth Press Ltd., 1949).

Froebel, *Chief Educational Writings*, Translated by Dr. Fletcher.

Gentile, G., *The Theory of Mind as Pure Act*, English translation by H. Wildon Carr (Macmillan).

Huxley, A., *Proper Studies* (London: Chatto & Windus, 1951).

——, *Ends and Means* (London: Chatto and Windus, 1951).

Hume, D., *Treatise on Human Nature*, Book II.

Huta, *Salutations* (1973).

Indrasen, Longings for *The Mother* (1978).

Iyengar, K.R. Srinivasa, *Tryst with The Divine*, (1974).

James, W., *The Will to Believe.*

——, *Varieties of Religious Experiences.*

Kant, I., *Critic of Pure Reason.*

Leuba, J.H., *The Psychology of Religious Mysticism* (London: Regan Paul, 1929).

—— , *Monis* (July, 1901).

Muirhead, J.H., *The Elements of Ethics* (London: John Murrey, 1865).

McTaggart, *Some Dogmas of Religion.*

Maclver, R.M. & Page, C.H., Society: *Introductory Societies.*

Marx, K., *Selected Works*, Vol. I (Moscow: Foreign Languages Publishing House, 1955).

Das Capital, Vol. I (Moscow: Foreign Languages Publishing House, 1958).

Nirodharan, *The Mother Sweetness and Light* (1978).

Pandit, M.P., *The Mother of Love I* (1973).

——, *The Mother of Love* II (1972).

——, *The Mother of Love* III (1972).

——, *Sidelights on The Mother*, 2nd Imp. (1977).

——, *Tell us of the The Mother* (1980).

——, *Under The Mother's Banner* (1975).

Prema, N.K. *Our Mother* (1978).

Plotinus, *The New Platonists.*

Plato, *Republic*, Jowett.

——, *Laws*, Jowett.

Ravindra, The White Lotus: *At the Feet of The Mother* (1978).

Rusk, R.R., *The Philosophical Bases of Education* (London: University of London Press, 1950).

Rishabhchand, *In the Mother's Light* (1967).

Russell, B., *Authority and The Individual* (London: George Allen & Unwin Ltd., 1949).

Rousseau, J.J., *Emile* (London: J.M. Dents & Sons, 1950).

Radhkrishnan, S., *An Idealist View of Life* (London: George Allen & Unwin Ltd., 1961).

Sarkar, M., Sweet Mother: Harmonies of Light I (1978).

——, *Sweet Mother*: *Harmonies of Light* II (1979).

Sastry, T.V.K., *Flames of White Light*, 2nd Edn. (1976).

Sethna, K.D., The Mother — *Past, Present and Future* (1977).

Sharma, G.R., *Trends in Contemporary Indian Philosophy of Education* (New Delhi: Atlantic Publishers, 1987).

Tagore, R.N., *Creative Unity* (London: Macmillan, 1917).

Whitehead, A.N., *Religion in the Making*.

Index